MATT KINDT ◆ MATT SMITH ◆ CHRIS O'HALLORAN

folklords™

Published by

Logo Design by
MARIE KRUPINA

Series Designer
MICHELLE ANKLEY

Collection Designer
SCOTT NEWMAN

Assistant Editors
RAMIRO PORTNOY & GAVIN GRONENTHAL

Editor
ERIC HARBURN

FOLKLORDS, July 2020. Published by BOOM! Studios, a division of Boom Entertainment, Inc. Folklords is ™ & © 2020 Matt Kindt & Matthew T. Smith. Originally published in single magazine form as Folklords No. 1-5. ™ & © 2019, 2020 Matt Kindt & Matthew T. Smith. All rights reserved. BOOM! Studios™ and the BOOM! Studios logo are trademarks of Boom Entertainment, Inc., registered in various countries and categories. All characters, events, and institutions depicted herein are fictional. Any similarity between any of the names, characters, persons, events, and/or institutions in this publication to actual names, characters, and persons, whether living or dead, events, and/or institutions is unintended and purely coincidental. BOOM! Studios does not read or accept unsolicited submissions of ideas, stories, or artwork.

BOOM! Studios, 5670 Wilshire Boulevard, Suite 400, Los Angeles, CA 90036-5679. Printed in China. First Printing.

ISBN: 978-1-68415-540-8, eISBN: 978-1-64144-706-5

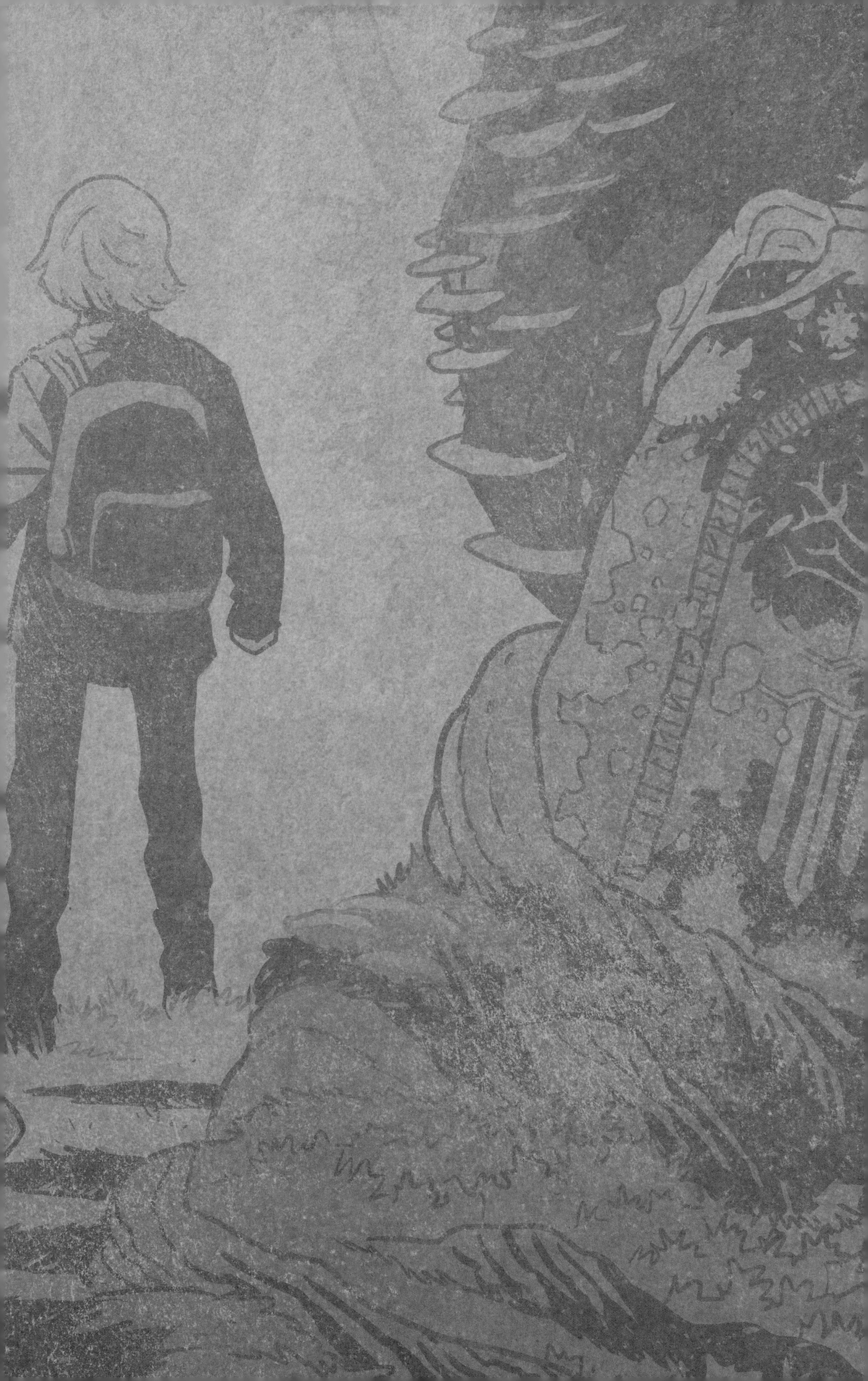

Written by
MATT KINDT

folklu

Colored by
CHRIS O'HALLORAN

Lettered by
JIM CAMPBELL

Illustrated by
MATT SMITH

ORDS ™

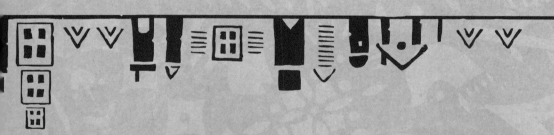

Cover by
MATT SMITH

Created by
MATT KINDT
& MATT SMITH

CHAPTER
ONE

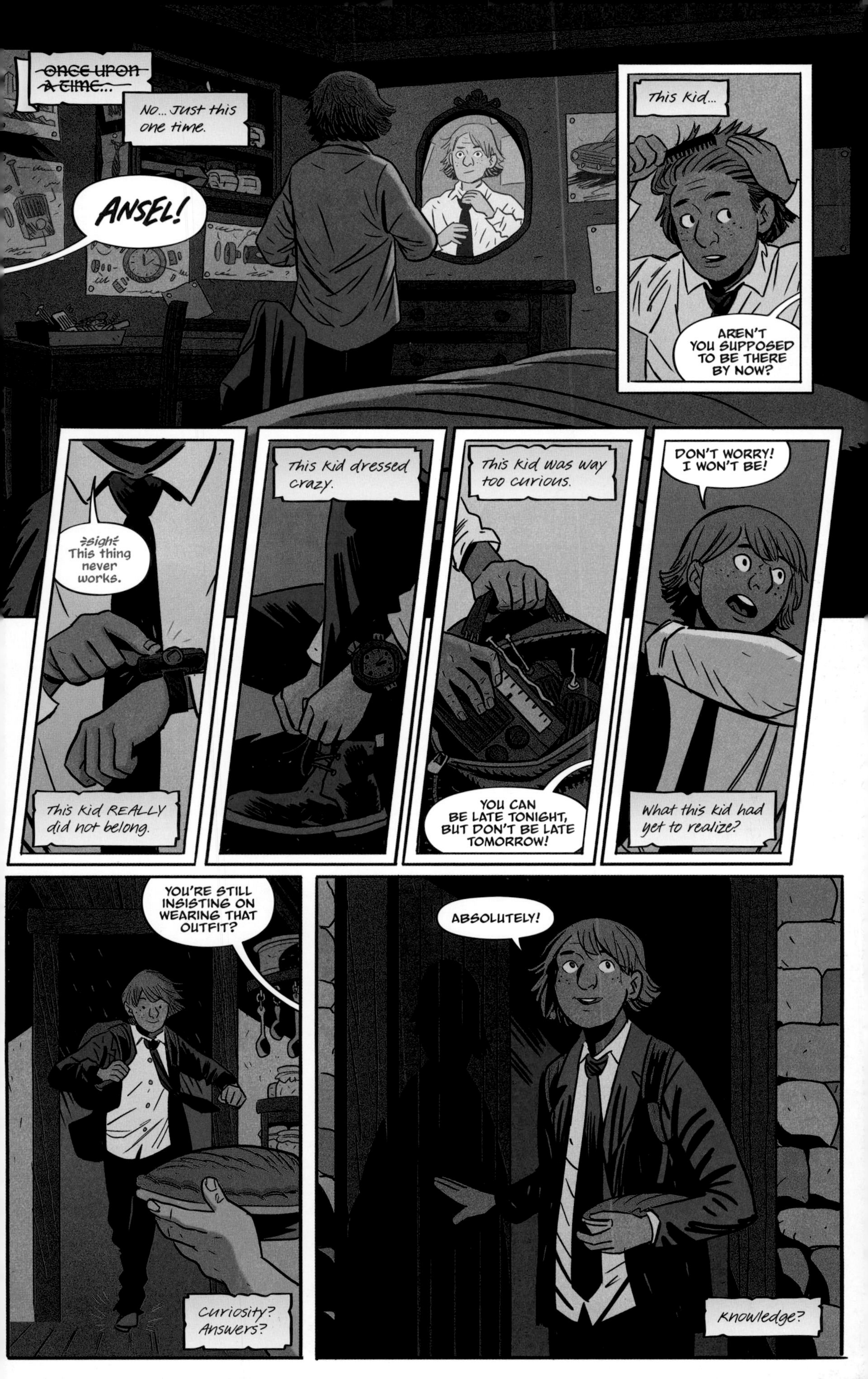
~~ONCE UPON A TIME...~~
No... Just this one time.
ANSEL!
This kid...
AREN'T YOU SUPPOSED TO BE THERE BY NOW?
sigh This thing never works.
This kid REALLY did not belong.
This kid dressed crazy.
This kid was way too curious.
YOU CAN BE LATE TONIGHT, BUT DON'T BE LATE TOMORROW!
DON'T WORRY! I WON'T BE!
What this kid had yet to realize?
YOU'RE STILL INSISTING ON WEARING THAT OUTFIT?
Curiosity? Answers?
ABSOLUTELY!
Knowledge?

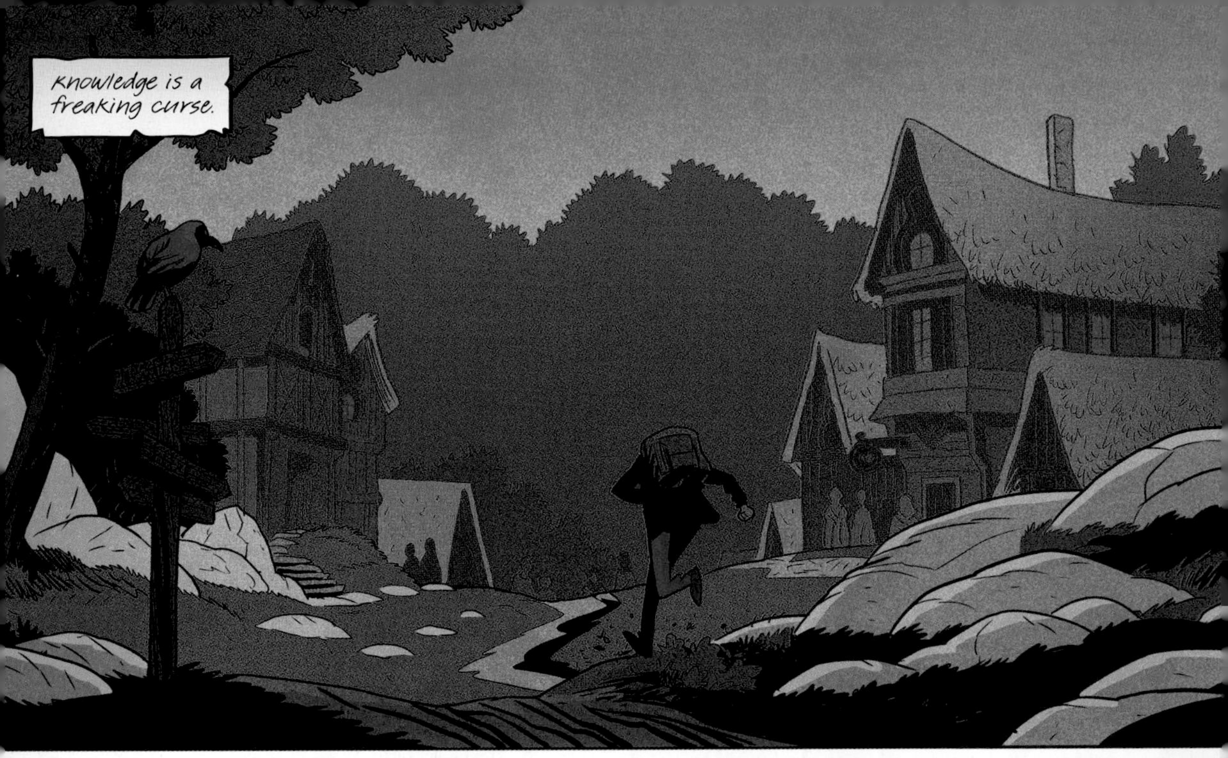
Knowledge is a freaking curse.

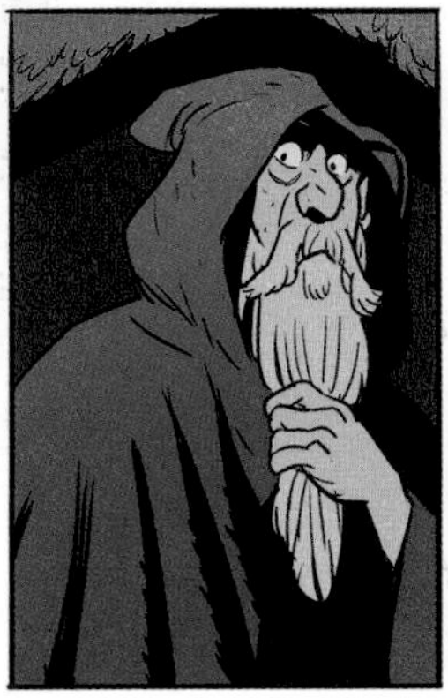

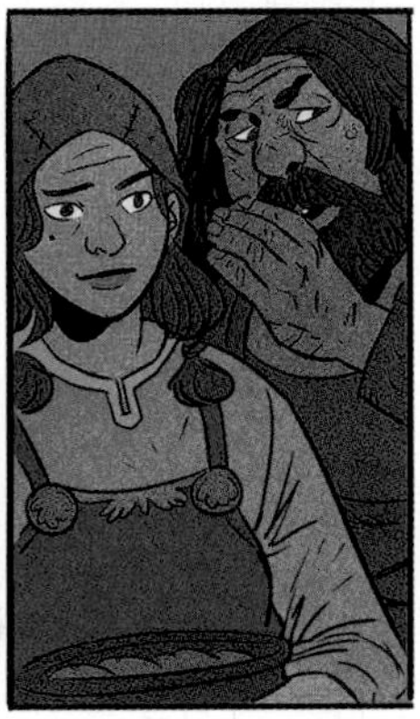

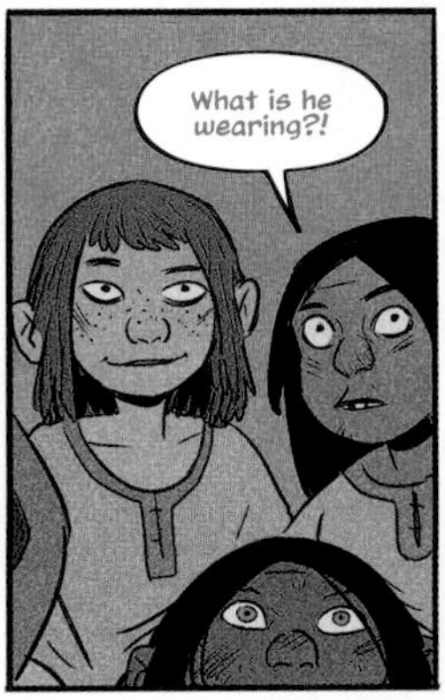
What is he wearing?!

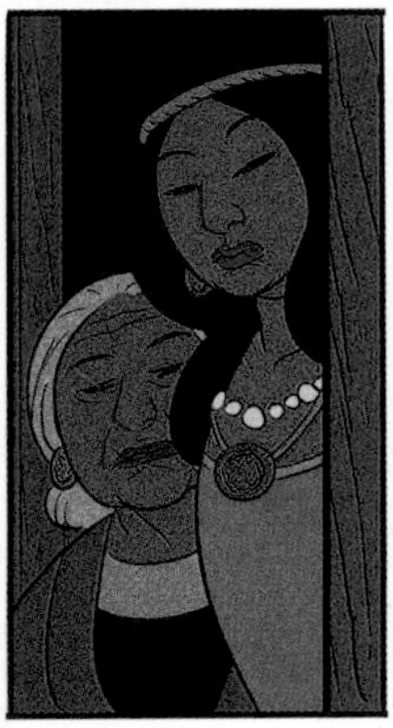

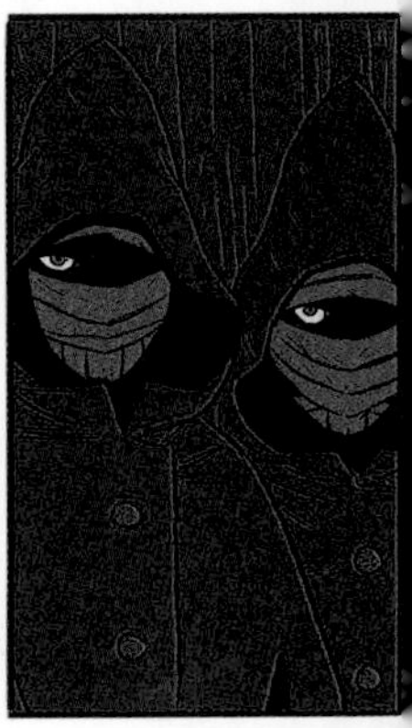

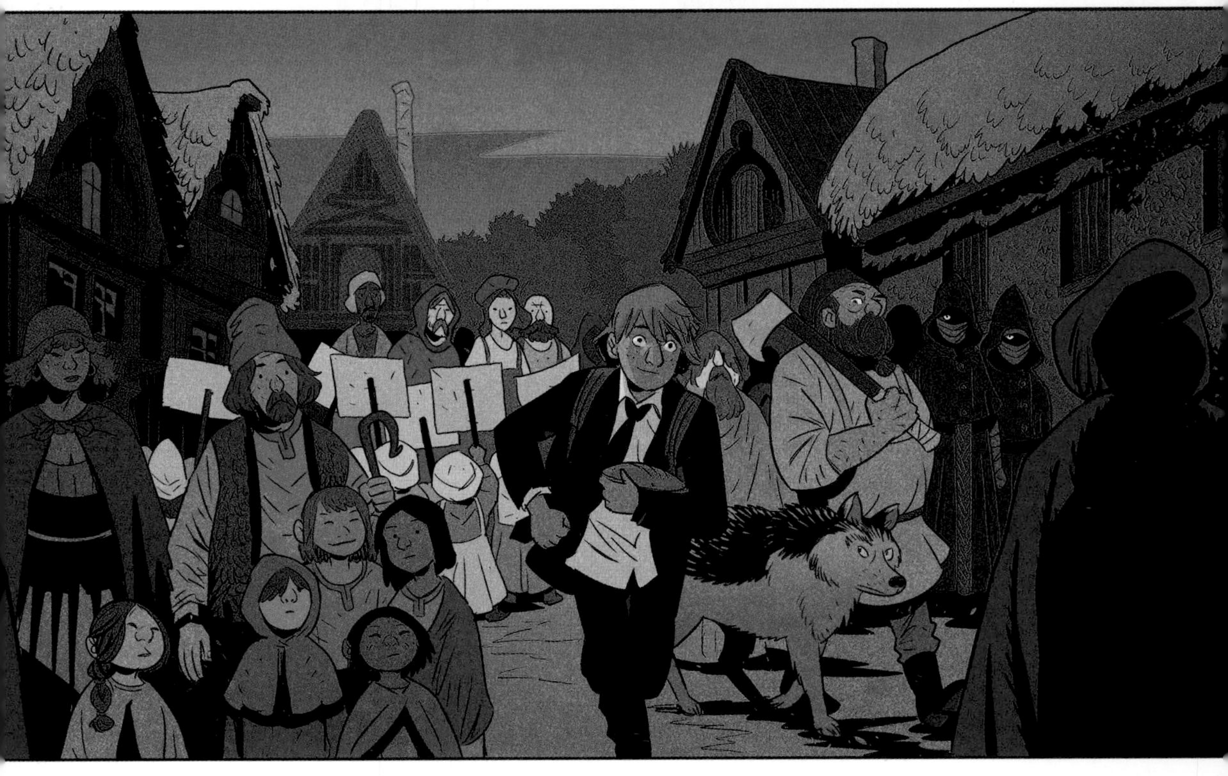

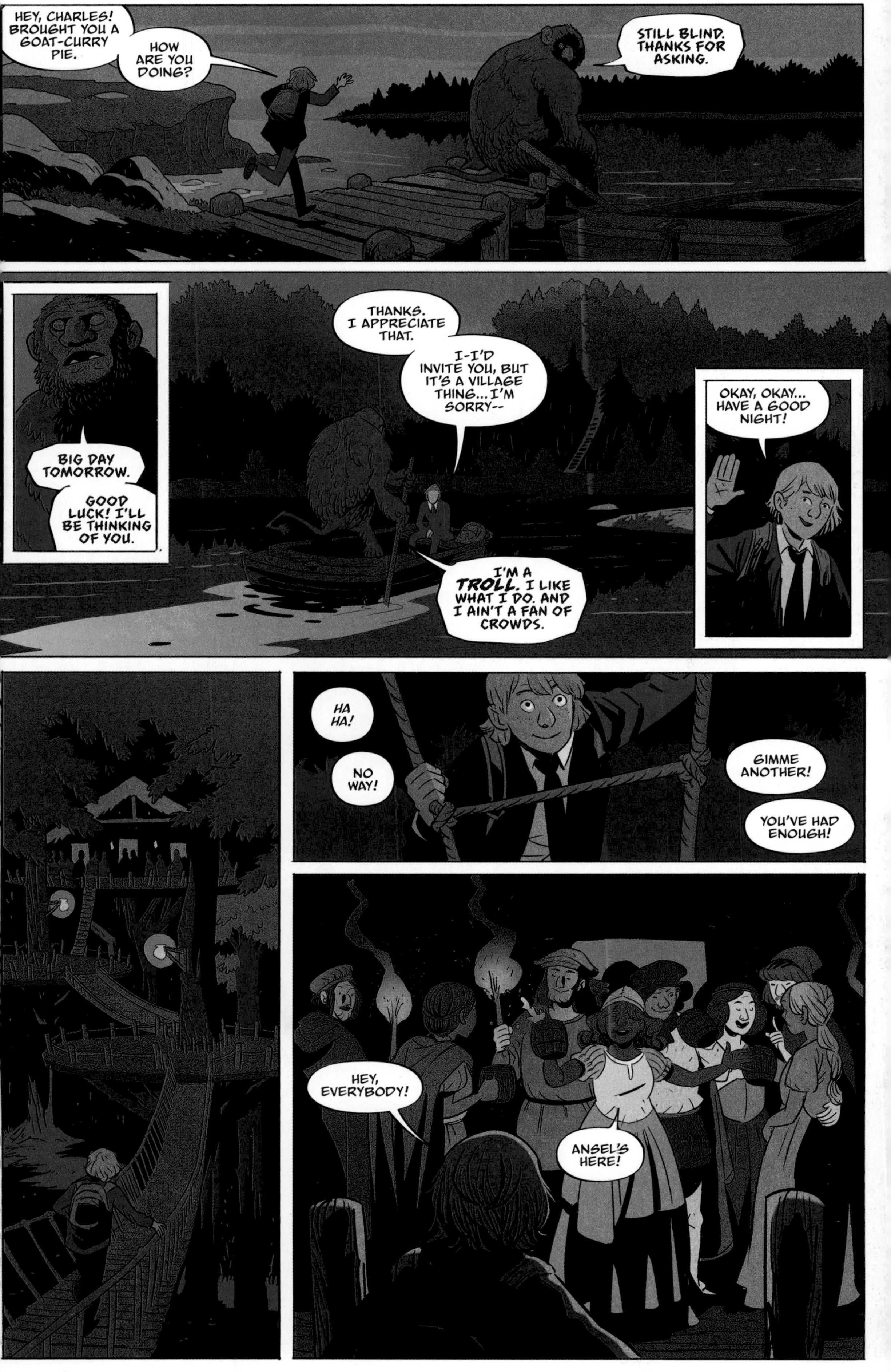
HEY, CHARLES! BROUGHT YOU A GOAT-CURRY PIE.
HOW ARE YOU DOING?
STILL BLIND. THANKS FOR ASKING.
BIG DAY TOMORROW.
GOOD LUCK! I'LL BE THINKING OF YOU.
THANKS. I APPRECIATE THAT.
I-I'D INVITE YOU, BUT IT'S A VILLAGE THING... I'M SORRY--
I'M A TROLL. I LIKE WHAT I DO. AND I AIN'T A FAN OF CROWDS.
OKAY, OKAY... HAVE A GOOD NIGHT!
HA HA!
NO WAY!
GIMME ANOTHER!
YOU'VE HAD ENOUGH!
HEY, EVERYBODY!
ANSEL'S HERE!

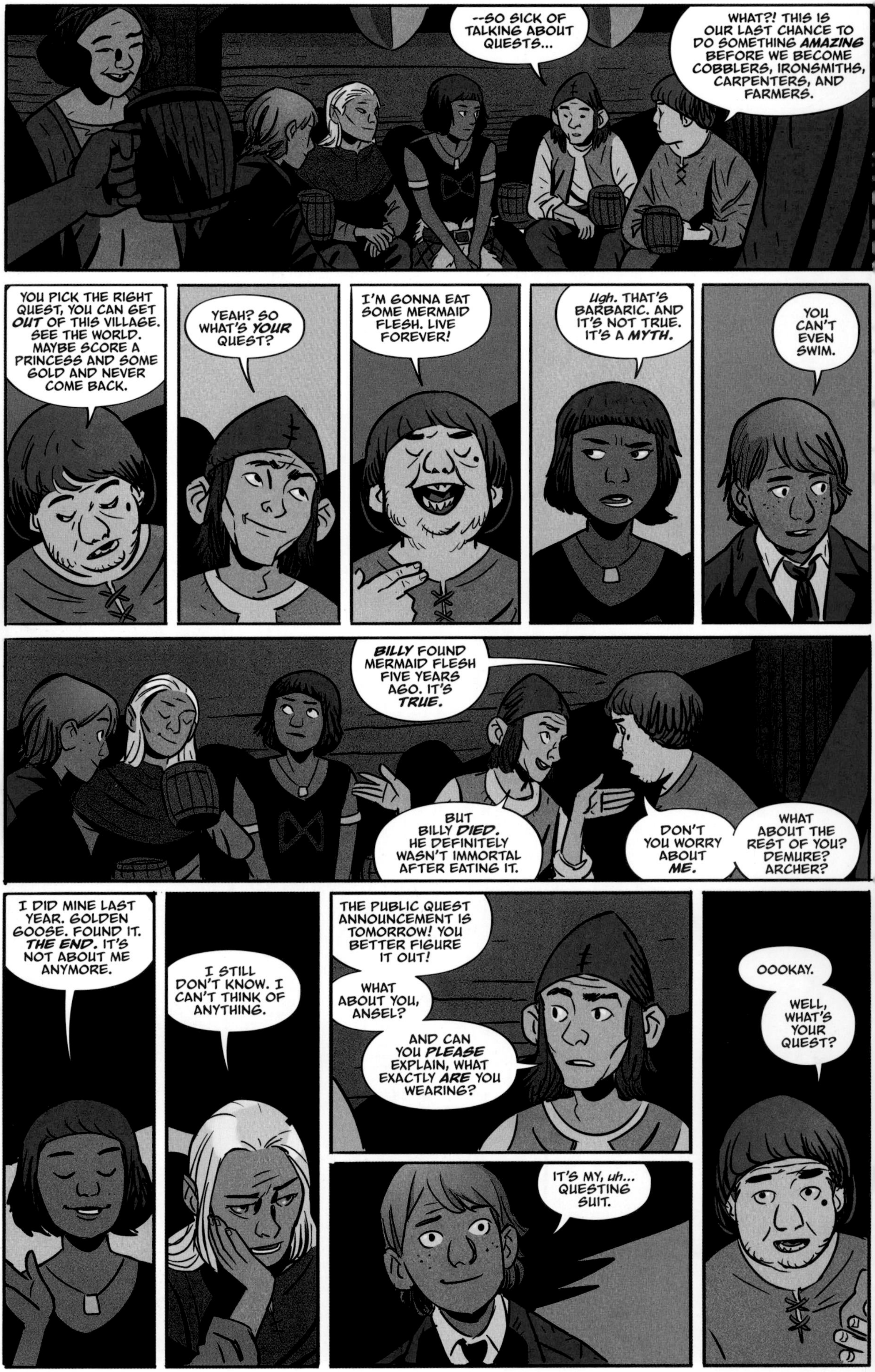
--SO SICK OF TALKING ABOUT QUESTS...
WHAT?! THIS IS OUR LAST CHANCE TO DO SOMETHING AMAZING BEFORE WE BECOME COBBLERS, IRONSMITHS, CARPENTERS, AND FARMERS.
YOU PICK THE RIGHT QUEST, YOU CAN GET OUT OF THIS VILLAGE. SEE THE WORLD. MAYBE SCORE A PRINCESS AND SOME GOLD AND NEVER COME BACK.
YEAH? SO WHAT'S YOUR QUEST?
I'M GONNA EAT SOME MERMAID FLESH. LIVE FOREVER!
Ugh. THAT'S BARBARIC. AND IT'S NOT TRUE. IT'S A MYTH.
YOU CAN'T EVEN SWIM.
BILLY FOUND MERMAID FLESH FIVE YEARS AGO. IT'S TRUE.
BUT BILLY DIED. HE DEFINITELY WASN'T IMMORTAL AFTER EATING IT.
DON'T YOU WORRY ABOUT ME.
WHAT ABOUT THE REST OF YOU? DEMURE? ARCHER?
I DID MINE LAST YEAR. GOLDEN GOOSE. FOUND IT. THE END. IT'S NOT ABOUT ME ANYMORE.
I STILL DON'T KNOW. I CAN'T THINK OF ANYTHING.
THE PUBLIC QUEST ANNOUNCEMENT IS TOMORROW! YOU BETTER FIGURE IT OUT!
WHAT ABOUT YOU, ANSEL?
AND CAN YOU PLEASE EXPLAIN, WHAT EXACTLY ARE YOU WEARING?
IT'S MY, uh... QUESTING SUIT.
OOOKAY.
WELL, WHAT'S YOUR QUEST?

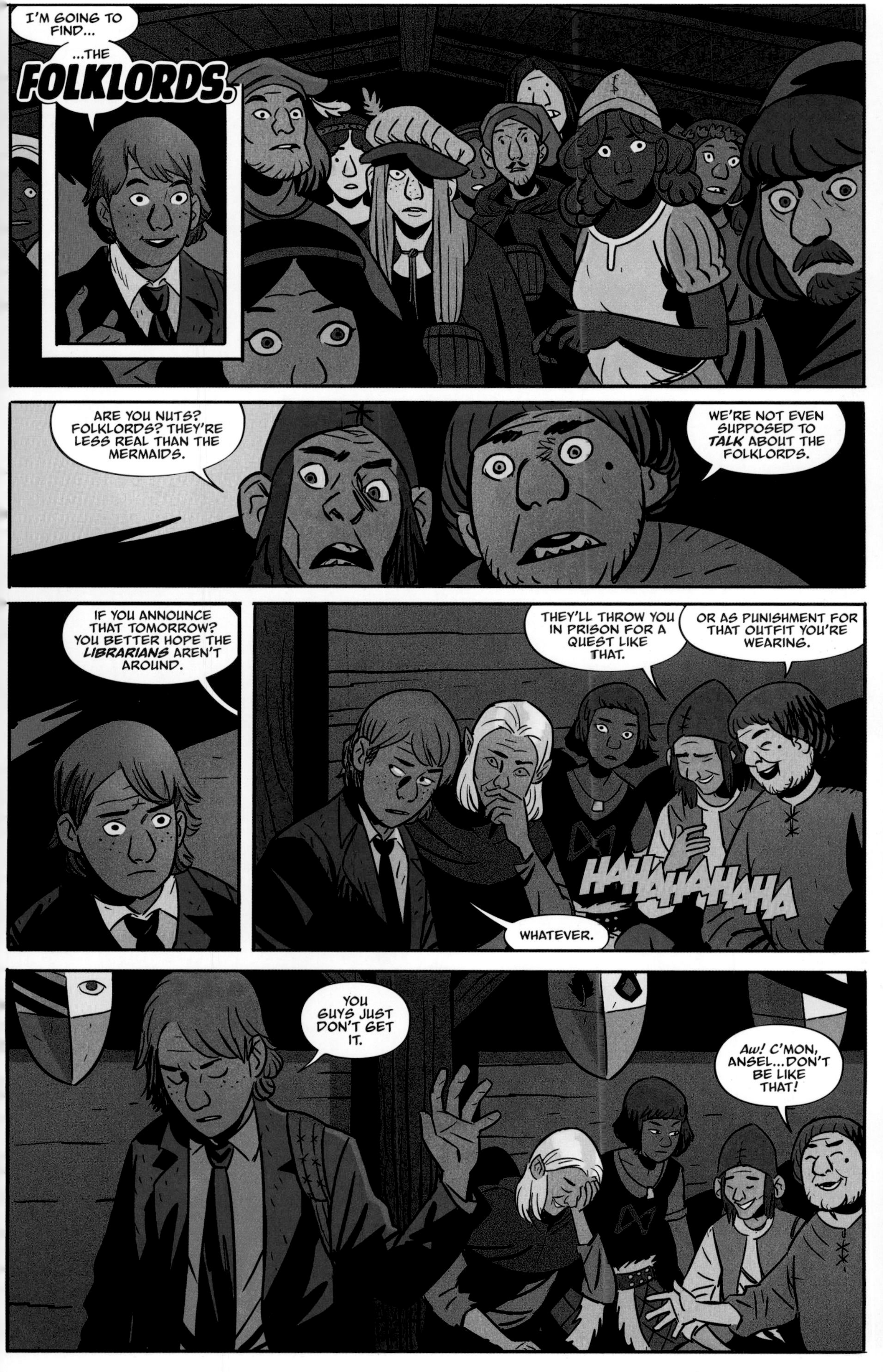
I'M GOING TO FIND...
...THE FOLKLORDS.
ARE YOU NUTS? FOLKLORDS? THEY'RE LESS REAL THAN THE MERMAIDS.
WE'RE NOT EVEN SUPPOSED TO TALK ABOUT THE FOLKLORDS.
IF YOU ANNOUNCE THAT TOMORROW? YOU BETTER HOPE THE LIBRARIANS AREN'T AROUND.
THEY'LL THROW YOU IN PRISON FOR A QUEST LIKE THAT.
OR AS PUNISHMENT FOR THAT OUTFIT YOU'RE WEARING.
HAHAHAHAHAHA
WHATEVER.
YOU GUYS JUST DON'T GET IT.
AW! C'MON, ANSEL...DON'T BE LIKE THAT!

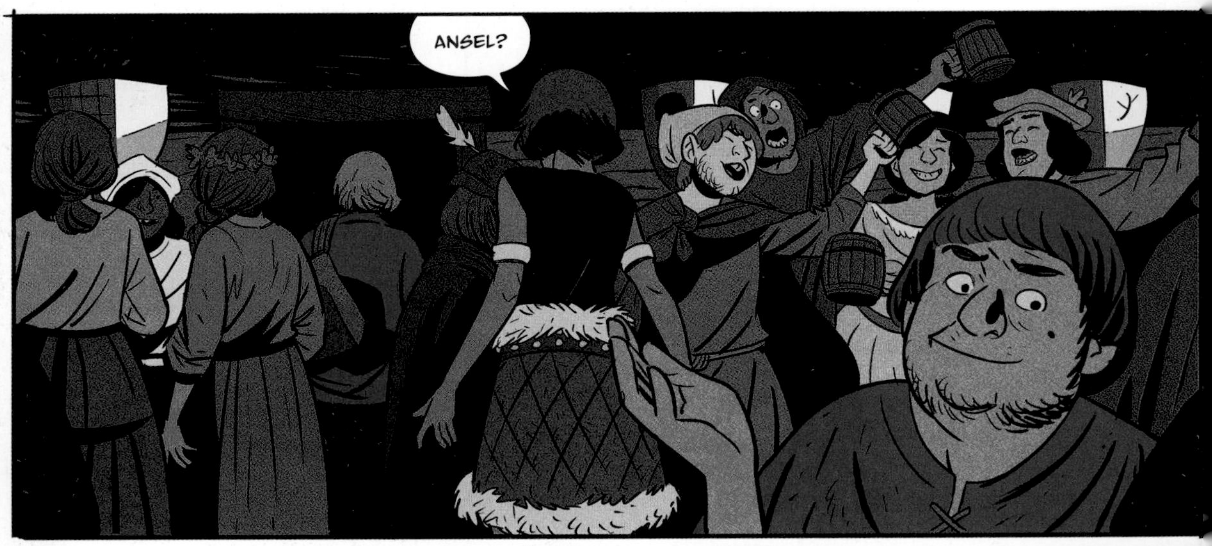
ANSEL?

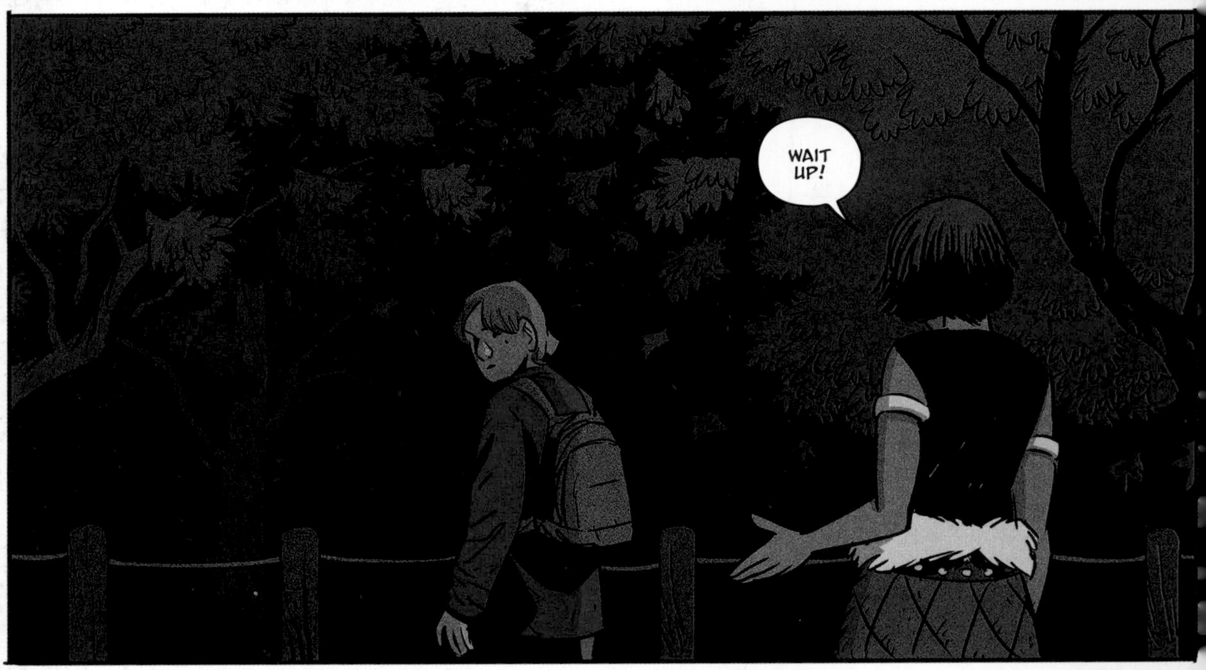
WAIT UP!

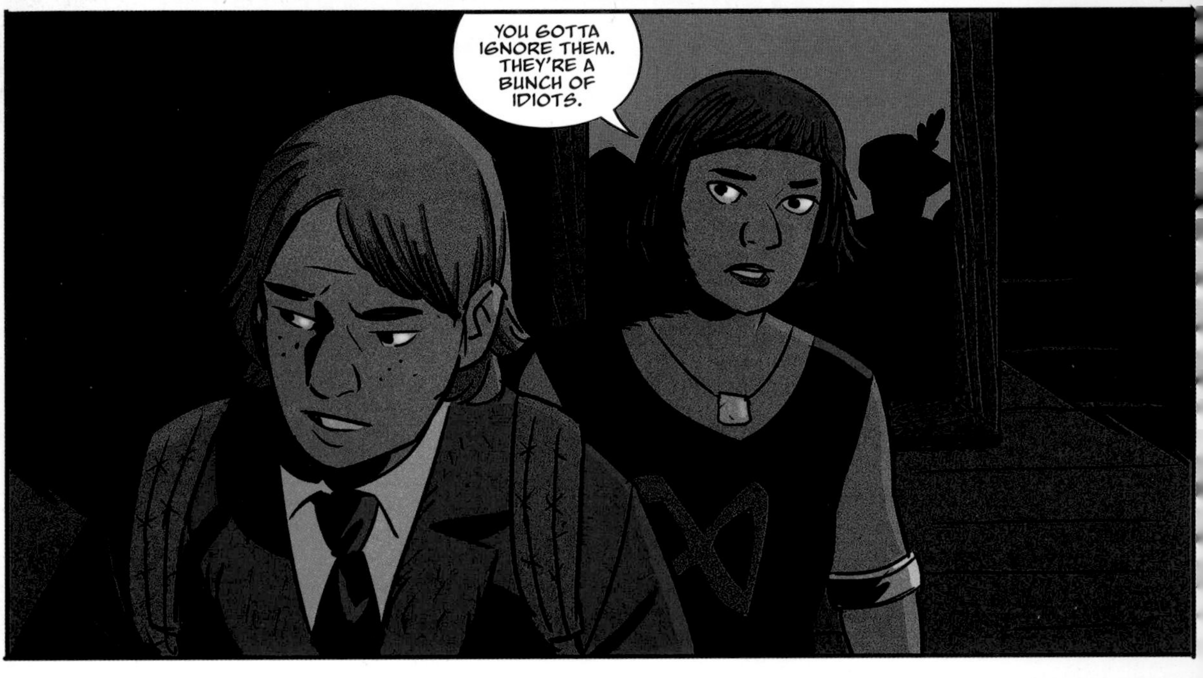
YOU GOTTA IGNORE THEM. THEY'RE A BUNCH OF IDIOTS.

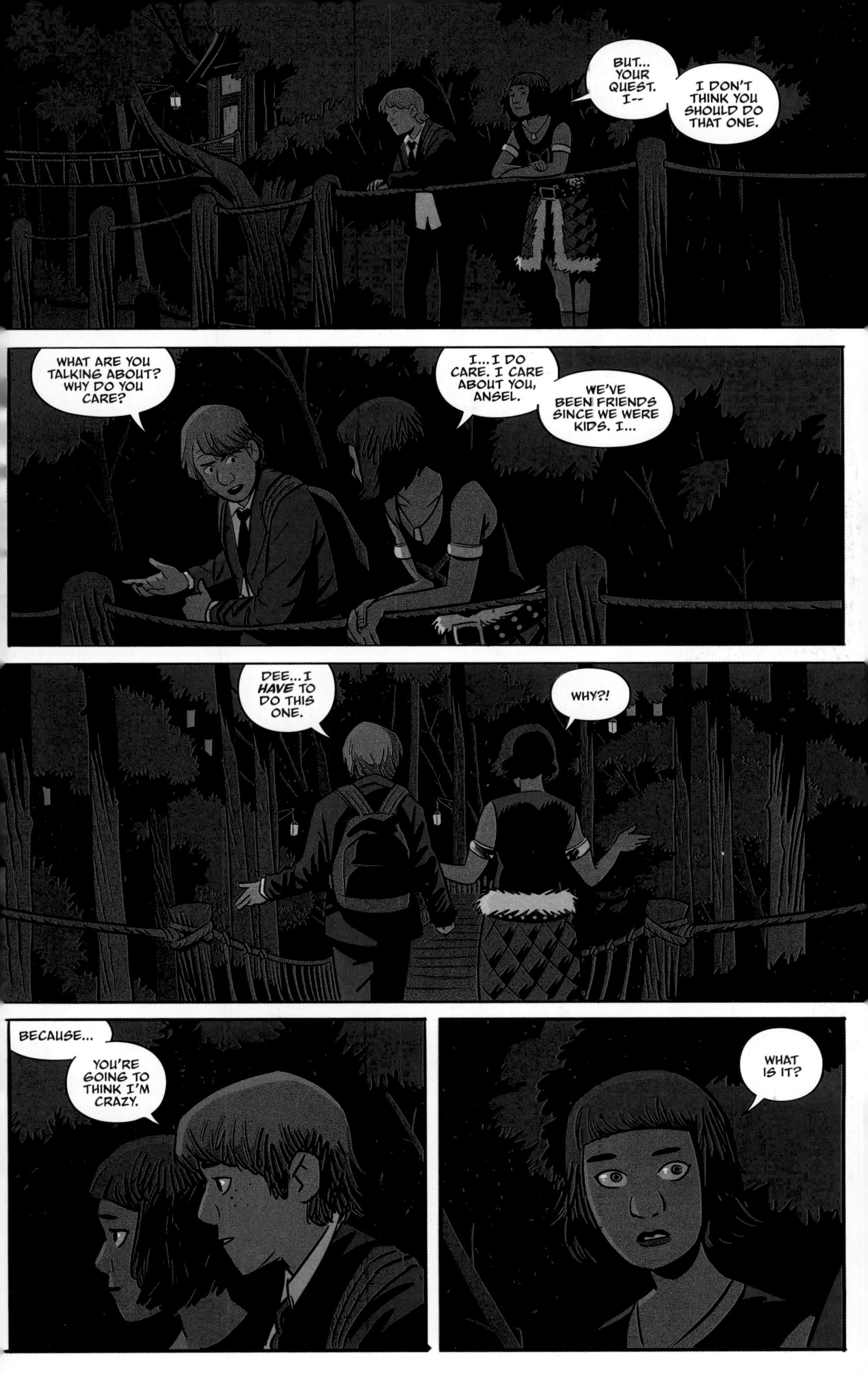
BUT... YOUR QUEST. I--
I DON'T THINK YOU SHOULD DO THAT ONE.
WHAT ARE YOU TALKING ABOUT? WHY DO YOU CARE?
I... I DO CARE. I CARE ABOUT YOU, ANSEL.
WE'VE BEEN FRIENDS SINCE WE WERE KIDS. I...
DEE... I *HAVE* TO DO THIS ONE.
WHY?!
BECAUSE...
YOU'RE GOING TO THINK I'M CRAZY.
WHAT IS IT?

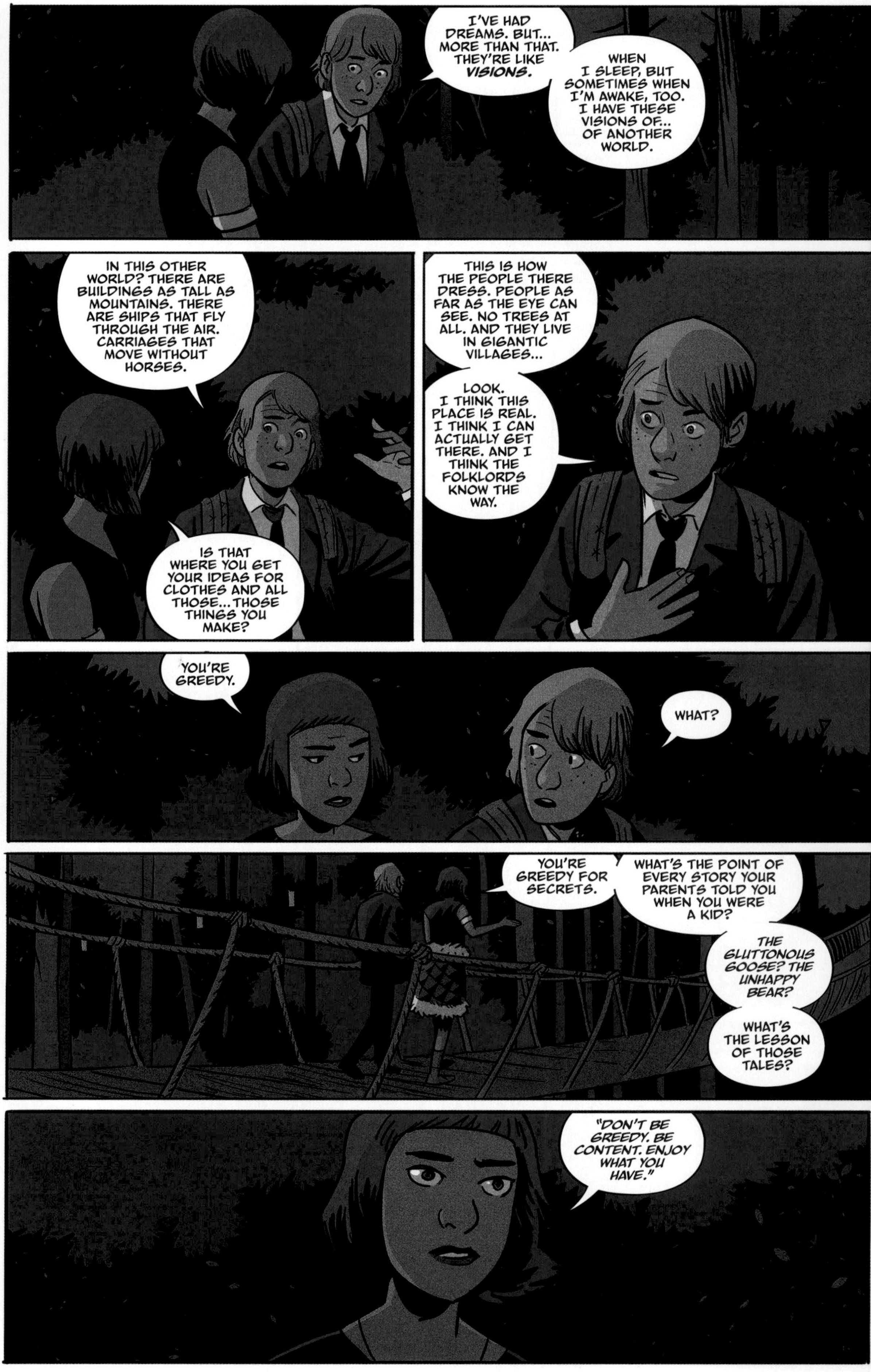
I'VE HAD DREAMS. BUT... MORE THAN THAT. THEY'RE LIKE *VISIONS.*
WHEN I SLEEP, BUT SOMETIMES WHEN I'M AWAKE, TOO. I HAVE THESE VISIONS OF... OF ANOTHER WORLD.
IN THIS OTHER WORLD? THERE ARE BUILDINGS AS TALL AS MOUNTAINS. THERE ARE SHIPS THAT FLY THROUGH THE AIR. CARRIAGES THAT MOVE WITHOUT HORSES.
IS THAT WHERE YOU GET YOUR IDEAS FOR CLOTHES AND ALL THOSE... THOSE THINGS YOU MAKE?
THIS IS HOW THE PEOPLE THERE DRESS. PEOPLE AS FAR AS THE EYE CAN SEE. NO TREES AT ALL. AND THEY LIVE IN GIGANTIC VILLAGES...
LOOK. I THINK THIS PLACE IS REAL. I THINK I CAN ACTUALLY GET THERE. AND I THINK THE FOLKLORDS KNOW THE WAY.
YOU'RE GREEDY.
WHAT?
YOU'RE GREEDY FOR SECRETS.
WHAT'S THE POINT OF EVERY STORY YOUR PARENTS TOLD YOU WHEN YOU WERE A KID?
THE GLUTTONOUS GOOSE? THE UNHAPPY BEAR?
WHAT'S THE LESSON OF THOSE TALES?
"DON'T BE GREEDY. BE CONTENT. ENJOY WHAT YOU HAVE."

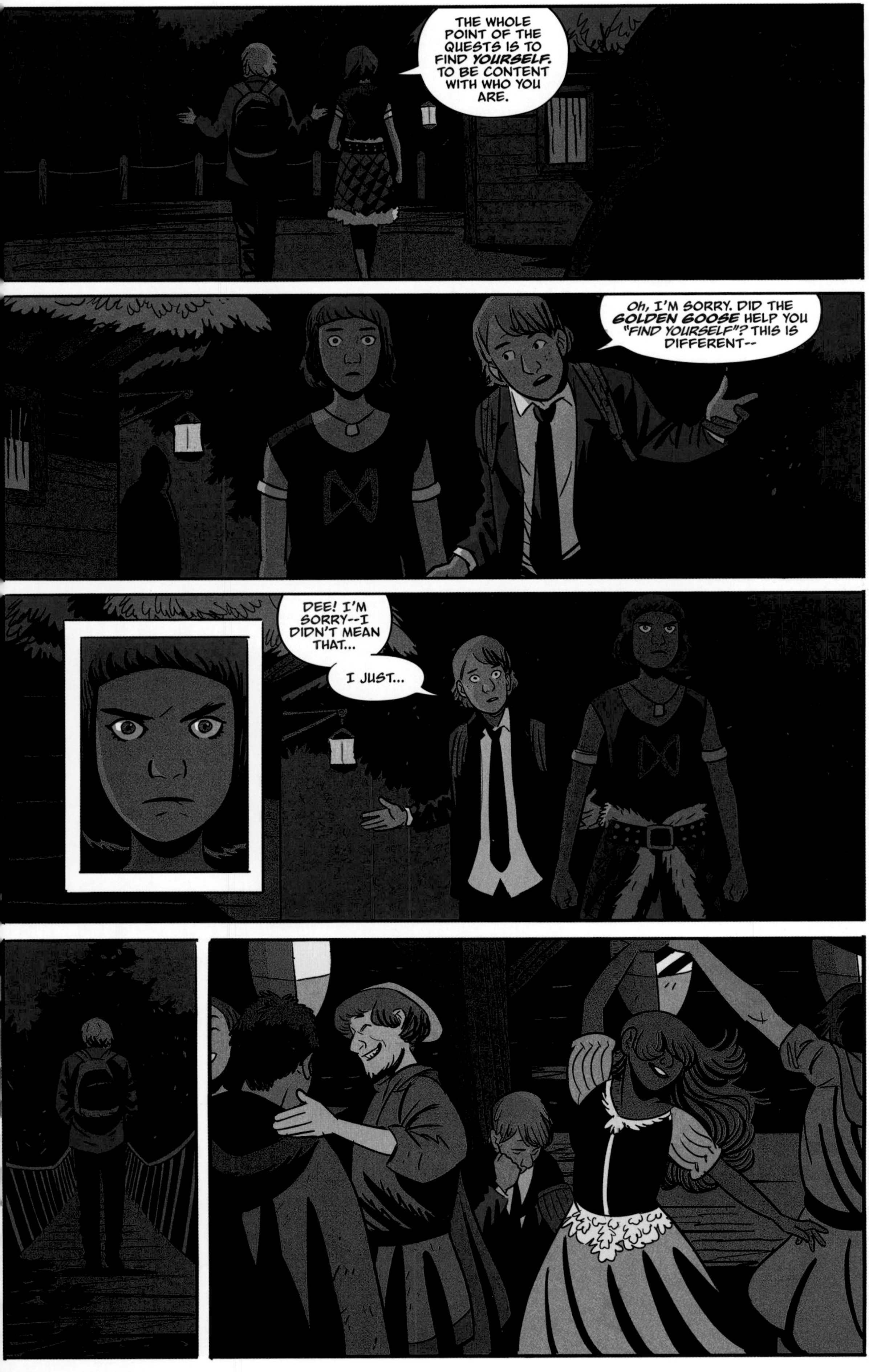
THE WHOLE POINT OF THE QUESTS IS TO FIND YOURSELF. TO BE CONTENT WITH WHO YOU ARE.
Oh, I'M SORRY. DID THE GOLDEN GOOSE HELP YOU "FIND YOURSELF"? THIS IS DIFFERENT--
DEE! I'M SORRY--I DIDN'T MEAN THAT...
I JUST...

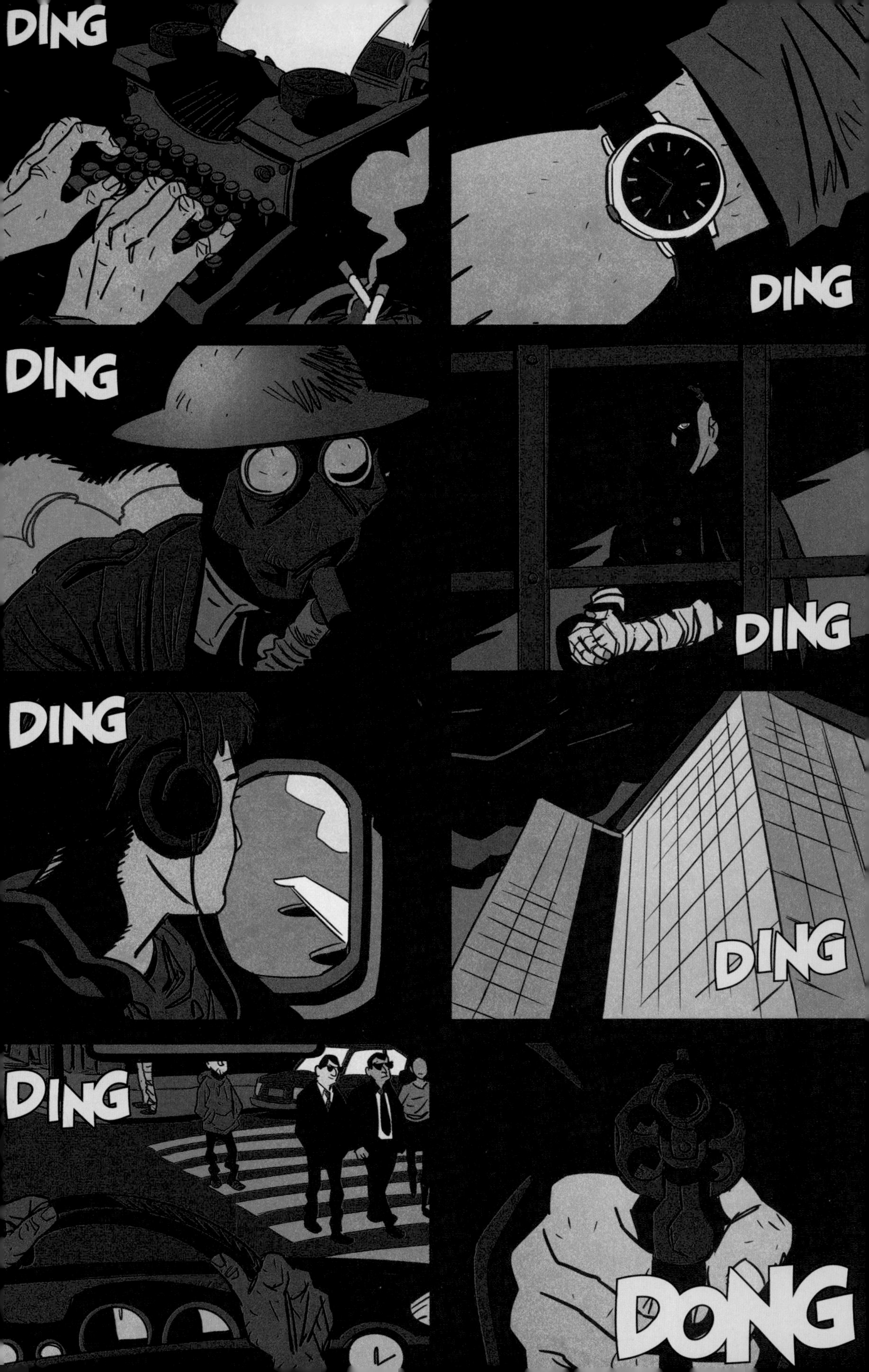
DING
DING
DING
DING
DING
DING
DING
DONG

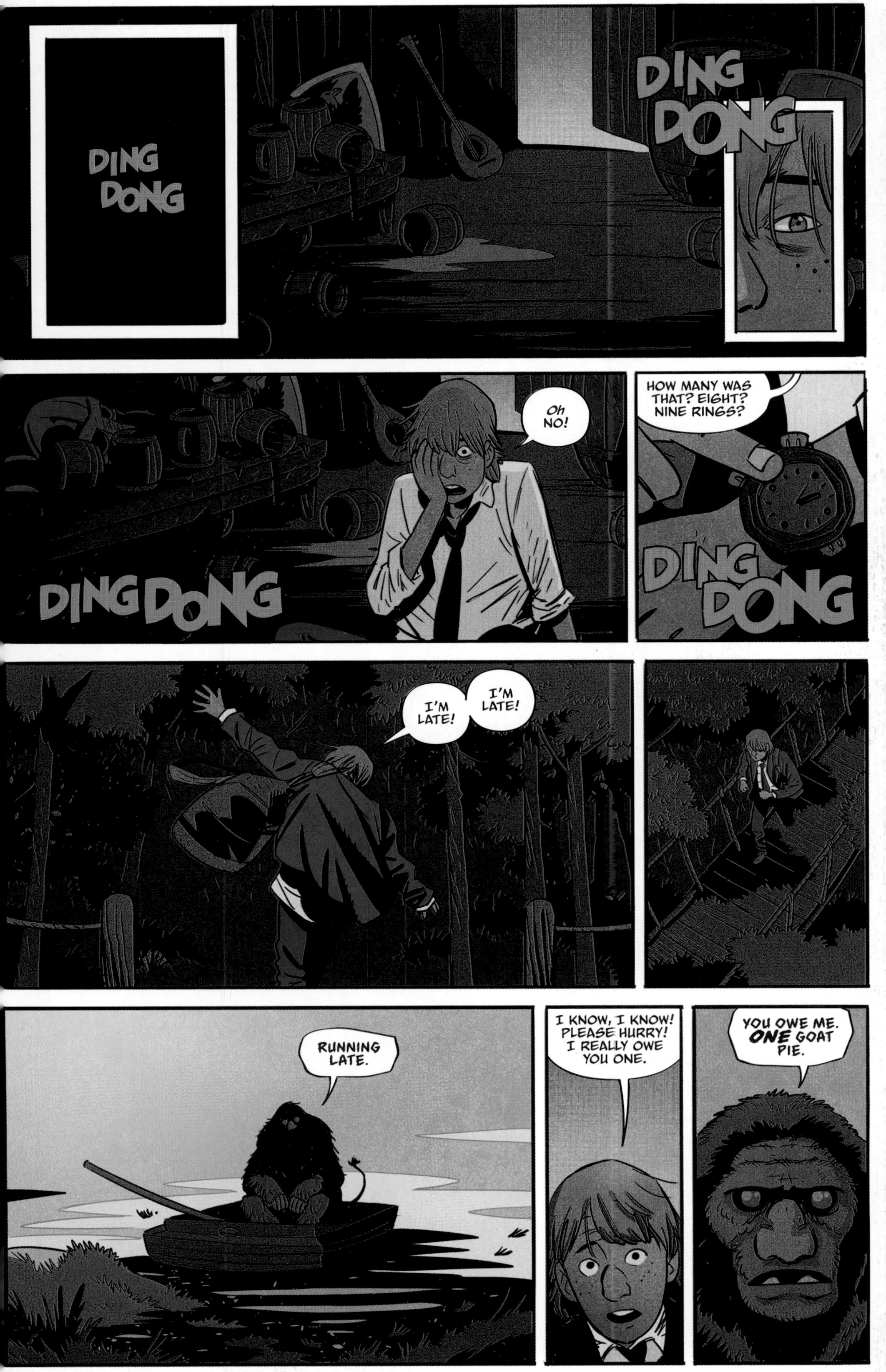
DING DONG
DING DONG
Oh NO!
DING DONG
HOW MANY WAS THAT? EIGHT? NINE RINGS?
DING DONG
I'M LATE!
I'M LATE!
RUNNING LATE.
I KNOW, I KNOW! PLEASE HURRY! I REALLY OWE YOU ONE.
YOU OWE ME. ONE GOAT PIE.

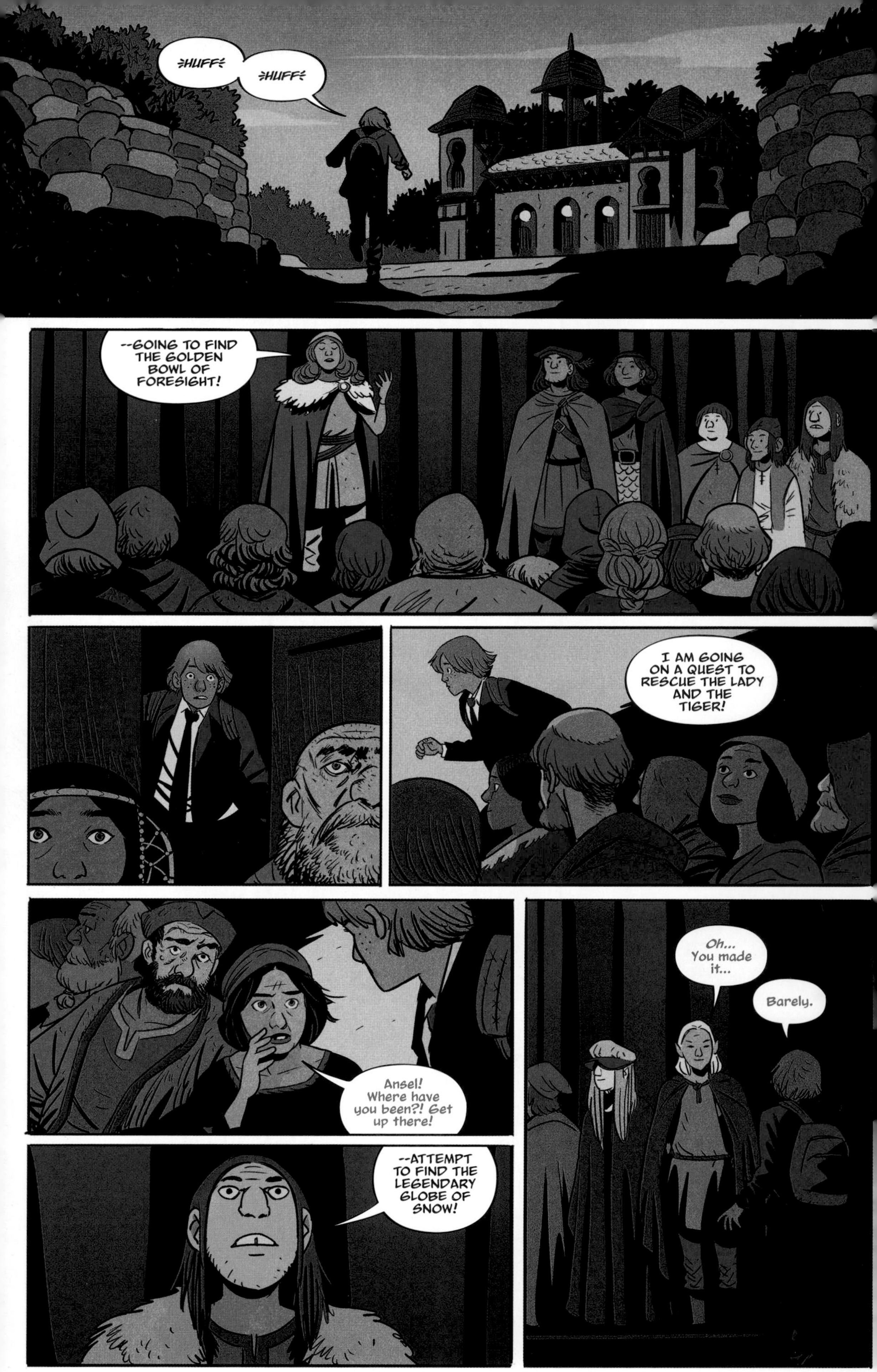
HUFF
HUFF
--GOING TO FIND THE GOLDEN BOWL OF FORESIGHT!
I AM GOING ON A QUEST TO RESCUE THE LADY AND THE TIGER!
Ansel! Where have you been?! Get up there!
--ATTEMPT TO FIND THE LEGENDARY GLOBE OF SNOW!
Oh... You made it...
Barely.

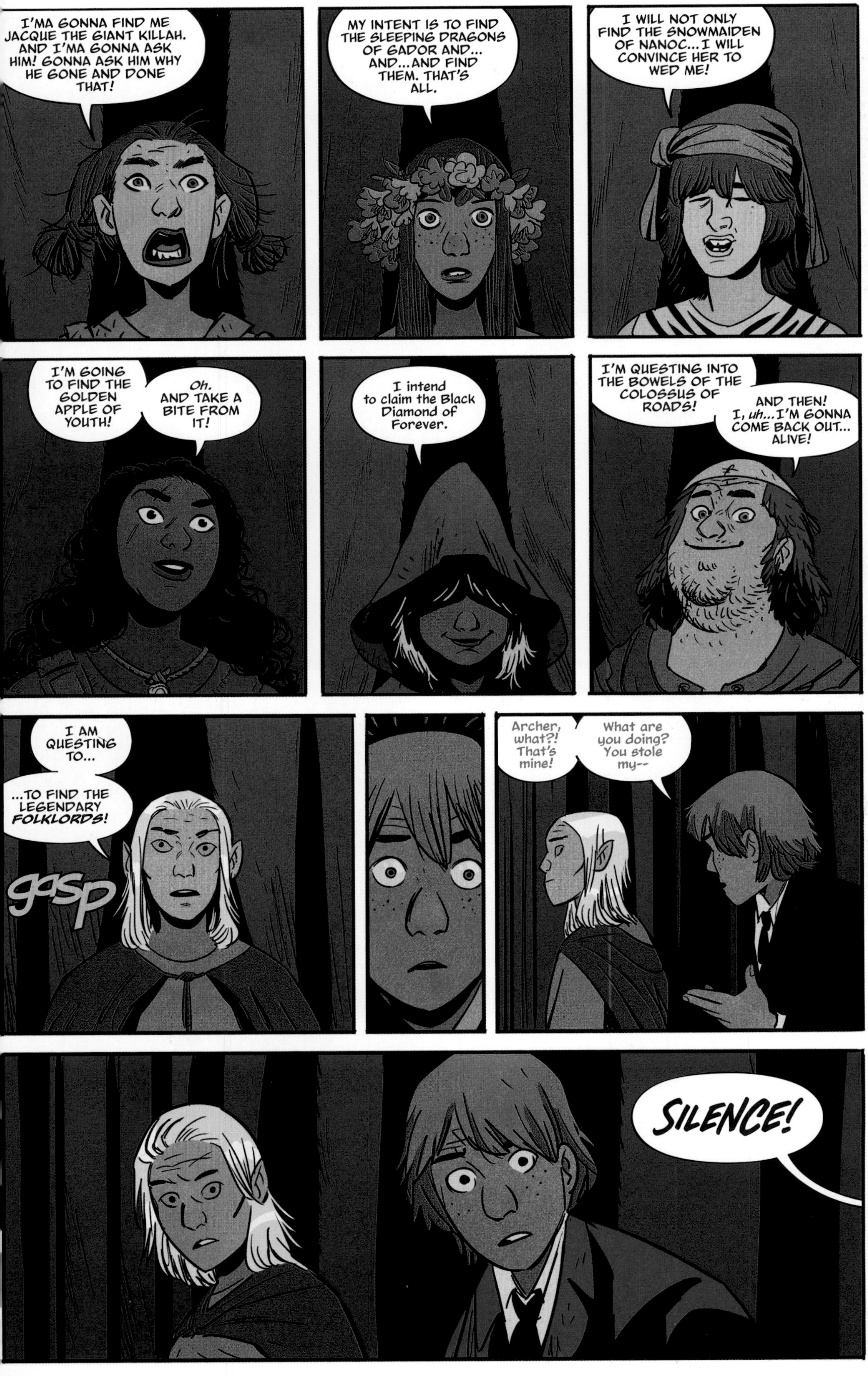
I'MA GONNA FIND ME JACQUE THE GIANT KILLAH. AND I'MA GONNA ASK HIM! GONNA ASK HIM WHY HE GONE AND DONE THAT!
MY INTENT IS TO FIND THE SLEEPING DRAGONS OF GADOR AND... AND...AND FIND THEM. THAT'S ALL.
I WILL NOT ONLY FIND THE SNOWMAIDEN OF NANOC...I WILL CONVINCE HER TO WED ME!
I'M GOING TO FIND THE GOLDEN APPLE OF YOUTH!
Oh. AND TAKE A BITE FROM IT!
I intend to claim the Black Diamond of Forever.
I'M QUESTING INTO THE BOWELS OF THE COLOSSUS OF ROADS!
AND THEN! I, uh... I'M GONNA COME BACK OUT... ALIVE!
I AM QUESTING TO...
...TO FIND THE LEGENDARY FOLKLORDS!
gasp
Archer, what?! That's mine!
What are you doing? You stole my--
SILENCE!

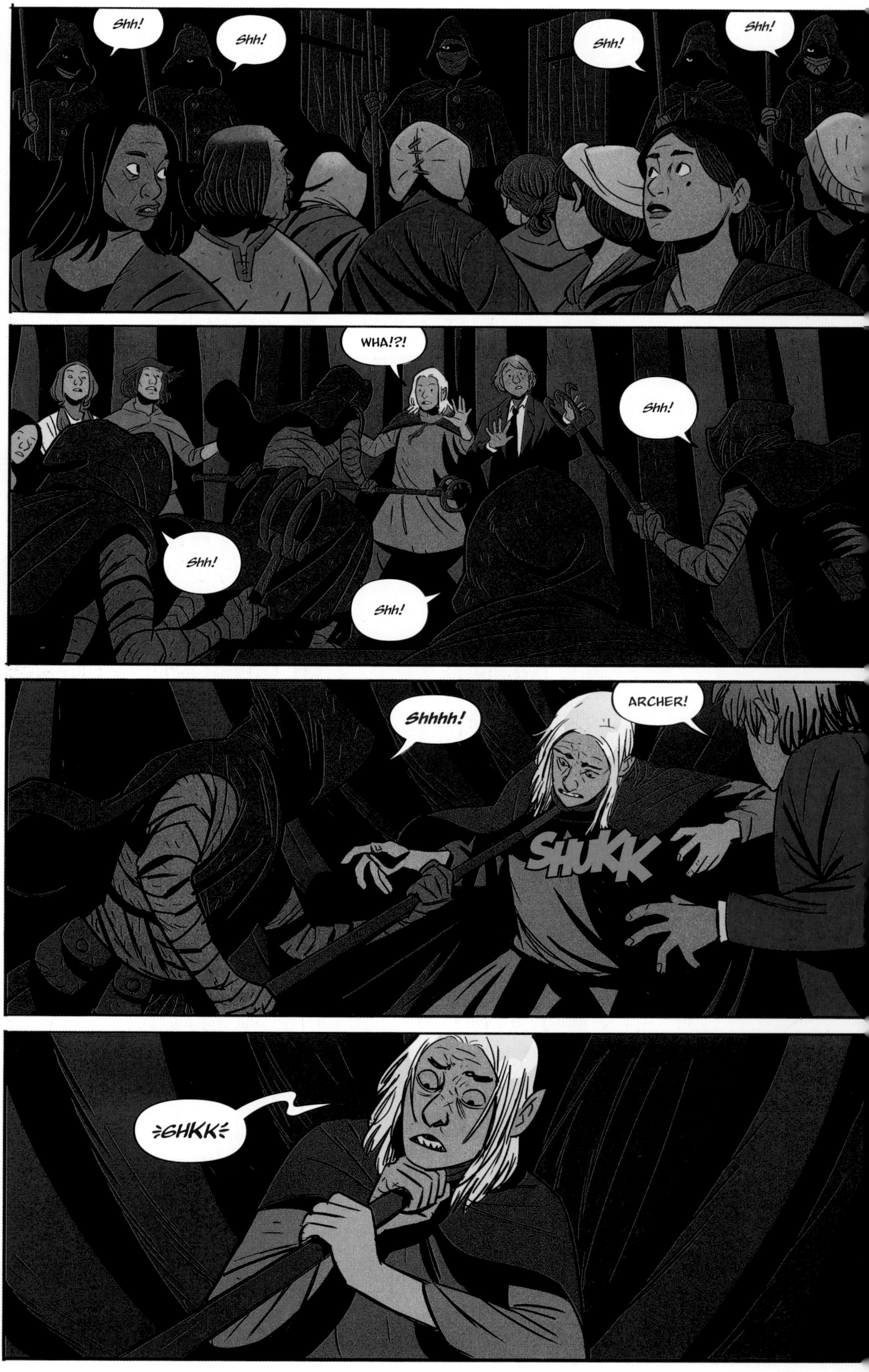
Shh!
Shh!
Shh!
Shh!
WHA!?!
Shh!
Shh!
Shh!
Shhhh!
ARCHER!
SHUKK
GHKK

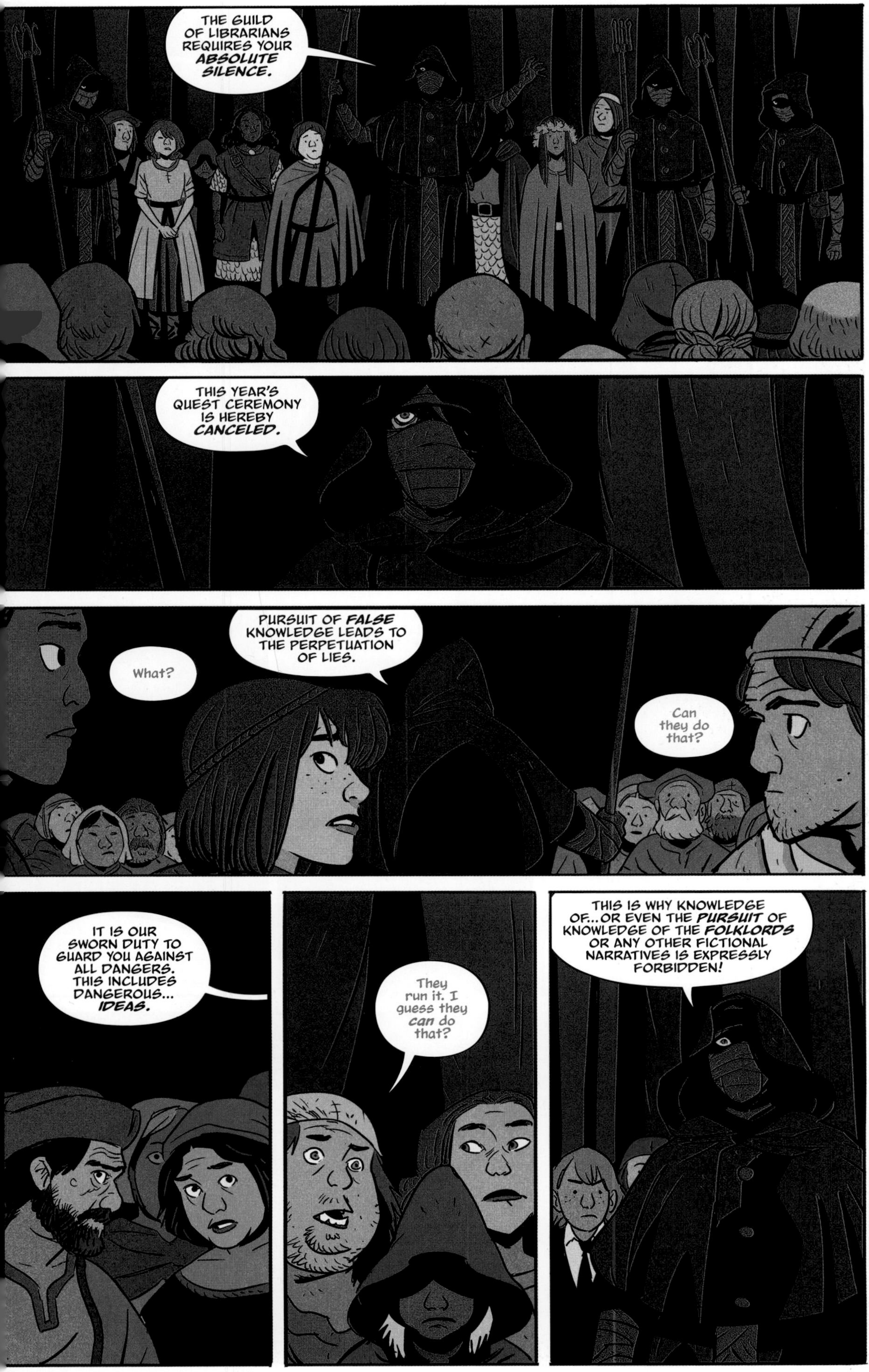
THE GUILD OF LIBRARIANS REQUIRES YOUR ABSOLUTE SILENCE.
THIS YEAR'S QUEST CEREMONY IS HEREBY CANCELED.
What?
PURSUIT OF FALSE KNOWLEDGE LEADS TO THE PERPETUATION OF LIES.
Can they do that?
IT IS OUR SWORN DUTY TO GUARD YOU AGAINST ALL DANGERS. THIS INCLUDES DANGEROUS... IDEAS.
They run it. I guess they can do that?
THIS IS WHY KNOWLEDGE OF... OR EVEN THE PURSUIT OF KNOWLEDGE OF THE FOLKLORDS OR ANY OTHER FICTIONAL NARRATIVES IS EXPRESSLY FORBIDDEN!

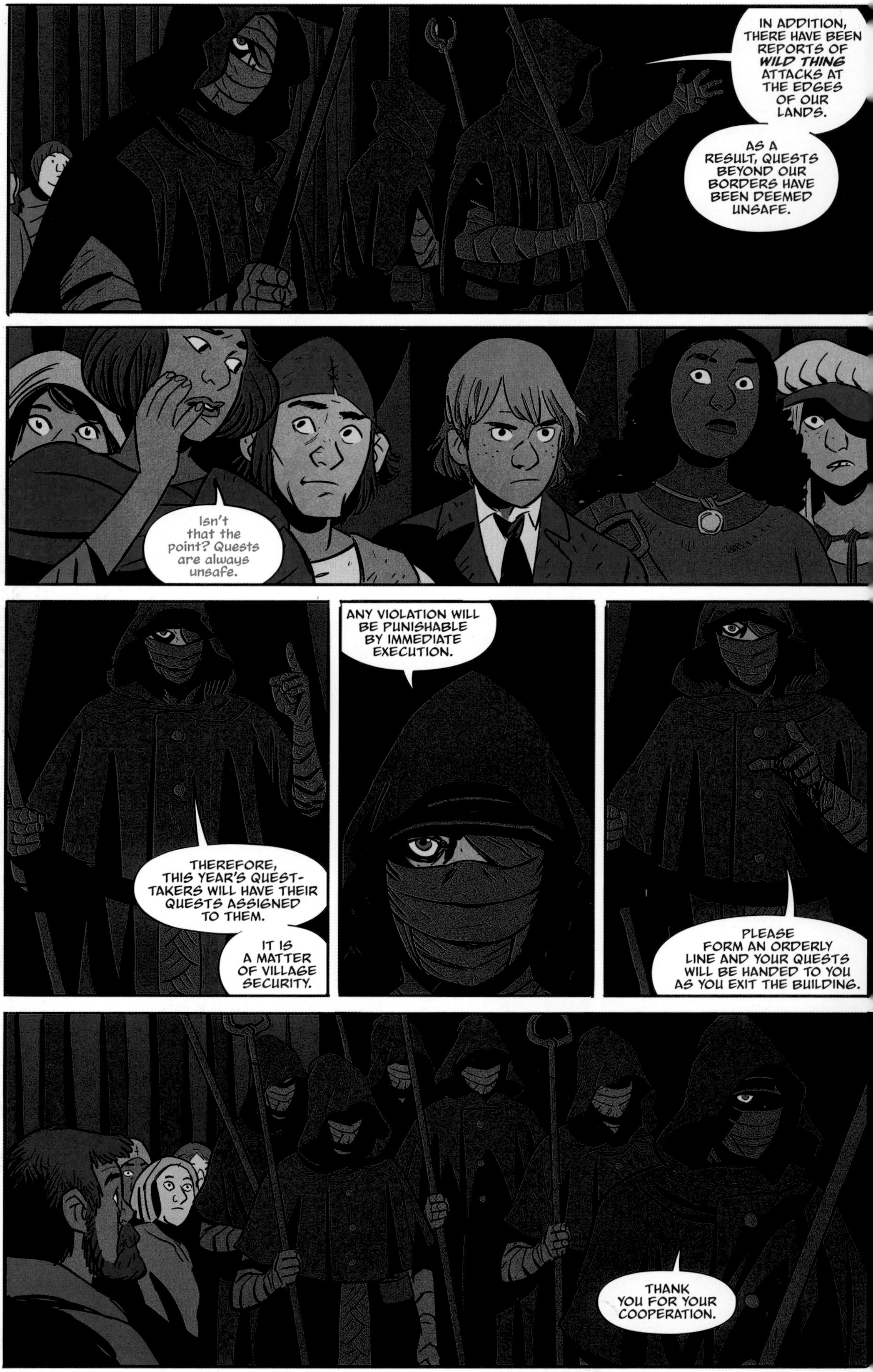
IN ADDITION, THERE HAVE BEEN REPORTS OF *WILD THING* ATTACKS AT THE EDGES OF OUR LANDS.
AS A RESULT, QUESTS BEYOND OUR BORDERS HAVE BEEN DEEMED UNSAFE.
Isn't that the point? Quests are always unsafe.
THEREFORE, THIS YEAR'S QUEST-TAKERS WILL HAVE THEIR QUESTS ASSIGNED TO THEM.
IT IS A MATTER OF VILLAGE SECURITY.
ANY VIOLATION WILL BE PUNISHABLE BY IMMEDIATE EXECUTION.
PLEASE FORM AN ORDERLY LINE AND YOUR QUESTS WILL BE HANDED TO YOU AS YOU EXIT THE BUILDING.
THANK YOU FOR YOUR COOPERATION.

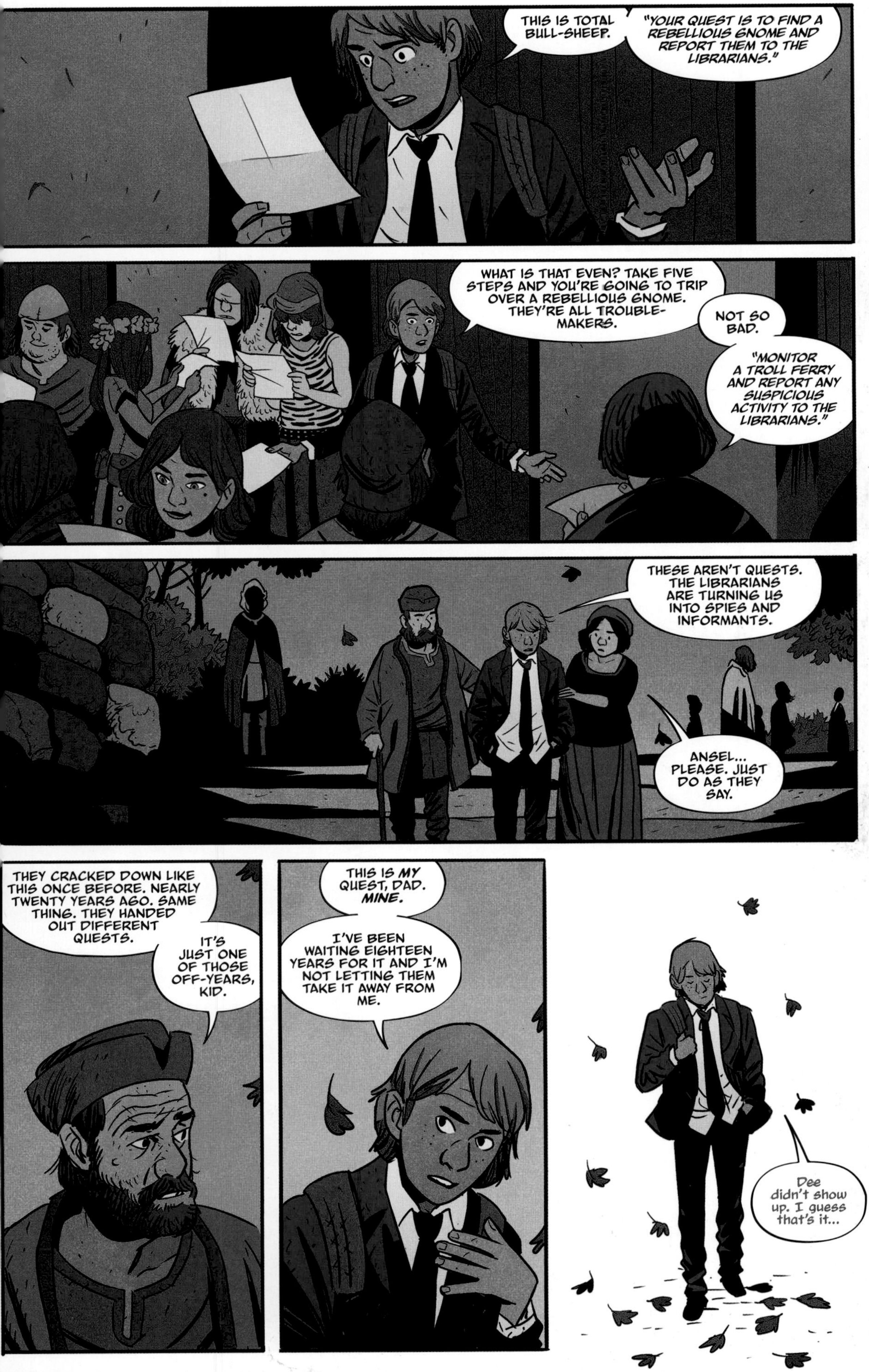
THIS IS TOTAL BULL-SHEEP.
"YOUR QUEST IS TO FIND A REBELLIOUS GNOME AND REPORT THEM TO THE LIBRARIANS."
WHAT IS THAT EVEN? TAKE FIVE STEPS AND YOU'RE GOING TO TRIP OVER A REBELLIOUS GNOME. THEY'RE ALL TROUBLE-MAKERS.
NOT SO BAD.
"MONITOR A TROLL FERRY AND REPORT ANY SUSPICIOUS ACTIVITY TO THE LIBRARIANS."
THESE AREN'T QUESTS. THE LIBRARIANS ARE TURNING US INTO SPIES AND INFORMANTS.
ANSEL... PLEASE. JUST DO AS THEY SAY.
THEY CRACKED DOWN LIKE THIS ONCE BEFORE. NEARLY TWENTY YEARS AGO. SAME THING. THEY HANDED OUT DIFFERENT QUESTS.
IT'S JUST ONE OF THOSE OFF-YEARS, KID.
THIS IS *MY* QUEST, DAD. *MINE.*
I'VE BEEN WAITING EIGHTEEN YEARS FOR IT AND I'M NOT LETTING THEM TAKE IT AWAY FROM ME.
Dee didn't show up. I guess that's it...

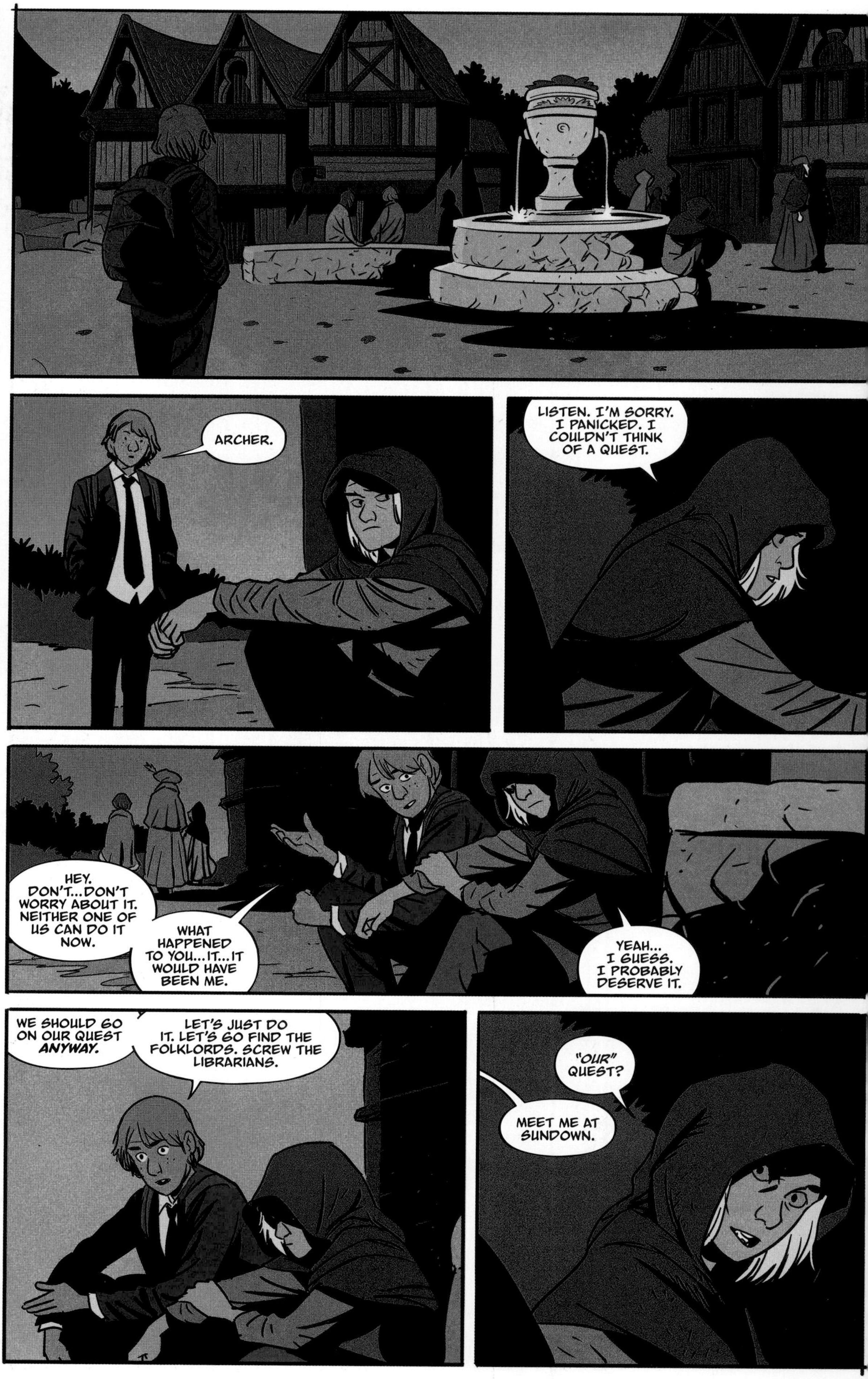
ARCHER.
LISTEN. I'M SORRY. I PANICKED. I COULDN'T THINK OF A QUEST.
HEY. DON'T...DON'T WORRY ABOUT IT. NEITHER ONE OF US CAN DO IT NOW.
WHAT HAPPENED TO YOU...IT...IT WOULD HAVE BEEN ME.
YEAH... I GUESS. I PROBABLY DESERVE IT.
WE SHOULD GO ON OUR QUEST *ANYWAY.*
LET'S JUST DO IT. LET'S GO FIND THE FOLKLORDS. SCREW THE LIBRARIANS.
"OUR" QUEST?
MEET ME AT SUNDOWN.

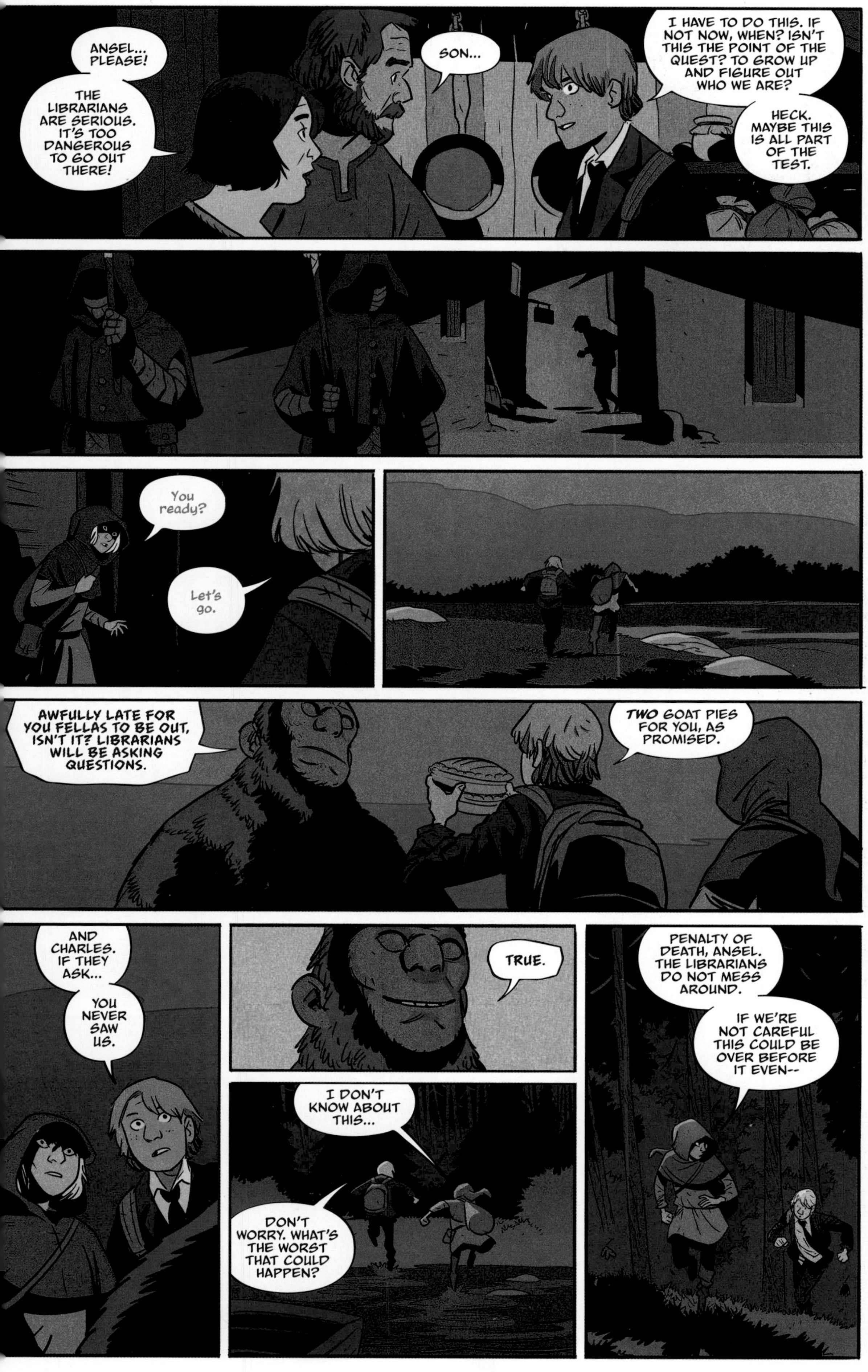
ANSEL... PLEASE!
THE LIBRARIANS ARE SERIOUS. IT'S TOO DANGEROUS TO GO OUT THERE!
SON...
I HAVE TO DO THIS. IF NOT NOW, WHEN? ISN'T THIS THE POINT OF THE QUEST? TO GROW UP AND FIGURE OUT WHO WE ARE?
HECK. MAYBE THIS IS ALL PART OF THE TEST.
You ready?
Let's go.
AWFULLY LATE FOR YOU FELLAS TO BE OUT, ISN'T IT? LIBRARIANS WILL BE ASKING QUESTIONS.
TWO GOAT PIES FOR YOU, AS PROMISED.
AND CHARLES. IF THEY ASK...
YOU NEVER SAW US.
TRUE.
I DON'T KNOW ABOUT THIS...
DON'T WORRY. WHAT'S THE WORST THAT COULD HAPPEN?
PENALTY OF DEATH, ANSEL. THE LIBRARIANS DO NOT MESS AROUND.
IF WE'RE NOT CAREFUL THIS COULD BE OVER BEFORE IT EVEN--

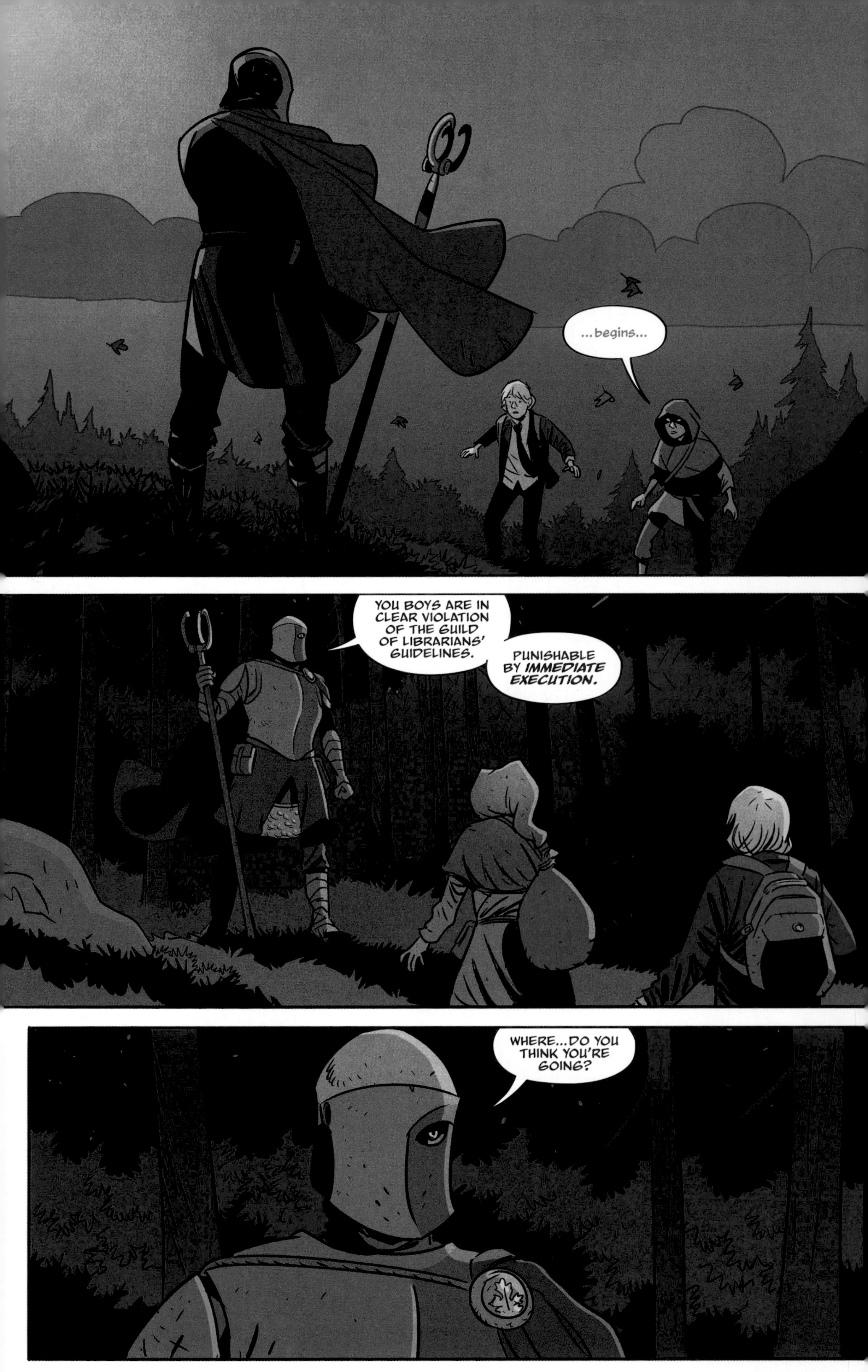
...begins...
YOU BOYS ARE IN CLEAR VIOLATION OF THE GUILD OF LIBRARIANS' GUIDELINES.
PUNISHABLE BY IMMEDIATE EXECUTION.
WHERE...DO YOU THINK YOU'RE GOING?

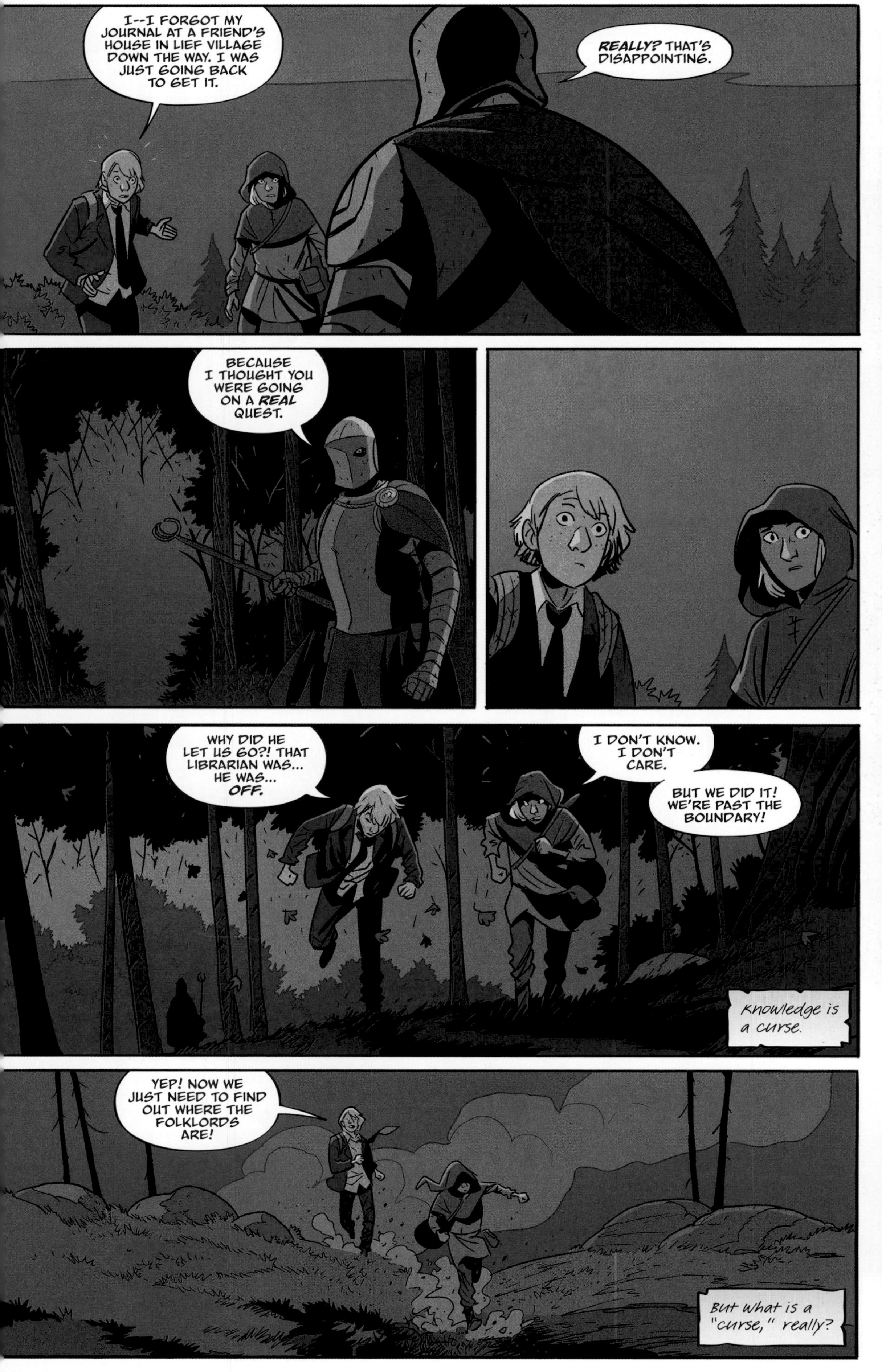

I--I FORGOT MY JOURNAL AT A FRIEND'S HOUSE IN LIEF VILLAGE DOWN THE WAY. I WAS JUST GOING BACK TO GET IT.
REALLY? THAT'S DISAPPOINTING.
BECAUSE I THOUGHT YOU WERE GOING ON A REAL QUEST.
WHY DID HE LET US GO?! THAT LIBRARIAN WAS... HE WAS... OFF.
I DON'T KNOW. I DON'T CARE.
BUT WE DID IT! WE'RE PAST THE BOUNDARY!
Knowledge is a curse.
YEP! NOW WE JUST NEED TO FIND OUT WHERE THE FOLKLORDS ARE!
But what is a "curse," really?

WAIT, WHAT?! YOU DON'T KNOW WHERE THE FOLKLORDS ARE?
NO. THAT'S THE FUN PART! THE JOURNEY IS THE QUEST!
Literally...literarily? A curse is just a word.
THIS IS OUR CHANCE. WE'RE GOING TO PROVE THE FOLKLORDS ARE REAL.
WE'RE GOING TO WRITE OURSELVES INTO LEGEND.
And what power do words really have, anyway?
To be continued...

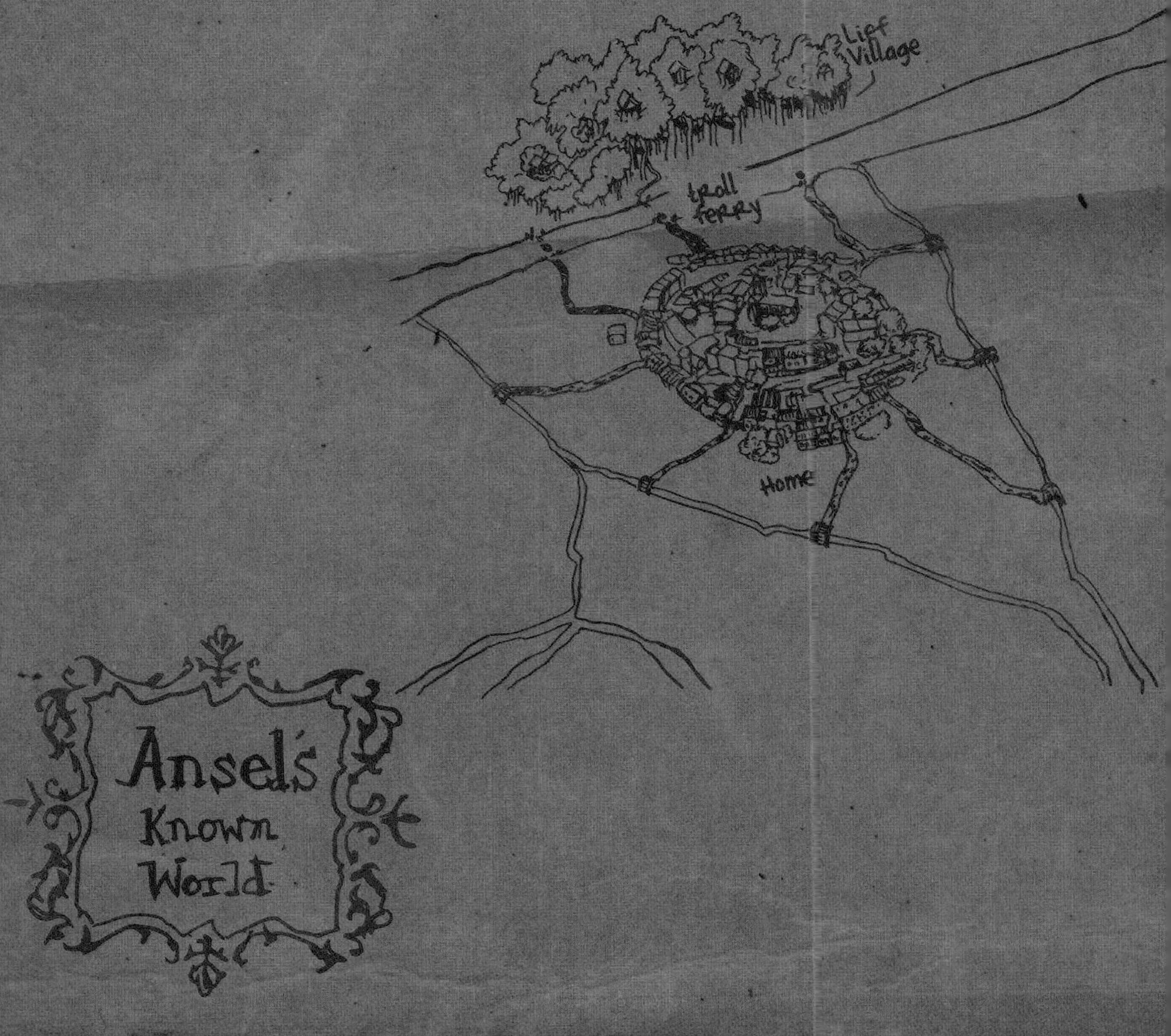
Lief Village
troll ferry
Home
Ansel's Known World

CHAPTER
TWO

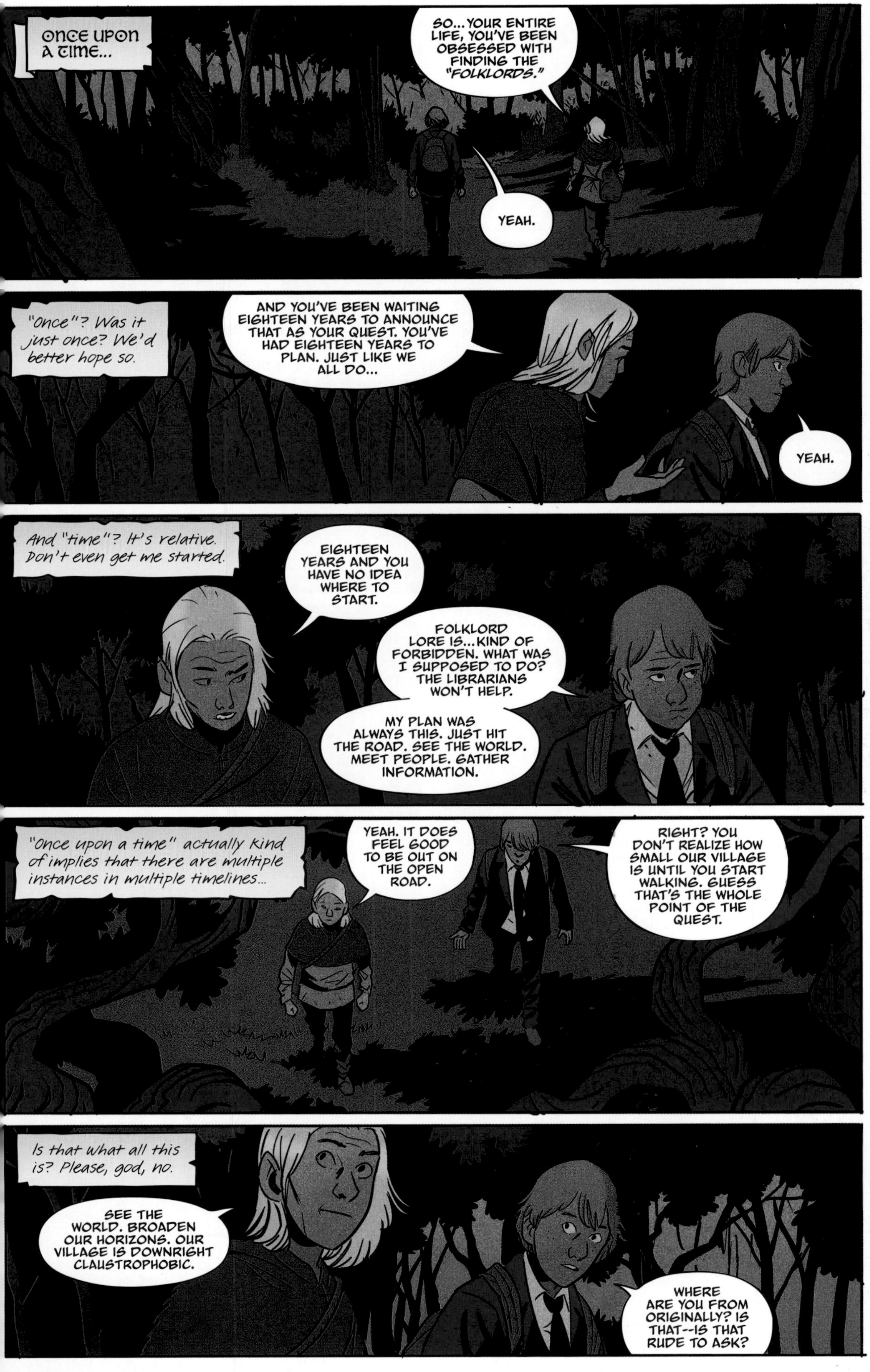

Once upon a time...
SO... YOUR ENTIRE LIFE, YOU'VE BEEN OBSESSED WITH FINDING THE "FOLKLORDS."
YEAH.
"Once"? Was it just once? We'd better hope so.
AND YOU'VE BEEN WAITING EIGHTEEN YEARS TO ANNOUNCE THAT AS YOUR QUEST. YOU'VE HAD EIGHTEEN YEARS TO PLAN. JUST LIKE WE ALL DO...
YEAH.
And "time"? It's relative. Don't even get me started.
EIGHTEEN YEARS AND YOU HAVE NO IDEA WHERE TO START.
FOLKLORD LORE IS...KIND OF FORBIDDEN. WHAT WAS I SUPPOSED TO DO? THE LIBRARIANS WON'T HELP.
MY PLAN WAS ALWAYS THIS. JUST HIT THE ROAD. SEE THE WORLD. MEET PEOPLE. GATHER INFORMATION.
"Once upon a time" actually kind of implies that there are multiple instances in multiple timelines...
YEAH. IT DOES FEEL GOOD TO BE OUT ON THE OPEN ROAD.
RIGHT? YOU DON'T REALIZE HOW SMALL OUR VILLAGE IS UNTIL YOU START WALKING. GUESS THAT'S THE WHOLE POINT OF THE QUEST.
Is that what all this is? Please, god, no.
SEE THE WORLD. BROADEN OUR HORIZONS. OUR VILLAGE IS DOWNRIGHT CLAUSTROPHOBIC.
WHERE ARE YOU FROM ORIGINALLY? IS THAT--IS THAT RUDE TO ASK?

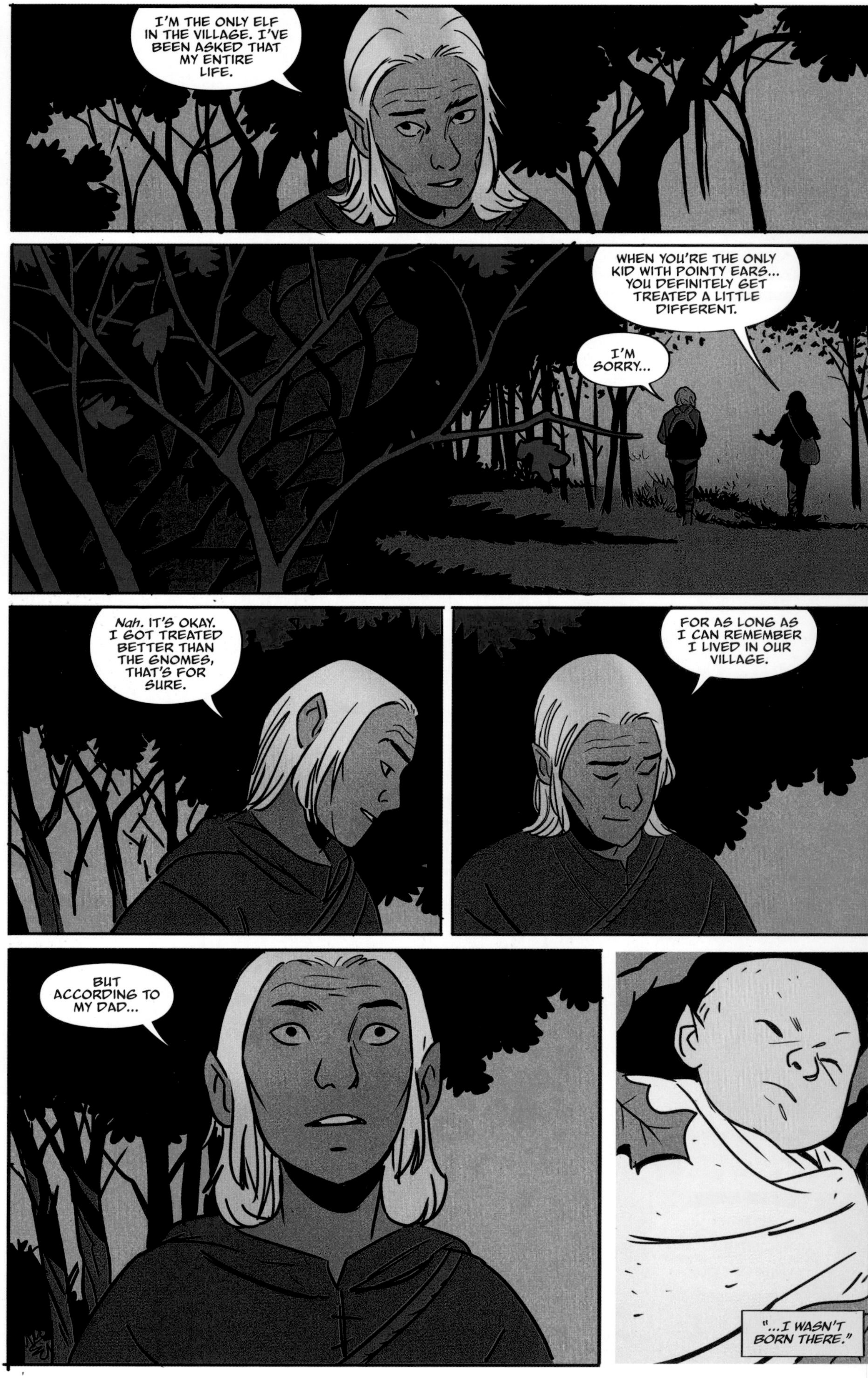
I'M THE ONLY ELF IN THE VILLAGE. I'VE BEEN ASKED THAT MY ENTIRE LIFE.
WHEN YOU'RE THE ONLY KID WITH POINTY EARS... YOU DEFINITELY GET TREATED A LITTLE DIFFERENT.
I'M SORRY...
Nah. IT'S OKAY. I GOT TREATED BETTER THAN THE GNOMES, THAT'S FOR SURE.
FOR AS LONG AS I CAN REMEMBER I LIVED IN OUR VILLAGE.
BUT ACCORDING TO MY DAD...
"...I WASN'T BORN THERE."

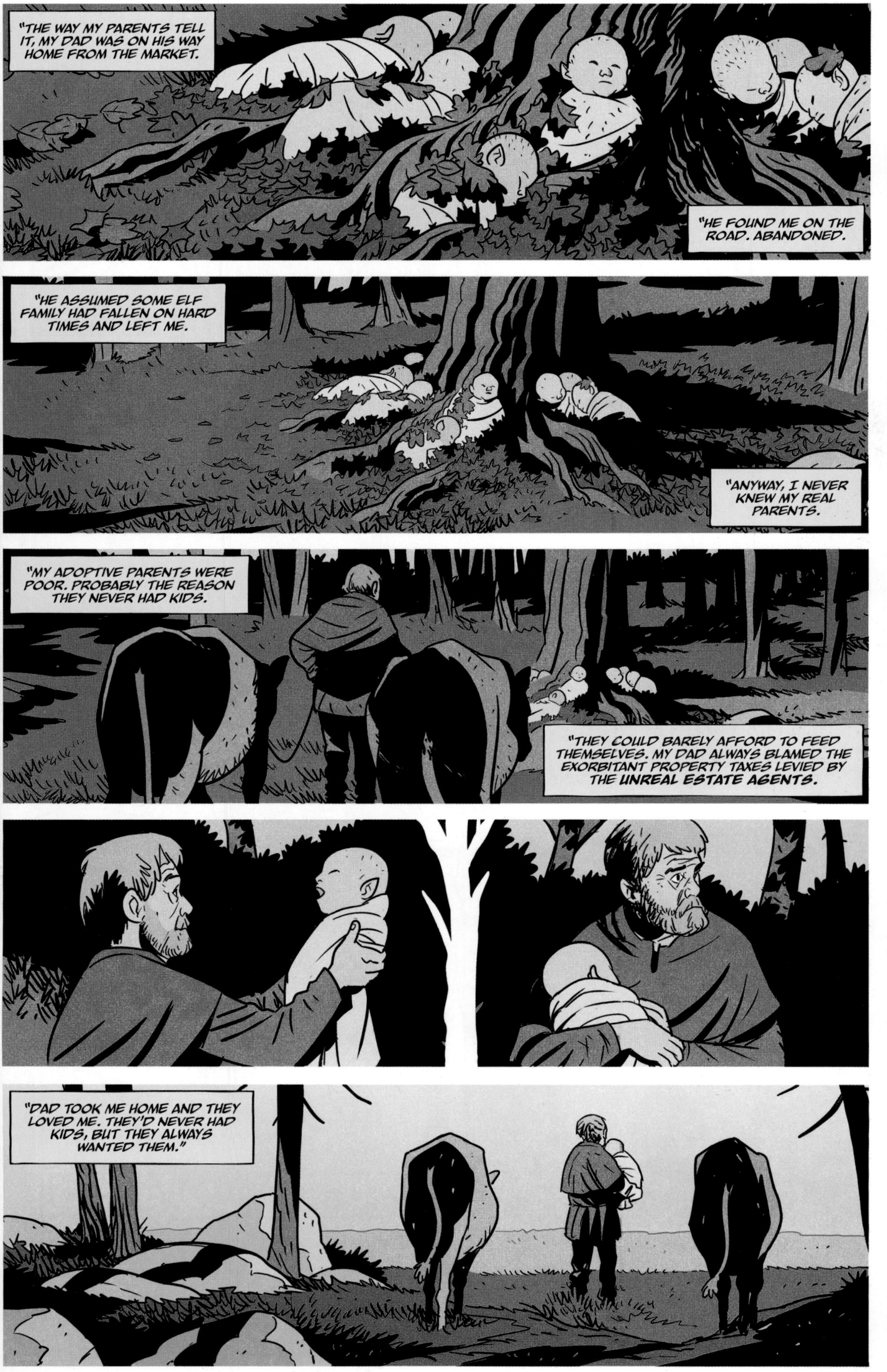
"THE WAY MY PARENTS TELL IT, MY DAD WAS ON HIS WAY HOME FROM THE MARKET.
"HE FOUND ME ON THE ROAD. ABANDONED.
"HE ASSUMED SOME ELF FAMILY HAD FALLEN ON HARD TIMES AND LEFT ME.
"ANYWAY, I NEVER KNEW MY REAL PARENTS.
"MY ADOPTIVE PARENTS WERE POOR. PROBABLY THE REASON THEY NEVER HAD KIDS.
"THEY COULD BARELY AFFORD TO FEED THEMSELVES. MY DAD ALWAYS BLAMED THE EXORBITANT PROPERTY TAXES LEVIED BY THE UNREAL ESTATE AGENTS.
"DAD TOOK ME HOME AND THEY LOVED ME. THEY'D NEVER HAD KIDS, BUT THEY ALWAYS WANTED THEM."

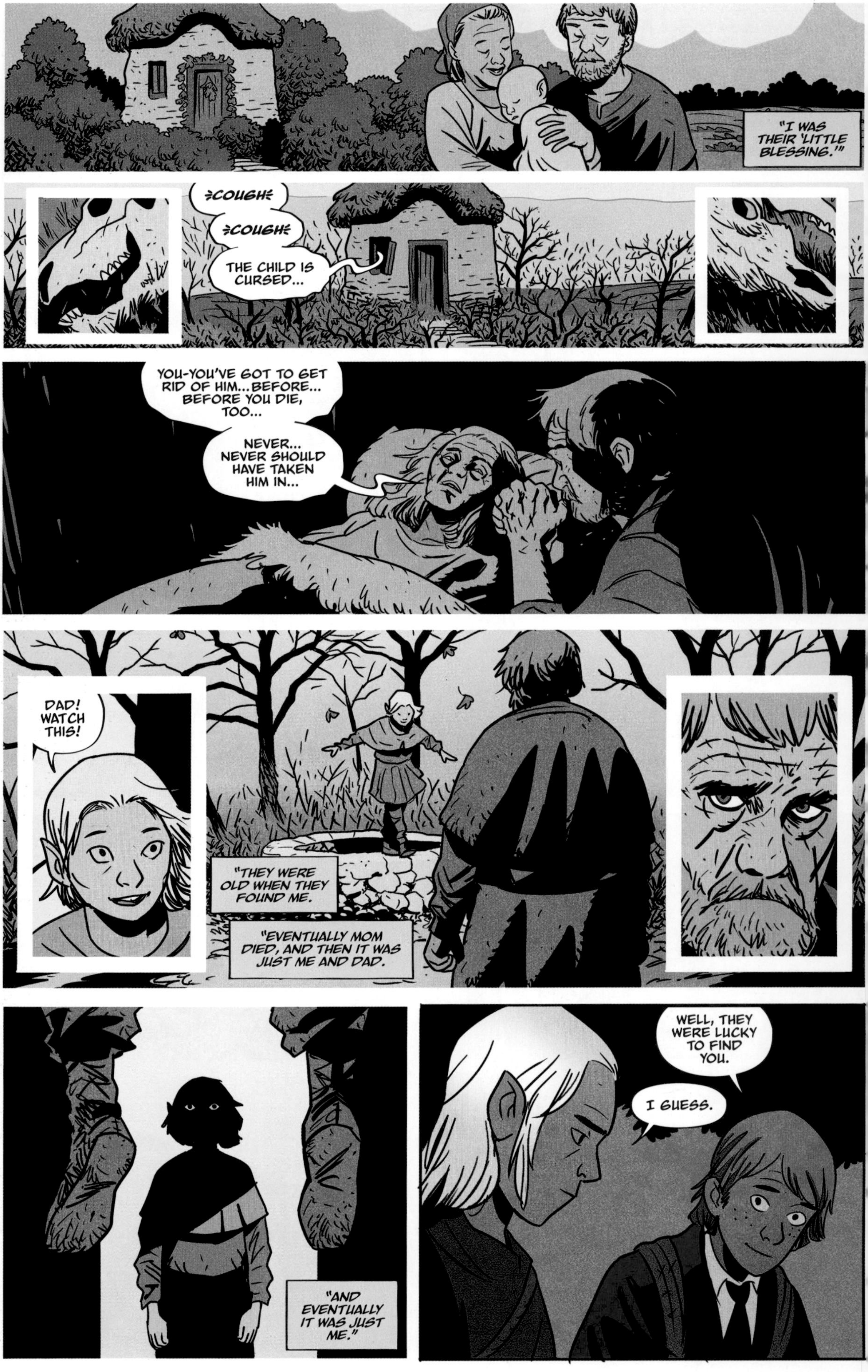
"I WAS THEIR 'LITTLE BLESSING.'"
COUGH
COUGH
THE CHILD IS CURSED...
YOU-YOU'VE GOT TO GET RID OF HIM...BEFORE... BEFORE YOU DIE, TOO...
NEVER... NEVER SHOULD HAVE TAKEN HIM IN...
DAD! WATCH THIS!
"THEY WERE OLD WHEN THEY FOUND ME.
"EVENTUALLY MOM DIED, AND THEN IT WAS JUST ME AND DAD.
"AND EVENTUALLY IT WAS JUST ME."
WELL, THEY WERE LUCKY TO FIND YOU.
I GUESS.

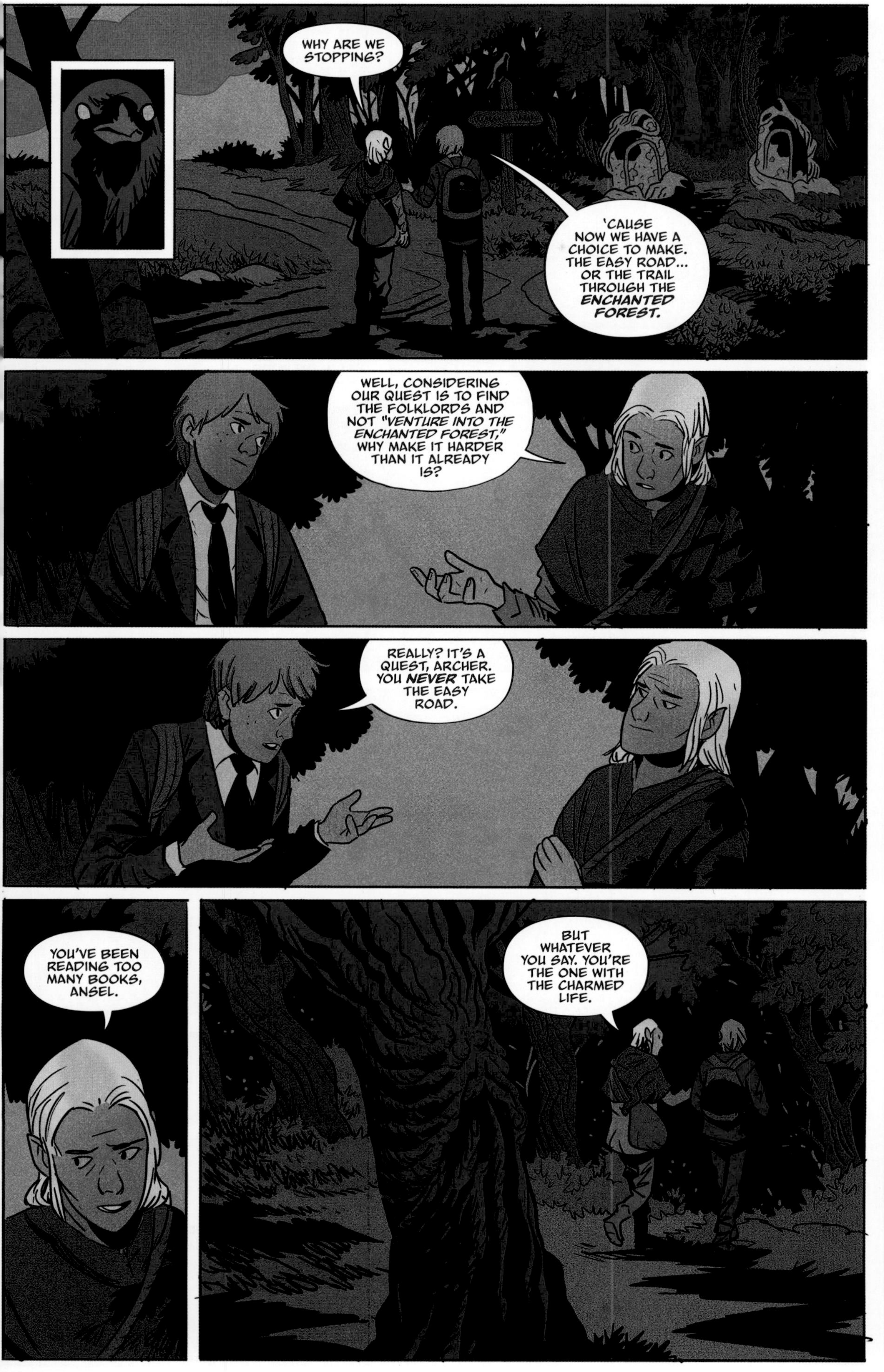
WHY ARE WE STOPPING?
'CAUSE NOW WE HAVE A CHOICE TO MAKE. THE EASY ROAD... OR THE TRAIL THROUGH THE *ENCHANTED FOREST.*
WELL, CONSIDERING OUR QUEST IS TO FIND THE FOLKLORDS AND NOT *"VENTURE INTO THE ENCHANTED FOREST,"* WHY MAKE IT HARDER THAN IT ALREADY IS?
REALLY? IT'S A QUEST, ARCHER. YOU ***NEVER*** TAKE THE EASY ROAD.
YOU'VE BEEN READING TOO MANY BOOKS, ANSEL.
BUT WHATEVER YOU SAY. YOU'RE THE ONE WITH THE CHARMED LIFE.

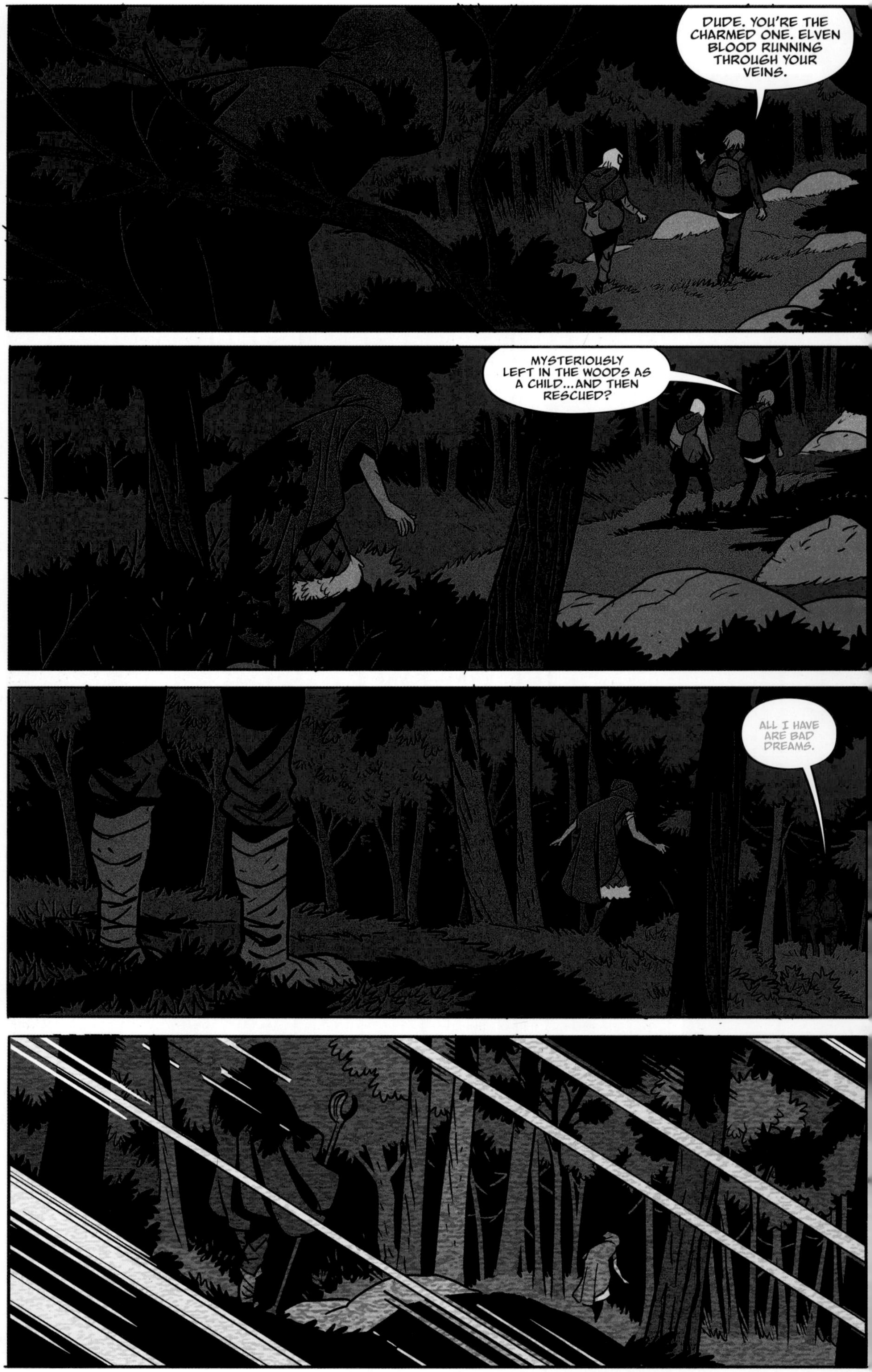
DUDE. YOU'RE THE CHARMED ONE. ELVEN BLOOD RUNNING THROUGH YOUR VEINS.
MYSTERIOUSLY LEFT IN THE WOODS AS A CHILD...AND THEN RESCUED?
ALL I HAVE ARE BAD DREAMS.

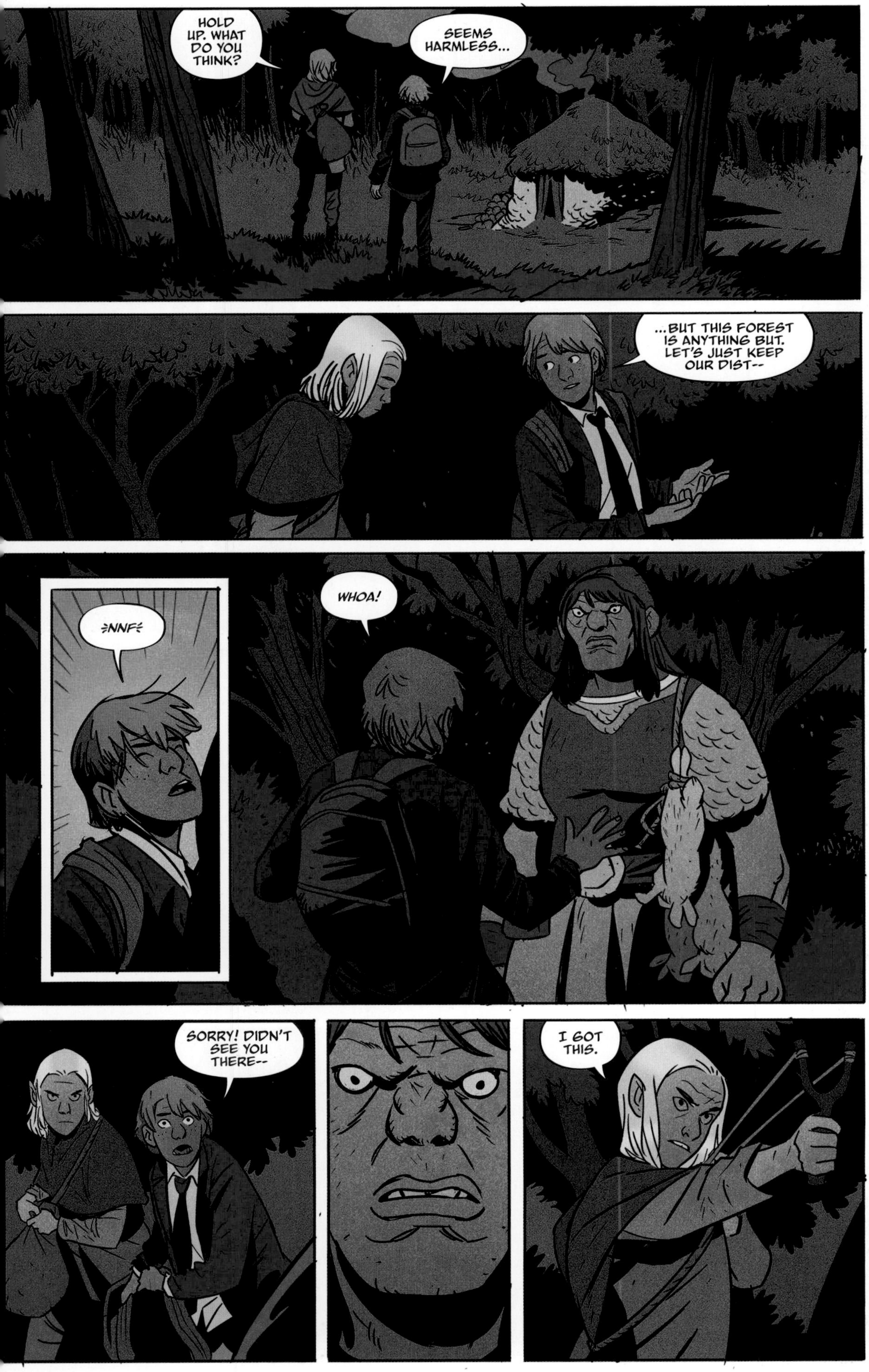
HOLD UP. WHAT DO YOU THINK?
SEEMS HARMLESS...
...BUT THIS FOREST IS ANYTHING BUT. LET'S JUST KEEP OUR DIST--
=NNF=
WHOA!
SORRY! DIDN'T SEE YOU THERE--
I GOT THIS.

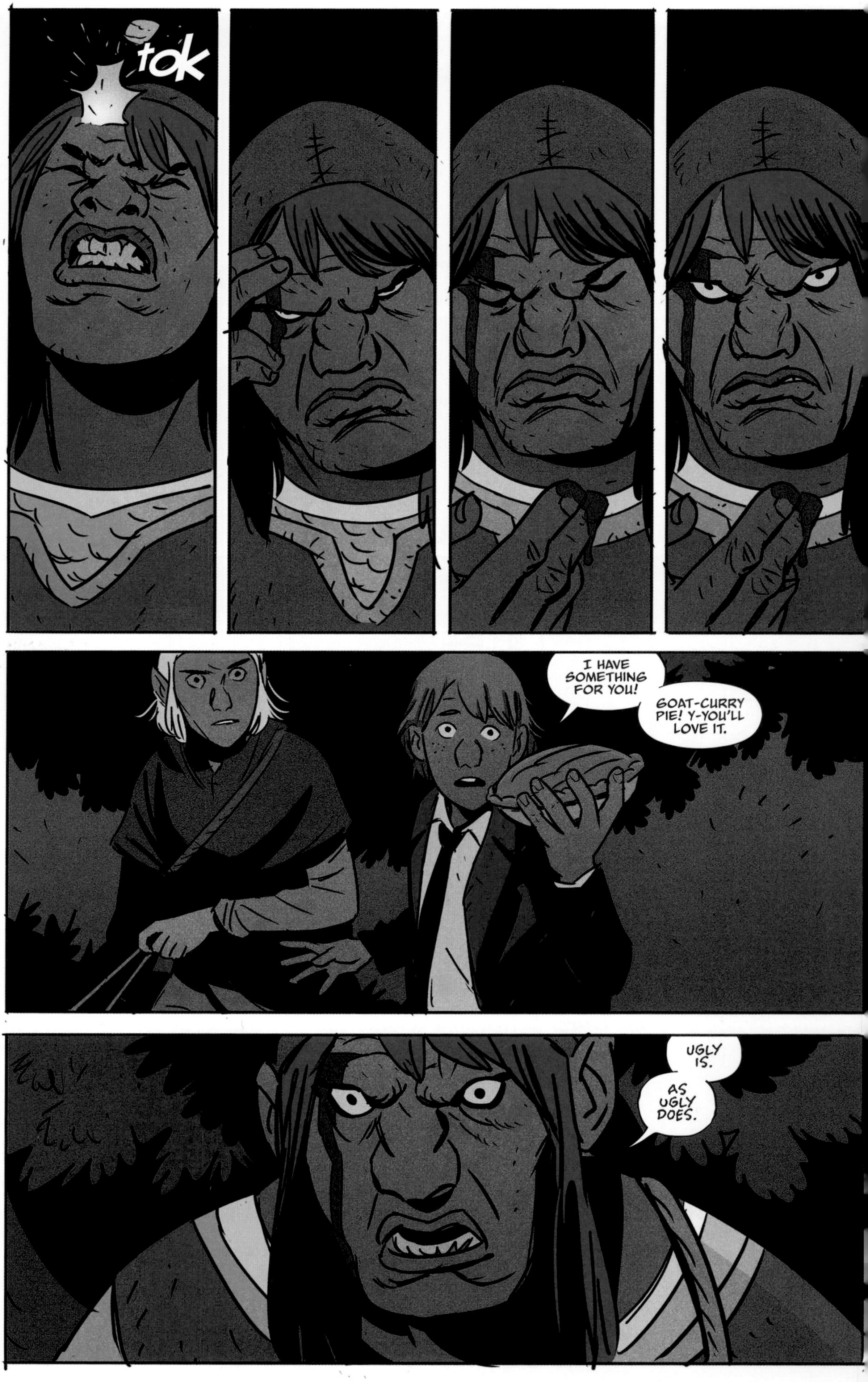
TOK
I HAVE SOMETHING FOR YOU!
GOAT-CURRY PIE! Y-YOU'LL LOVE IT.
UGLY IS.
AS UGLY DOES.

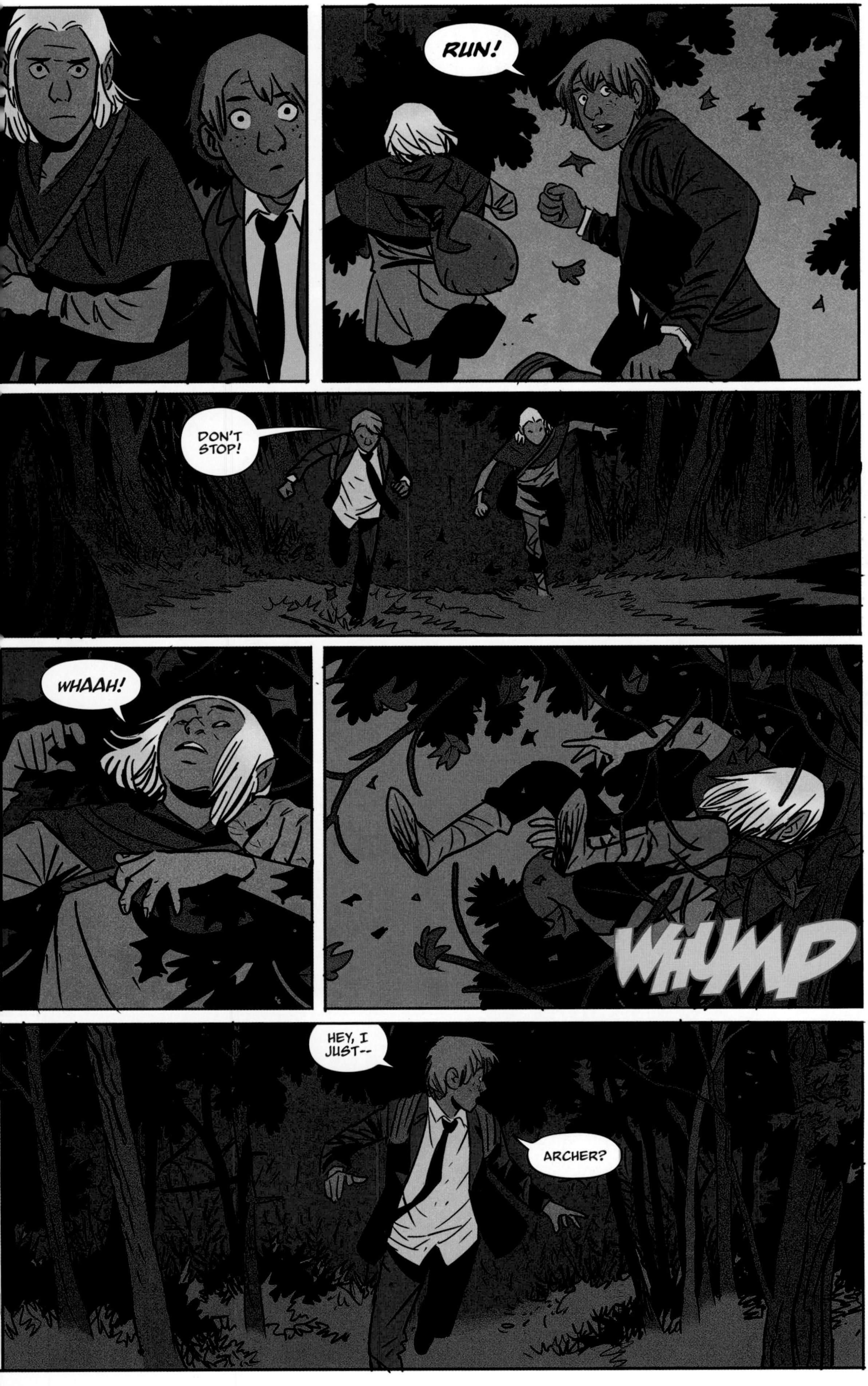
RUN!
DON'T STOP!
WHAAH!
WHUMP
HEY, I JUST--
ARCHER?

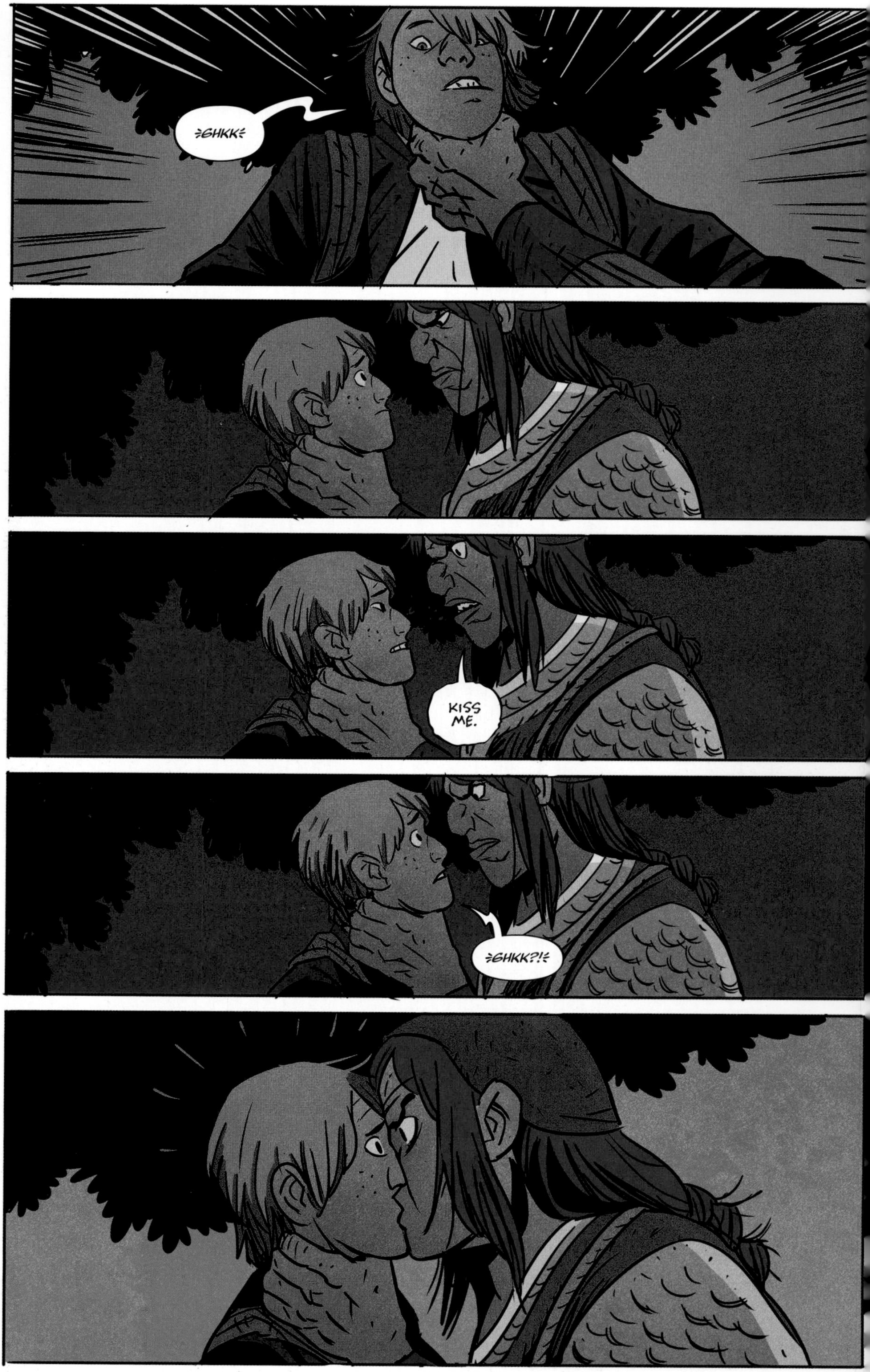

⚡GHKK⚡
KISS ME.
⚡GHKK?!⚡

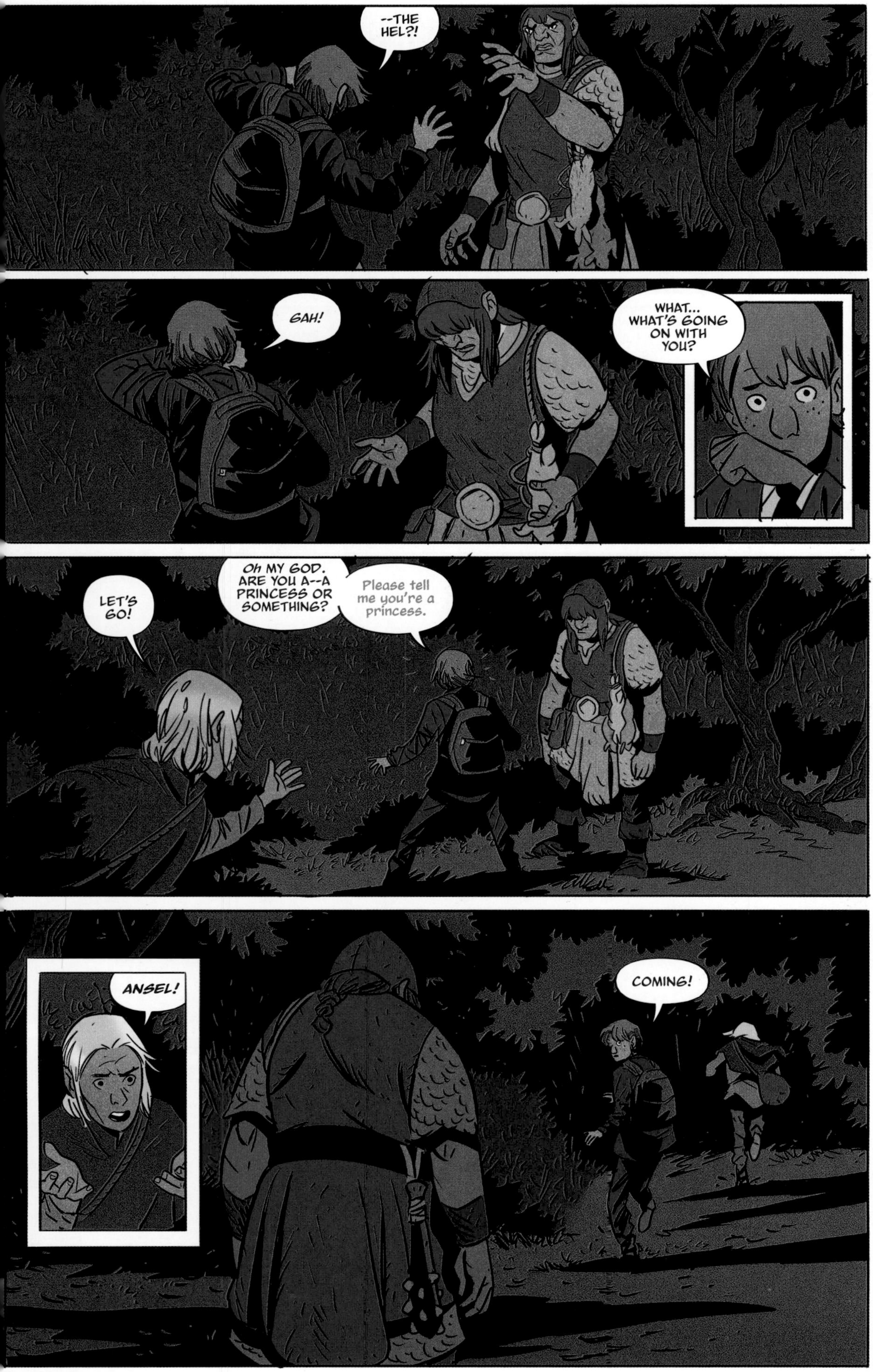
--THE HEL?!
GAH!
WHAT... WHAT'S GOING ON WITH YOU?
LET'S GO!
Oh MY GOD. ARE YOU A--A PRINCESS OR SOMETHING?
Please tell me you're a princess.
ANSEL!
COMING!

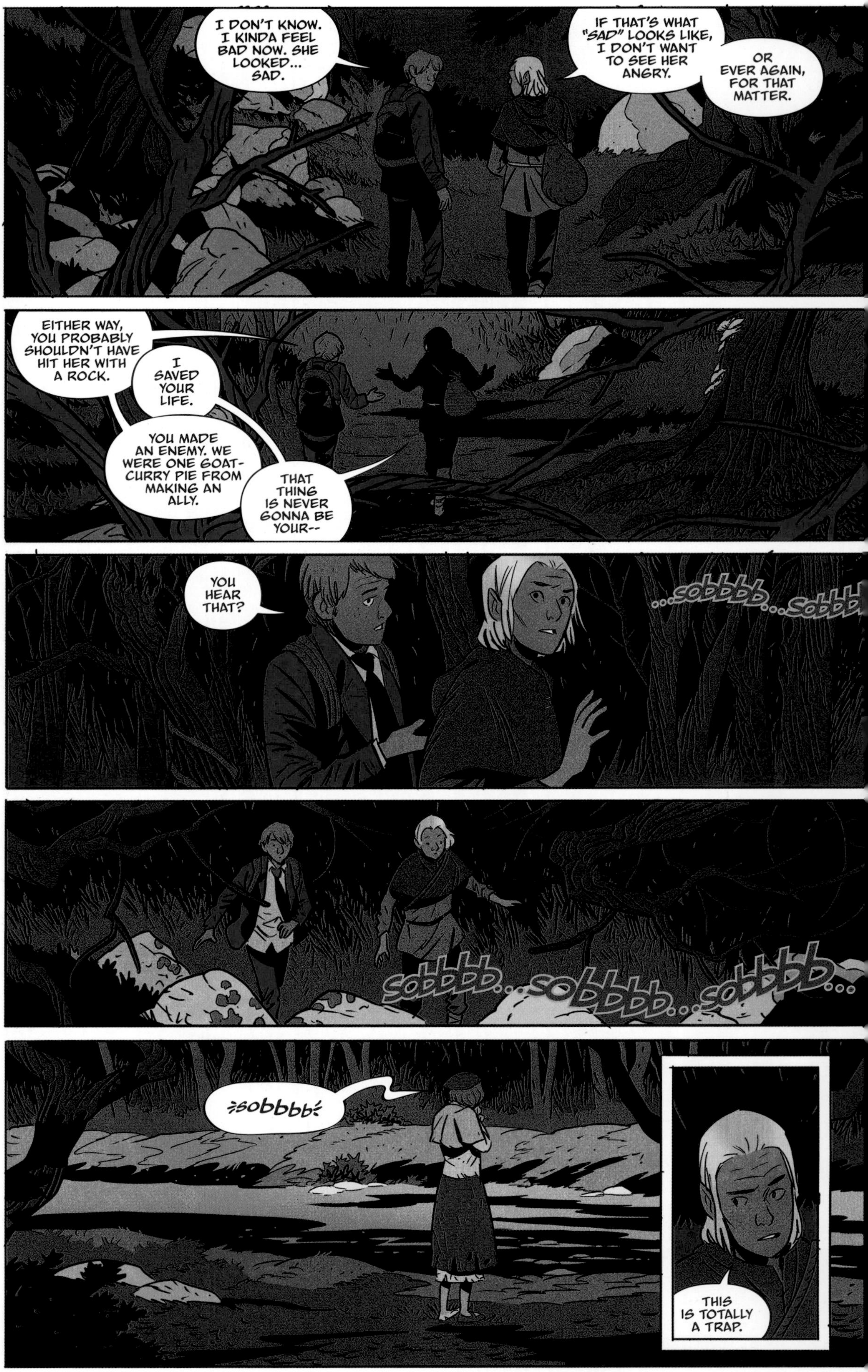
I DON'T KNOW. I KINDA FEEL BAD NOW. SHE LOOKED... SAD.
IF THAT'S WHAT "SAD" LOOKS LIKE, I DON'T WANT TO SEE HER ANGRY.
OR EVER AGAIN, FOR THAT MATTER.
EITHER WAY, YOU PROBABLY SHOULDN'T HAVE HIT HER WITH A ROCK.
I SAVED YOUR LIFE.
YOU MADE AN ENEMY. WE WERE ONE GOAT-CURRY PIE FROM MAKING AN ALLY.
THAT THING IS NEVER GONNA BE YOUR--
YOU HEAR THAT?
...SOBBBB...SOBBB
SOBBBB...SOBBBB...SOBBBB...
SOBBBB
THIS IS TOTALLY A TRAP.

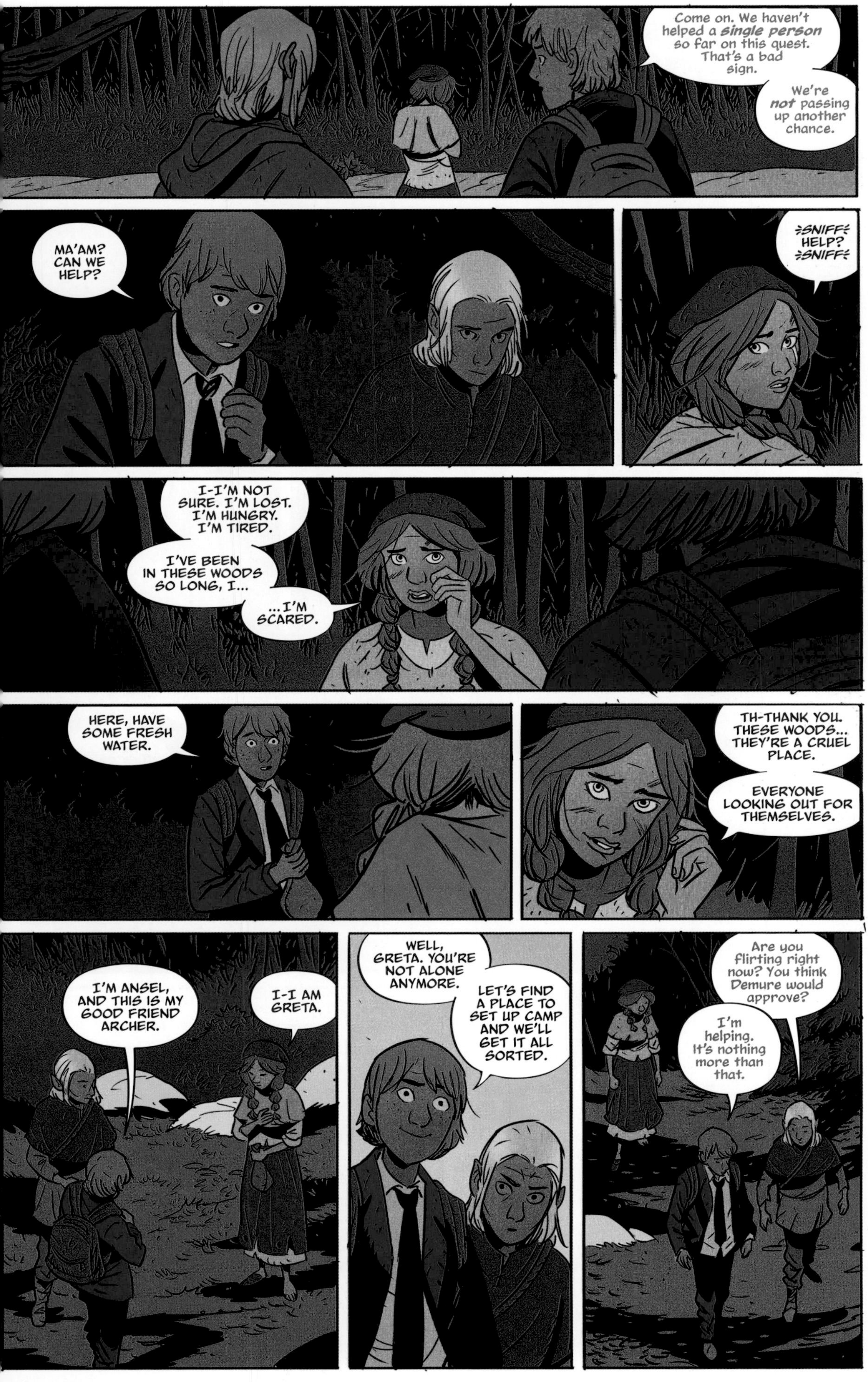
Come on. We haven't helped a *single person* so far on this quest. That's a bad sign.
We're *not* passing up another chance.
MA'AM? CAN WE HELP?
SNIFF HELP? *SNIFF*
I-I'M NOT SURE. I'M LOST. I'M HUNGRY. I'M TIRED.
I'VE BEEN IN THESE WOODS SO LONG, I...
...I'M SCARED.
HERE, HAVE SOME FRESH WATER.
TH-THANK YOU. THESE WOODS... THEY'RE A CRUEL PLACE.
EVERYONE LOOKING OUT FOR THEMSELVES.
I'M ANSEL, AND THIS IS MY GOOD FRIEND ARCHER.
I-I AM GRETA.
WELL, GRETA. YOU'RE NOT ALONE ANYMORE.
LET'S FIND A PLACE TO SET UP CAMP AND WE'LL GET IT ALL SORTED.
Are you flirting right now? You think Demure would approve?
I'm helping. It's nothing more than that.

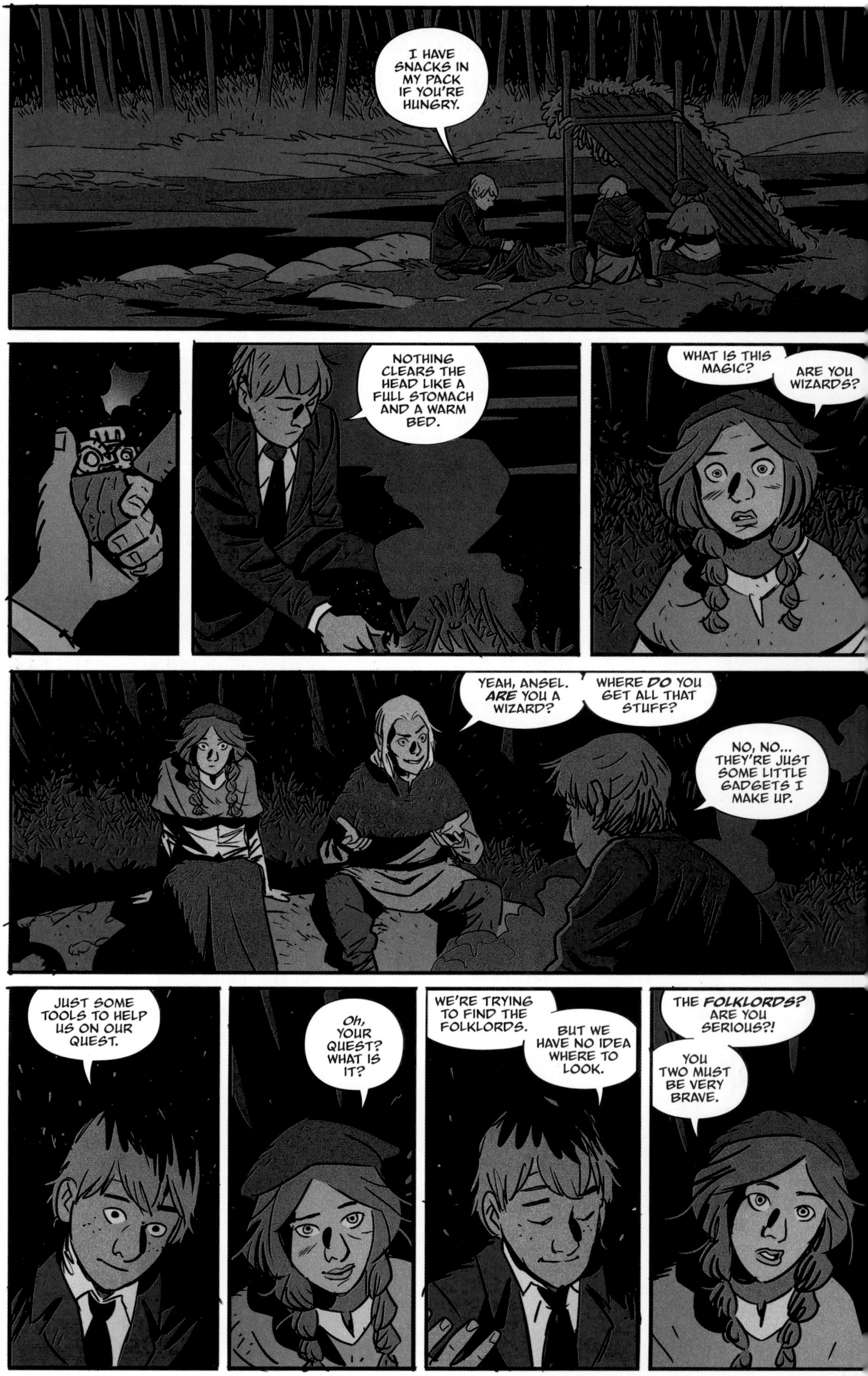
I HAVE SNACKS IN MY PACK IF YOU'RE HUNGRY.
NOTHING CLEARS THE HEAD LIKE A FULL STOMACH AND A WARM BED.
WHAT IS THIS MAGIC?
ARE YOU WIZARDS?
YEAH, ANSEL. *ARE* YOU A WIZARD?
WHERE *DO* YOU GET ALL THAT STUFF?
NO, NO... THEY'RE JUST SOME LITTLE GADGETS I MAKE UP.
JUST SOME TOOLS TO HELP US ON OUR QUEST.
Oh, YOUR QUEST? WHAT IS IT?
WE'RE TRYING TO FIND THE FOLKLORDS.
BUT WE HAVE NO IDEA WHERE TO LOOK.
THE *FOLKLORDS?* ARE YOU SERIOUS?!
YOU TWO MUST BE VERY BRAVE.

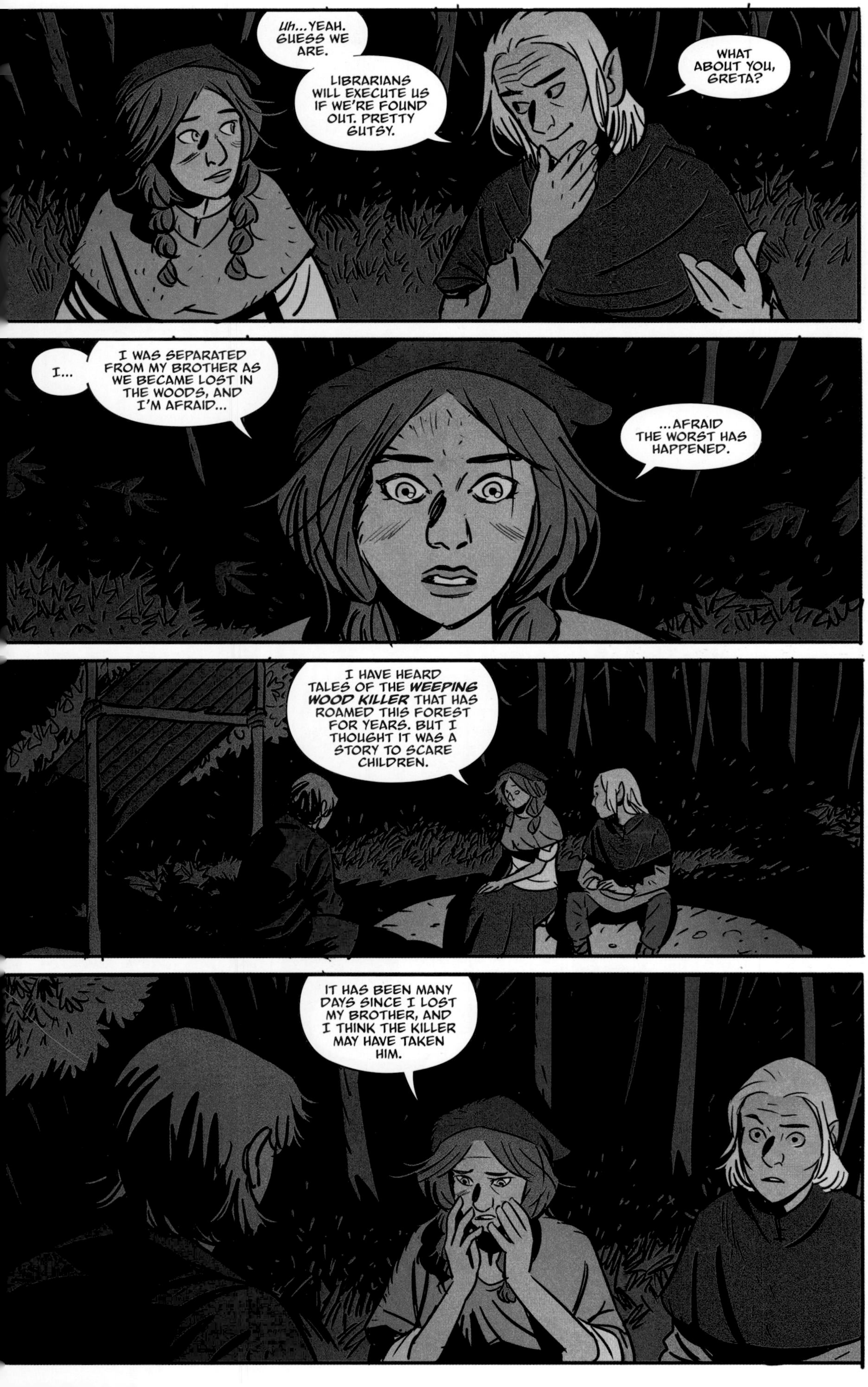
UH...YEAH. GUESS WE ARE.
LIBRARIANS WILL EXECUTE US IF WE'RE FOUND OUT. PRETTY GUTSY.
WHAT ABOUT YOU, GRETA?
I...
I WAS SEPARATED FROM MY BROTHER AS WE BECAME LOST IN THE WOODS, AND I'M AFRAID...
...AFRAID THE WORST HAS HAPPENED.
I HAVE HEARD TALES OF THE WEEPING WOOD KILLER THAT HAS ROAMED THIS FOREST FOR YEARS. BUT I THOUGHT IT WAS A STORY TO SCARE CHILDREN.
IT HAS BEEN MANY DAYS SINCE I LOST MY BROTHER, AND I THINK THE KILLER MAY HAVE TAKEN HIM.

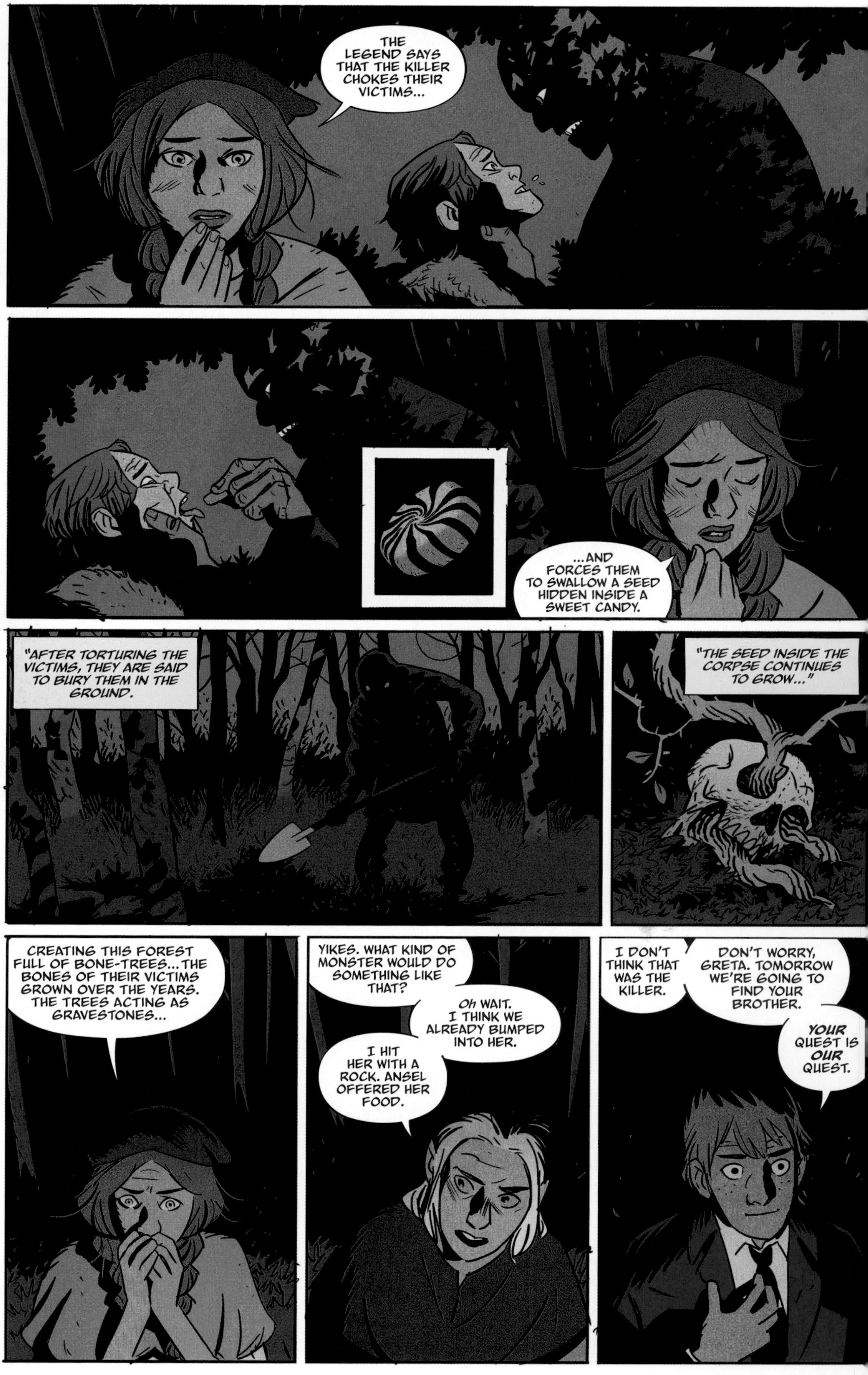

THE LEGEND SAYS THAT THE KILLER CHOKES THEIR VICTIMS...
...AND FORCES THEM TO SWALLOW A SEED HIDDEN INSIDE A SWEET CANDY.
"AFTER TORTURING THE VICTIMS, THEY ARE SAID TO BURY THEM IN THE GROUND.
"THE SEED INSIDE THE CORPSE CONTINUES TO GROW..."
CREATING THIS FOREST FULL OF BONE-TREES... THE BONES OF THEIR VICTIMS GROWN OVER THE YEARS. THE TREES ACTING AS GRAVESTONES...
YIKES. WHAT KIND OF MONSTER WOULD DO SOMETHING LIKE THAT?
Oh WAIT. I THINK WE ALREADY BUMPED INTO HER.
I HIT HER WITH A ROCK. ANSEL OFFERED HER FOOD.
I DON'T THINK THAT WAS THE KILLER.
DON'T WORRY, GRETA. TOMORROW WE'RE GOING TO FIND YOUR BROTHER.
YOUR QUEST IS OUR QUEST.

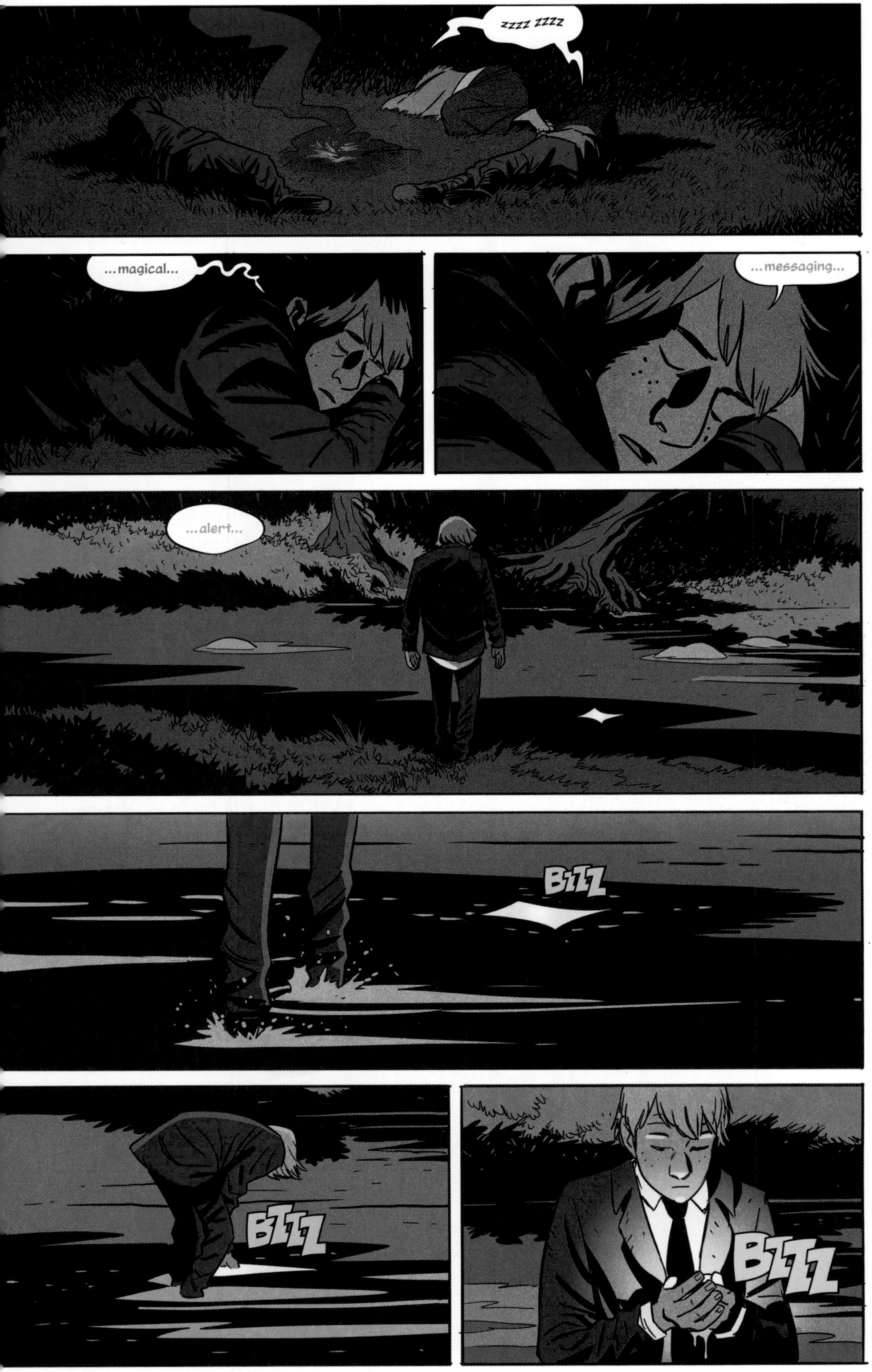
zzzz zzzz
...magical...
...messaging...
...alert...
BZZZ
BZZZ
BZZZ

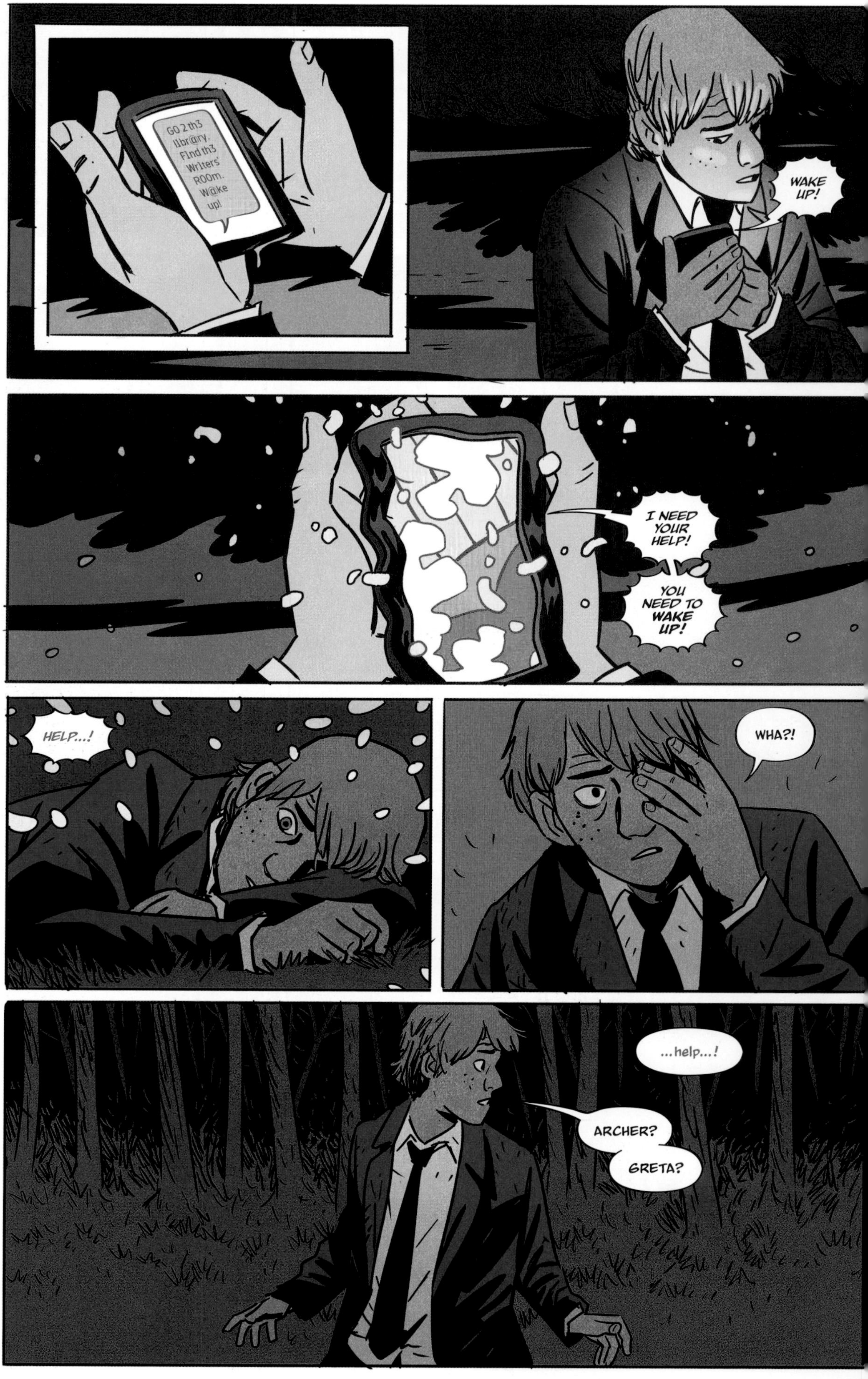
GO 2 th3 l1br@ry. F1nd th3 Wr1ters' ROOm. W@ke up!
WAKE UP!
I NEED YOUR HELP!
YOU NEED TO WAKE UP!
HELP...!
WHA?!
...help...!
ARCHER?
GRETA?

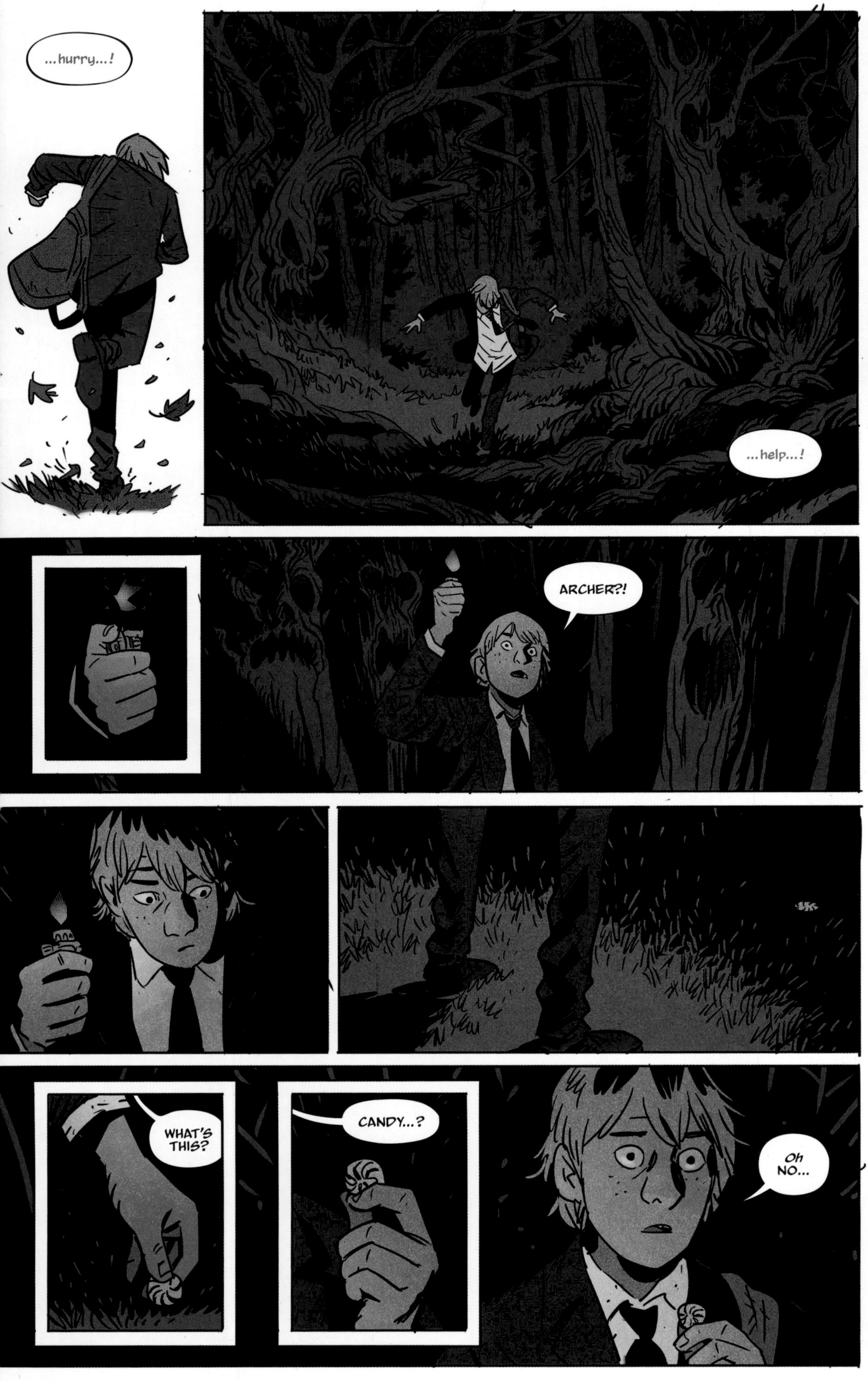

...hurry...!
...help...!
ARCHER?!
WHAT'S THIS?
CANDY...?
Oh NO...

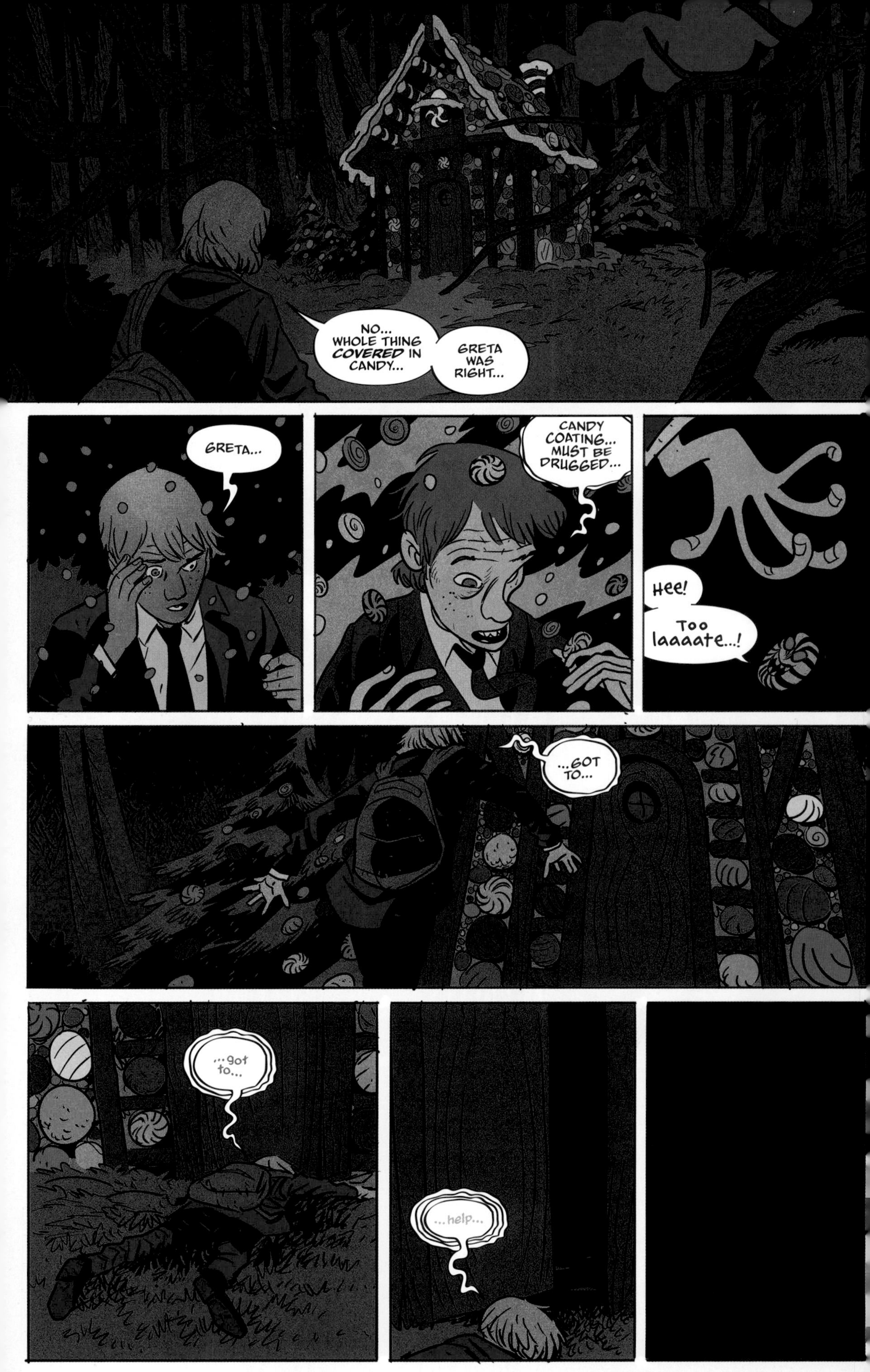
NO... WHOLE THING *COVERED* IN CANDY...
GRETA WAS RIGHT...
GRETA...
CANDY COATING... MUST BE DRUGGED...
Hee!
Too laaaate...!
...GOT TO...
...got to...
...help...

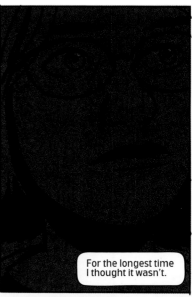

folklords is just a clever title. To intrigue you. A hook.

The ONCE UPON A TIME... is real. Trust me.

Are you reading this? Or are you living it?

For the longest time I thought it wasn't.

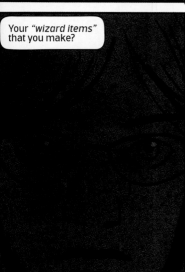

Your *"wizard items"* that you make?

You're going to need them.

You're going to need all of that and more...

...if you want to make it to your *real home*...alive.

WAKEY?

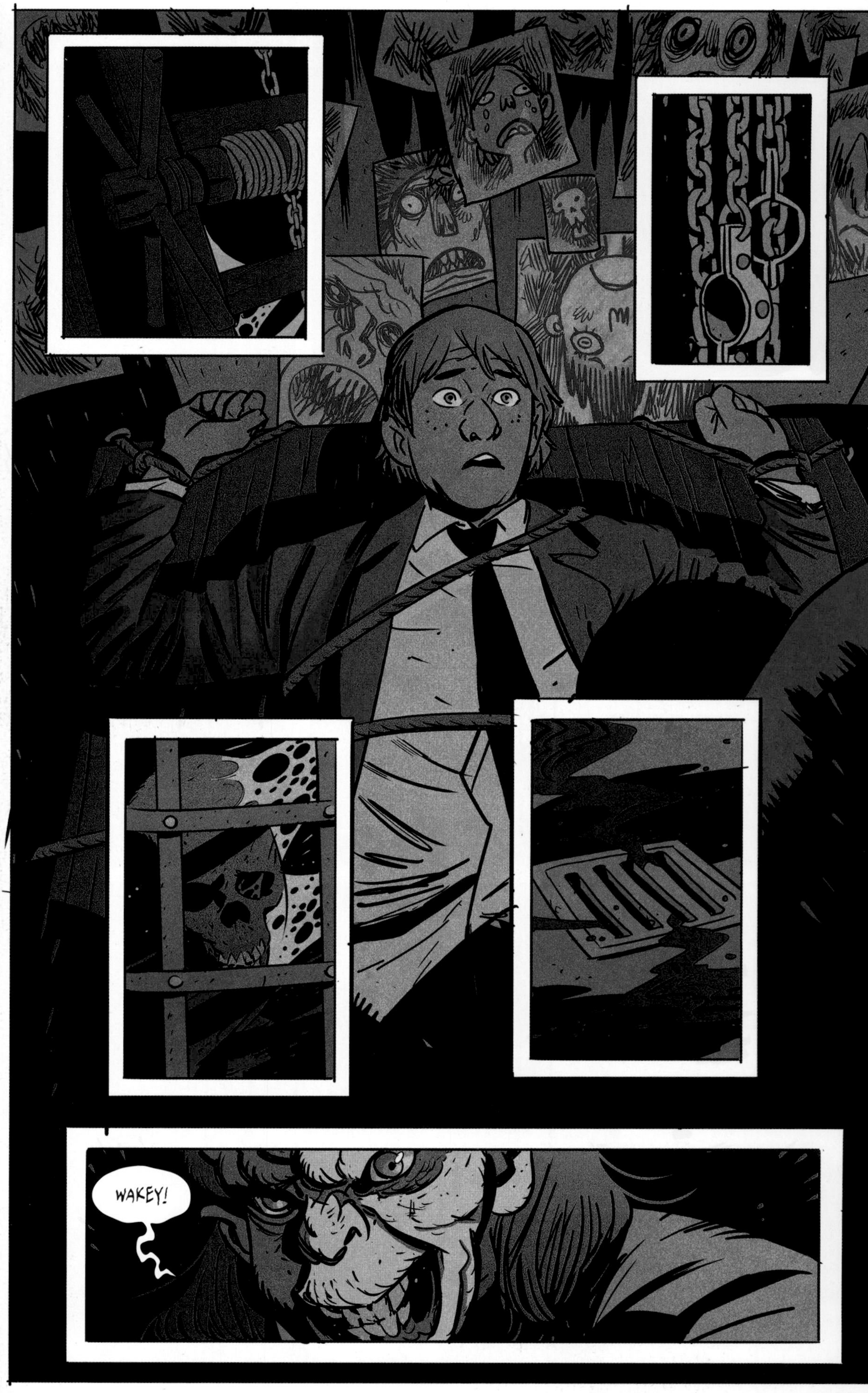
WAKEY!

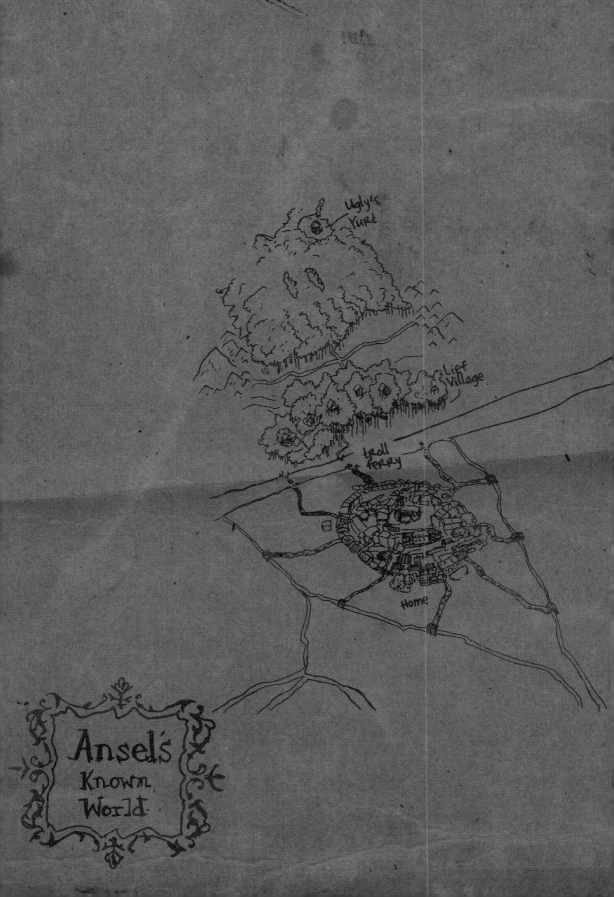

Ugly's Yurt

Lief Village

troll ferry

Home

Ansel's Known World

CHAPTER

THREE

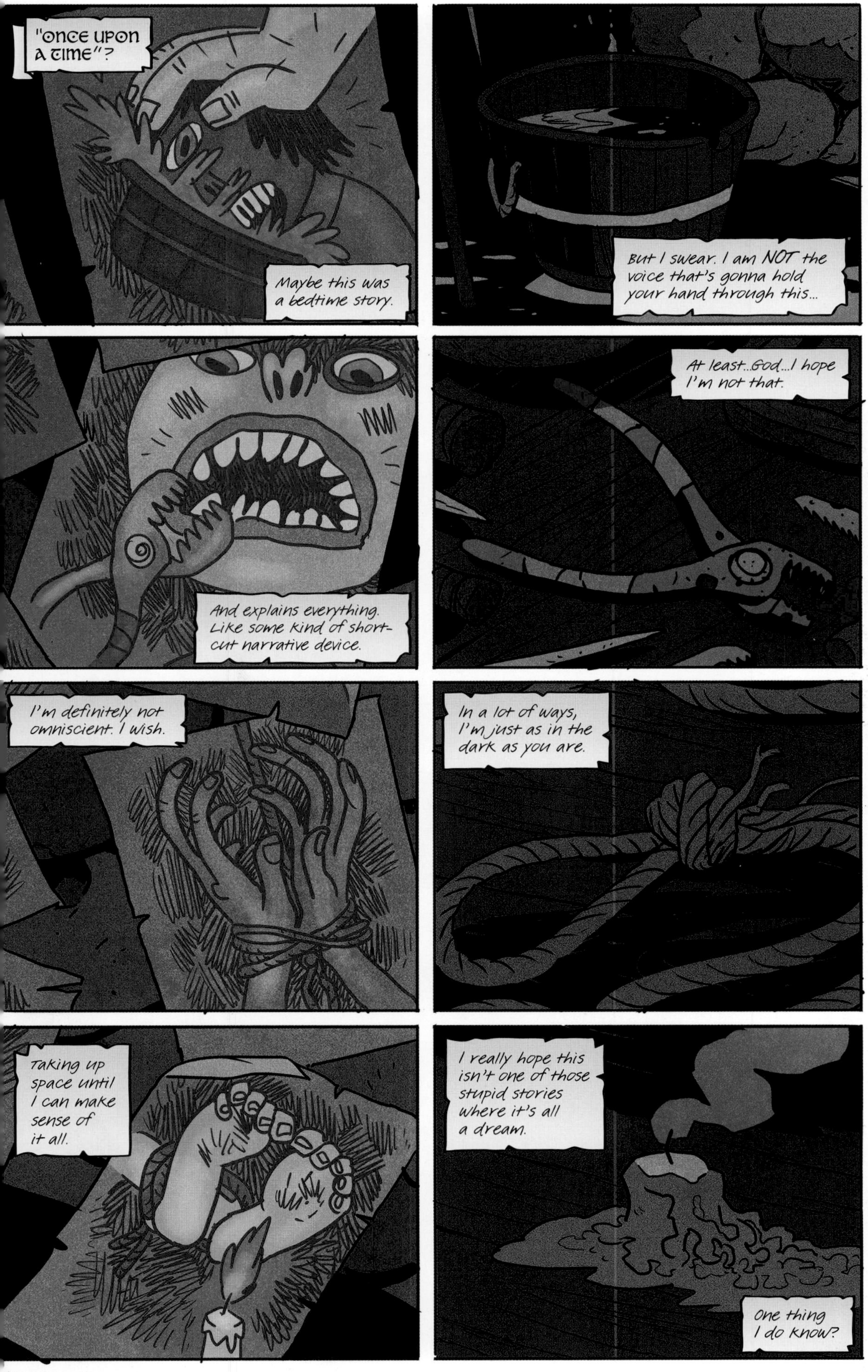
"Once upon a time"?
Maybe this was a bedtime story.
And explains everything. Like some kind of short-cut narrative device.
I'm definitely not omniscient. I wish.
Taking up space until I can make sense of it all.
But I swear. I am NOT the voice that's gonna hold your hand through this...
At least...God...I hope I'm not that.
In a lot of ways, I'm just as in the dark as you are.
I really hope this isn't one of those stupid stories where it's all a dream.
One thing I do know?

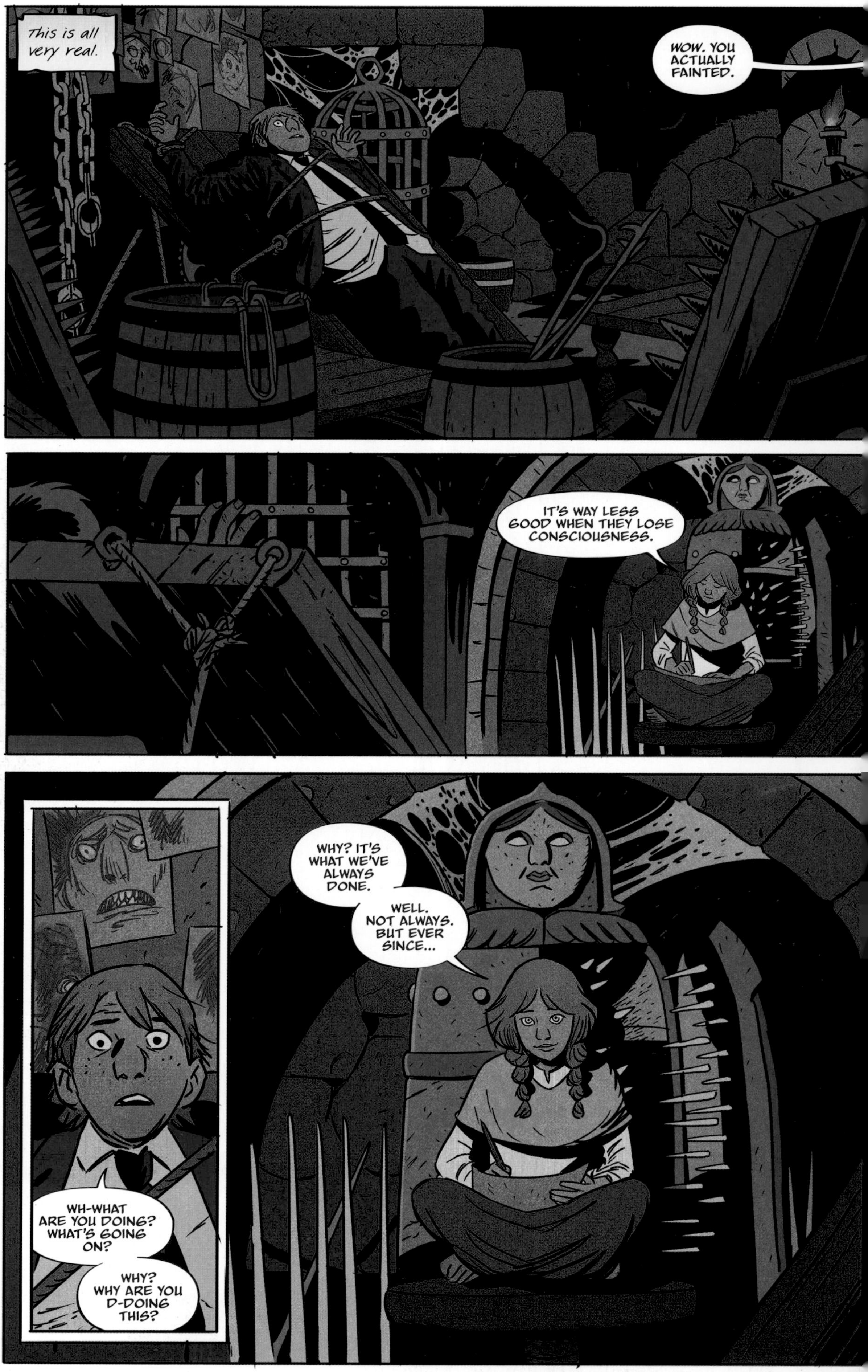
This is all very real.
WOW. YOU ACTUALLY FAINTED.
IT'S WAY LESS GOOD WHEN THEY LOSE CONSCIOUSNESS.
WH-WHAT ARE YOU DOING? WHAT'S GOING ON?
WHY? WHY ARE YOU D-DOING THIS?
WHY? IT'S WHAT WE'VE ALWAYS DONE.
WELL. NOT ALWAYS. BUT EVER SINCE...

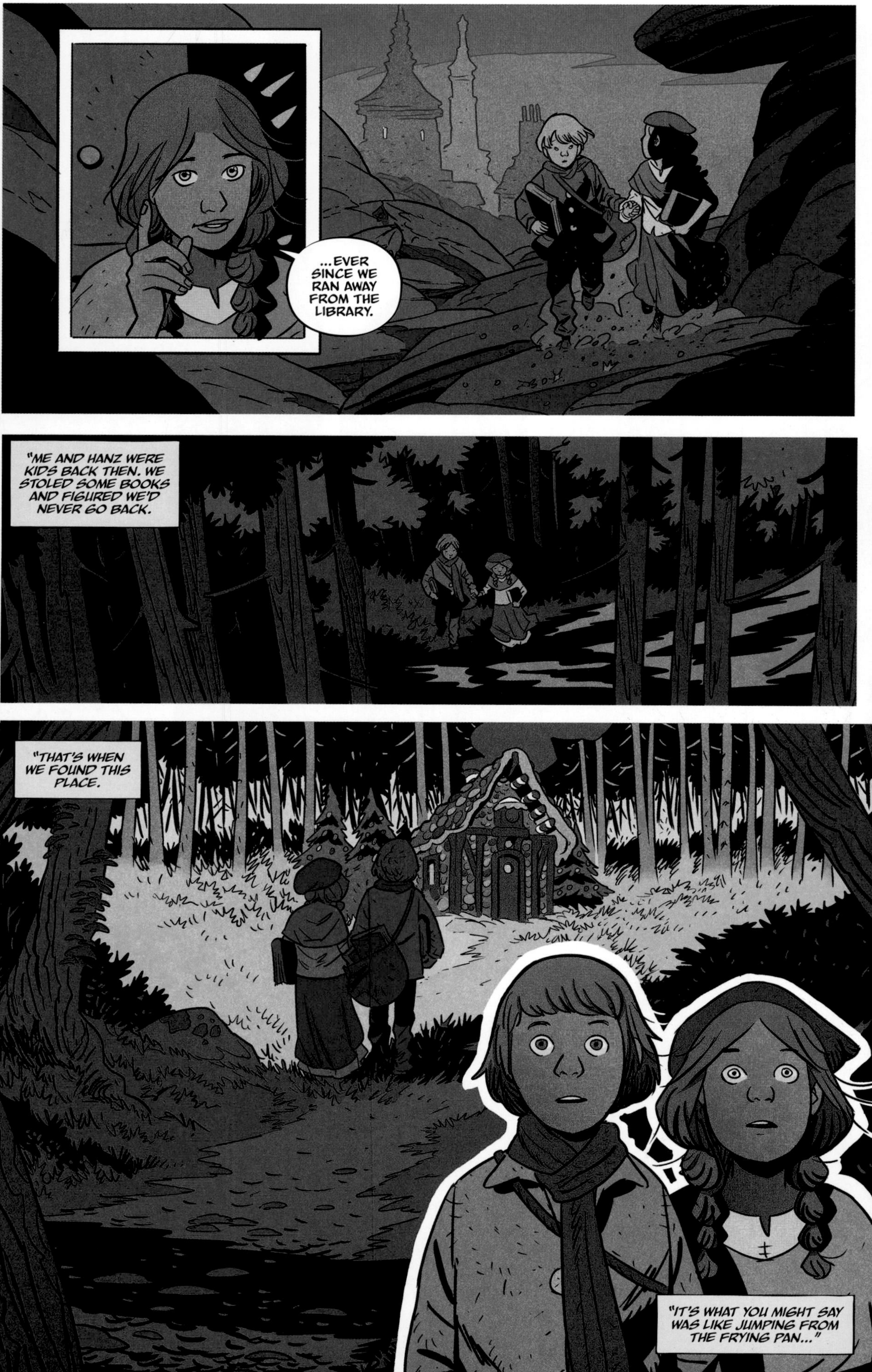
...EVER SINCE WE RAN AWAY FROM THE LIBRARY.
"ME AND HANZ WERE KIDS BACK THEN. WE STOLED SOME BOOKS AND FIGURED WE'D NEVER GO BACK.
"THAT'S WHEN WE FOUND THIS PLACE.
"IT'S WHAT YOU MIGHT SAY WAS LIKE JUMPING FROM THE FRYING PAN..."

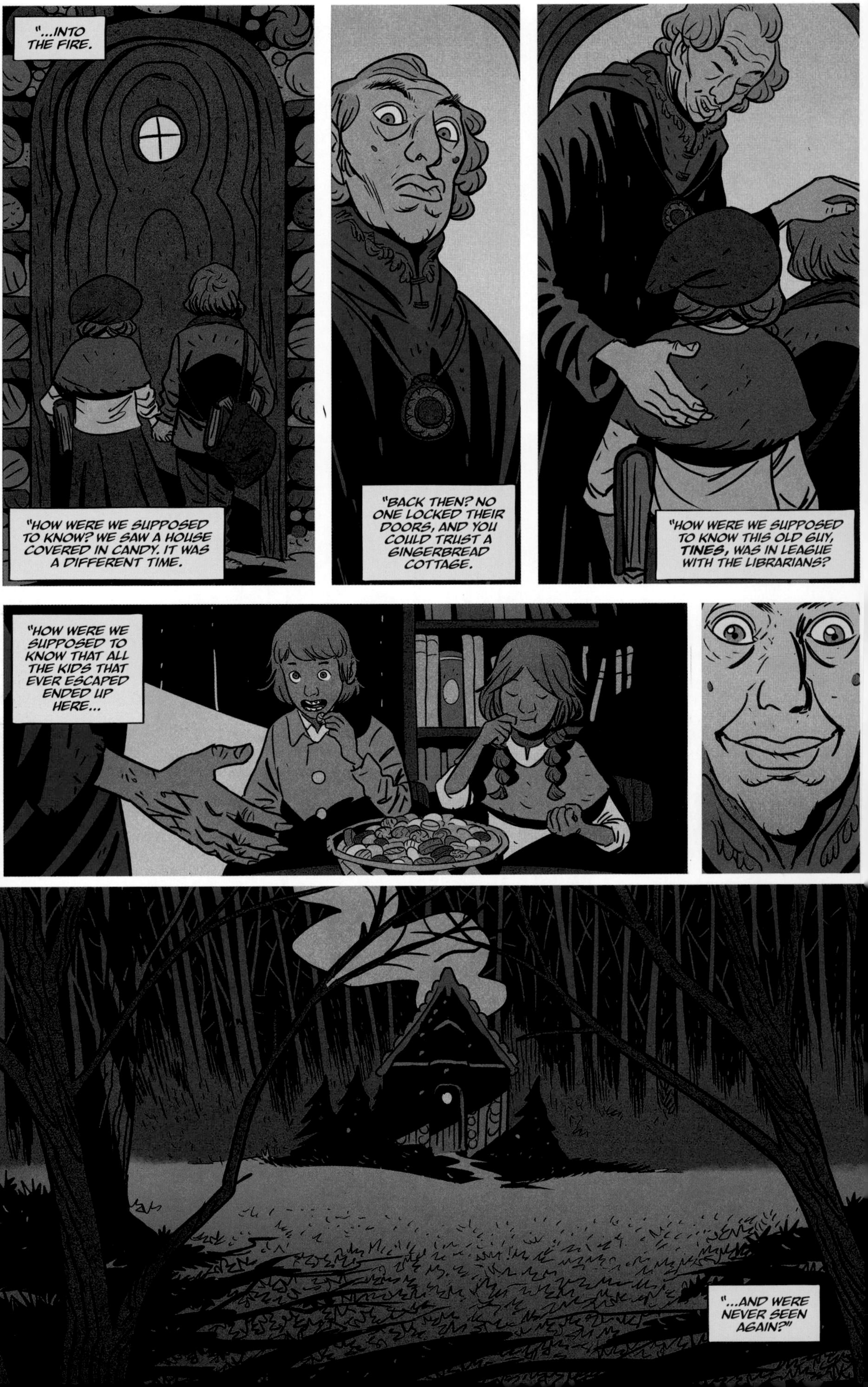
"...INTO THE FIRE.
"HOW WERE WE SUPPOSED TO KNOW? WE SAW A HOUSE COVERED IN CANDY. IT WAS A DIFFERENT TIME.
"BACK THEN? NO ONE LOCKED THEIR DOORS, AND YOU COULD TRUST A GINGERBREAD COTTAGE.
"HOW WERE WE SUPPOSED TO KNOW THIS OLD GUY, TINES, WAS IN LEAGUE WITH THE LIBRARIANS?
"HOW WERE WE SUPPOSED TO KNOW THAT ALL THE KIDS THAT EVER ESCAPED ENDED UP HERE...
"...AND WERE NEVER SEEN AGAIN?"

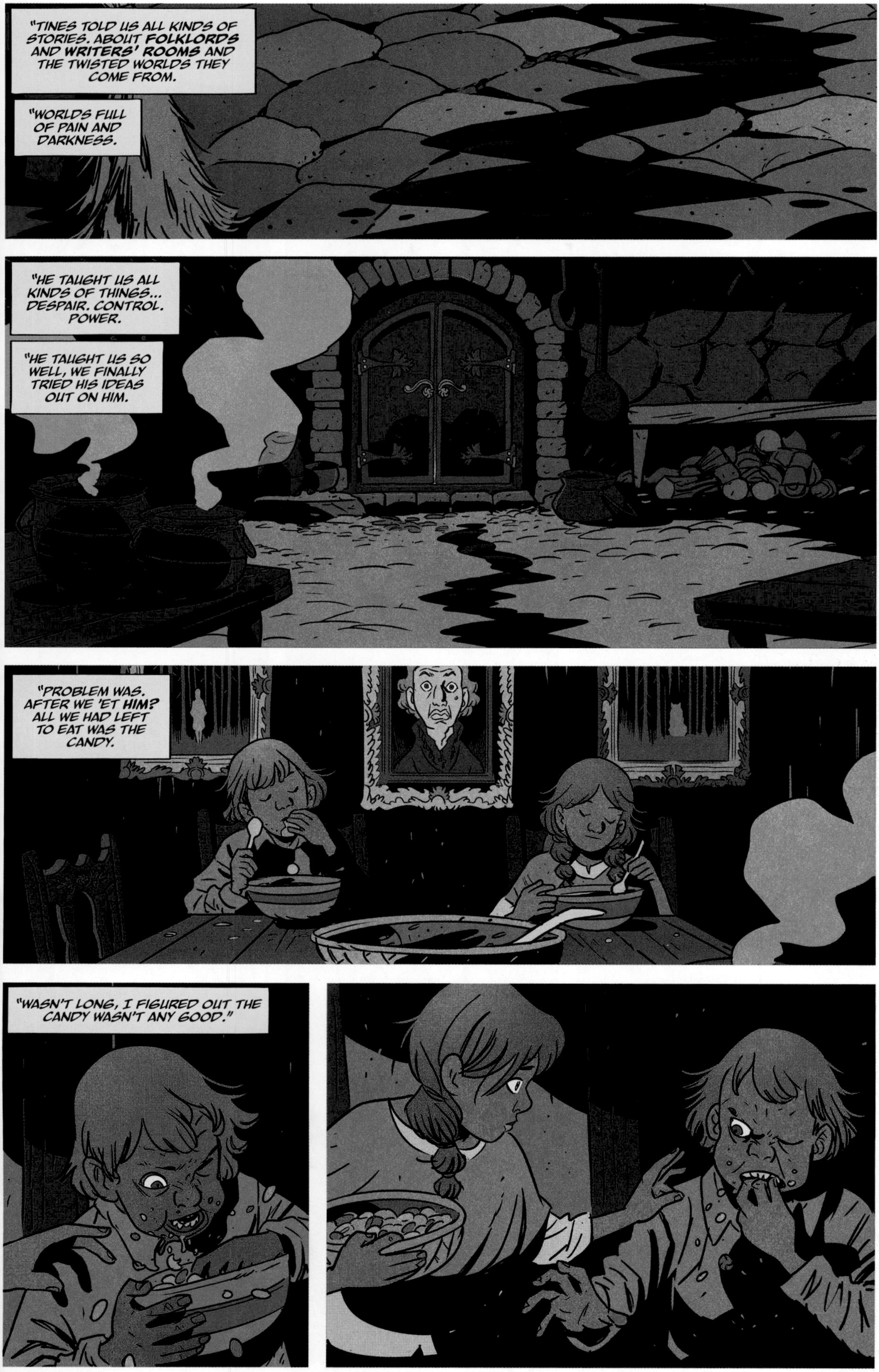
"TINES TOLD US ALL KINDS OF STORIES. ABOUT **FOLKLORDS** AND **WRITERS' ROOMS** AND THE TWISTED WORLDS THEY COME FROM.
"WORLDS FULL OF PAIN AND DARKNESS.
"HE TAUGHT US ALL KINDS OF THINGS... DESPAIR. CONTROL. POWER.
"HE TAUGHT US SO WELL, WE FINALLY TRIED HIS IDEAS OUT ON HIM.
"PROBLEM WAS. AFTER WE 'ET **HIM**? ALL WE HAD LEFT TO EAT WAS THE CANDY.
"WASN'T LONG, I FIGURED OUT THE CANDY WASN'T ANY GOOD."

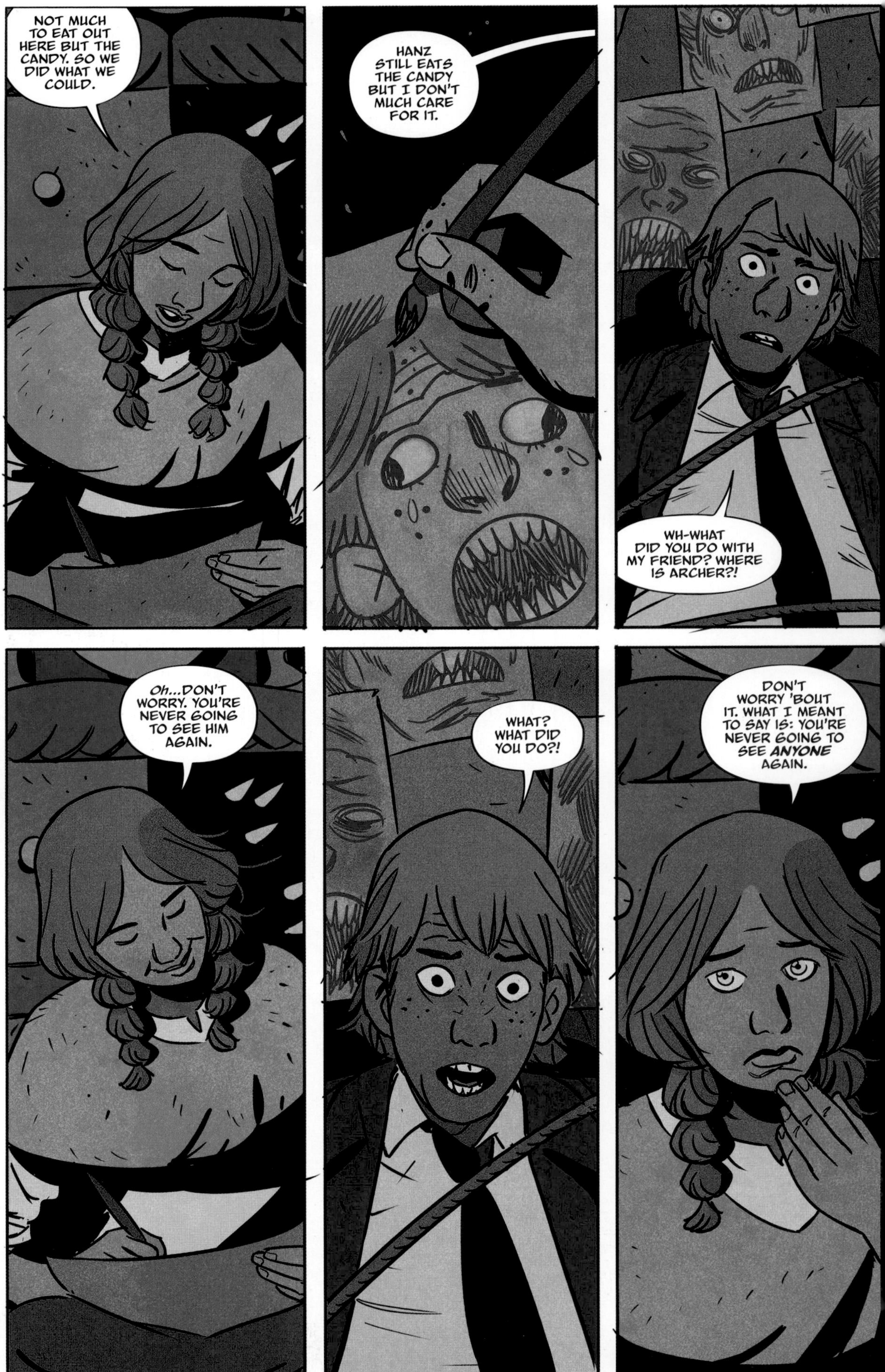
NOT MUCH TO EAT OUT HERE BUT THE CANDY. SO WE DID WHAT WE COULD.
HANZ STILL EATS THE CANDY BUT I DON'T MUCH CARE FOR IT.
WH-WHAT DID YOU DO WITH MY FRIEND? WHERE IS ARCHER?!
Oh...DON'T WORRY. YOU'RE NEVER GOING TO SEE HIM AGAIN.
WHAT? WHAT DID YOU DO?!
DON'T WORRY 'BOUT IT. WHAT I MEANT TO SAY IS: YOU'RE NEVER GOING TO SEE *ANYONE* AGAIN.

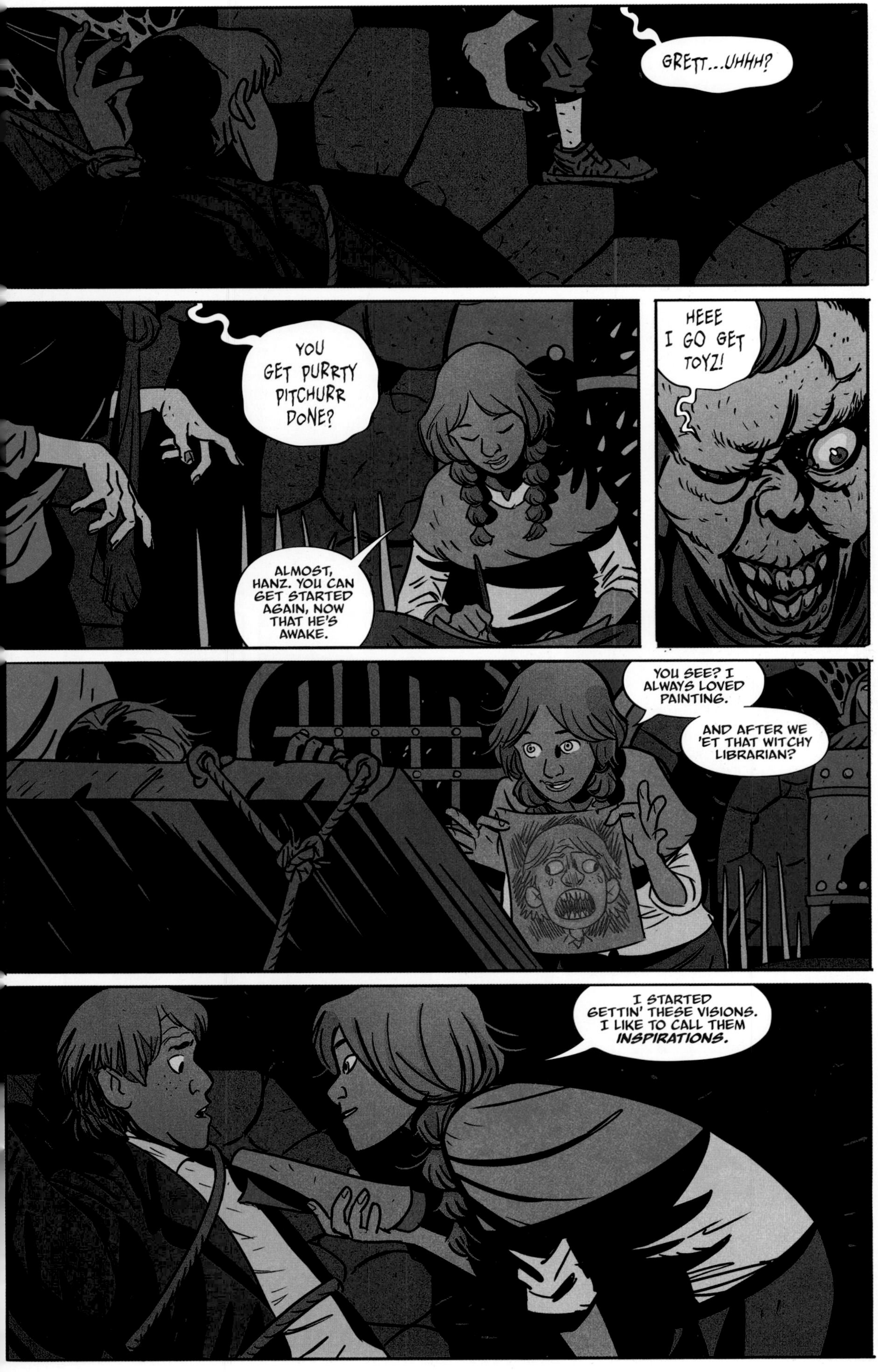
GRETT...UHHH?
YOU GET PURRTY PITCHURR DONE?
ALMOST, HANZ. YOU CAN GET STARTED AGAIN, NOW THAT HE'S AWAKE.
HEEE I GO GET TOYZ!
YOU SEE? I ALWAYS LOVED PAINTING.
AND AFTER WE 'ET THAT WITCHY LIBRARIAN?
I STARTED GETTIN' THESE VISIONS. I LIKE TO CALL THEM *INSPIRATIONS*.

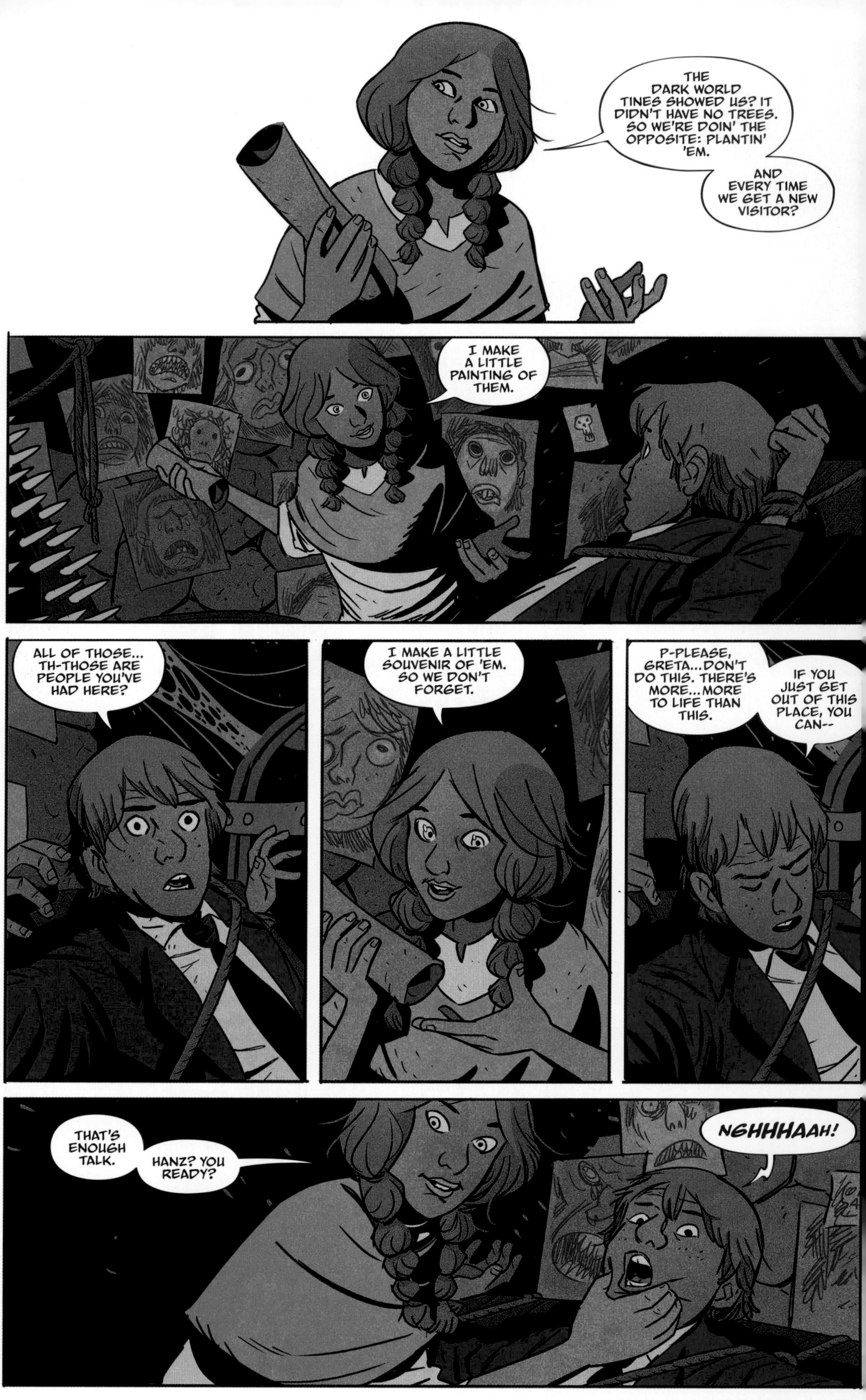
THE DARK WORLD TINES SHOWED US? IT DIDN'T HAVE NO TREES. SO WE'RE DOIN' THE OPPOSITE: PLANTIN' 'EM.
AND EVERY TIME WE GET A NEW VISITOR?
I MAKE A LITTLE PAINTING OF THEM.
ALL OF THOSE... TH-THOSE ARE PEOPLE YOU'VE HAD HERE?
I MAKE A LITTLE SOUVENIR OF 'EM. SO WE DON'T FORGET.
P-PLEASE, GRETA...DON'T DO THIS. THERE'S MORE...MORE TO LIFE THAN THIS.
IF YOU JUST GET OUT OF THIS PLACE, YOU CAN--
THAT'S ENOUGH TALK.
HANZ? YOU READY?
NGHHHAAH!

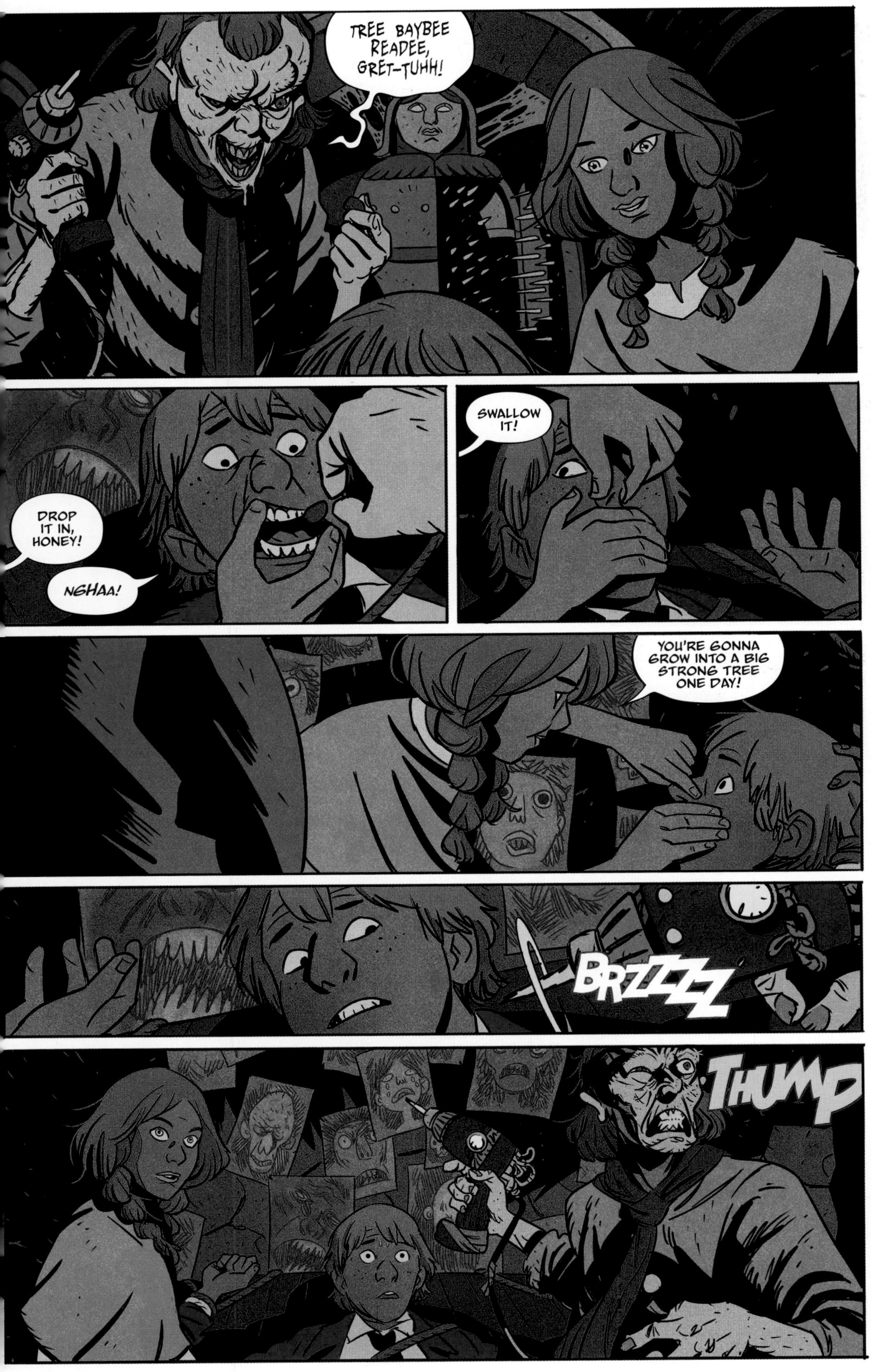
TREE BAYBEE READEE, GRET-TUHH!
DROP IT IN, HONEY!
NGHAA!
SWALLOW IT!
YOU'RE GONNA GROW INTO A BIG STRONG TREE ONE DAY!
BRZZZZ
THUMP

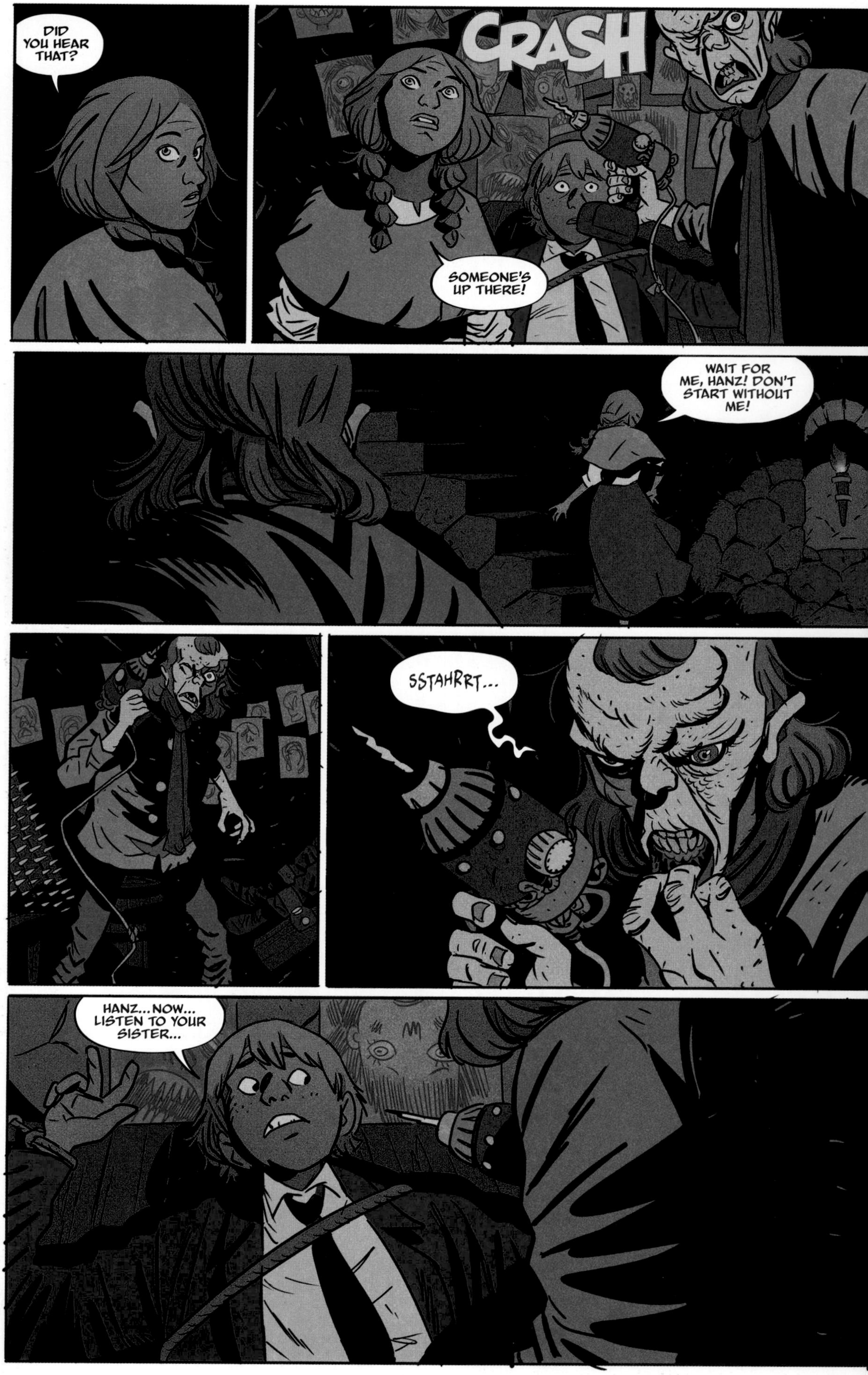

DID YOU HEAR THAT?
CRASH
SOMEONE'S UP THERE!
WAIT FOR ME, HANZ! DON'T START WITHOUT ME!
SSTAHRRT...
HANZ...NOW... LISTEN TO YOUR SISTER...

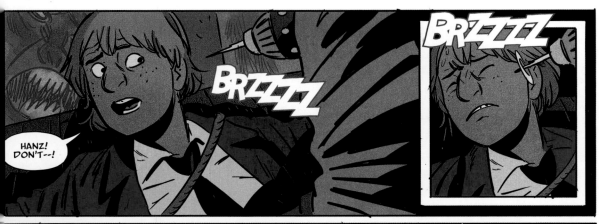

BRZZZZ

BRZZZZ

HANZ! DON'T--!

KERASHH

Oh. THAT SOUNDED BAD. POOR GRETA...

HOPE SHE'S OKAY.

GRET...TUHHHH?

GRETTUHHHH!

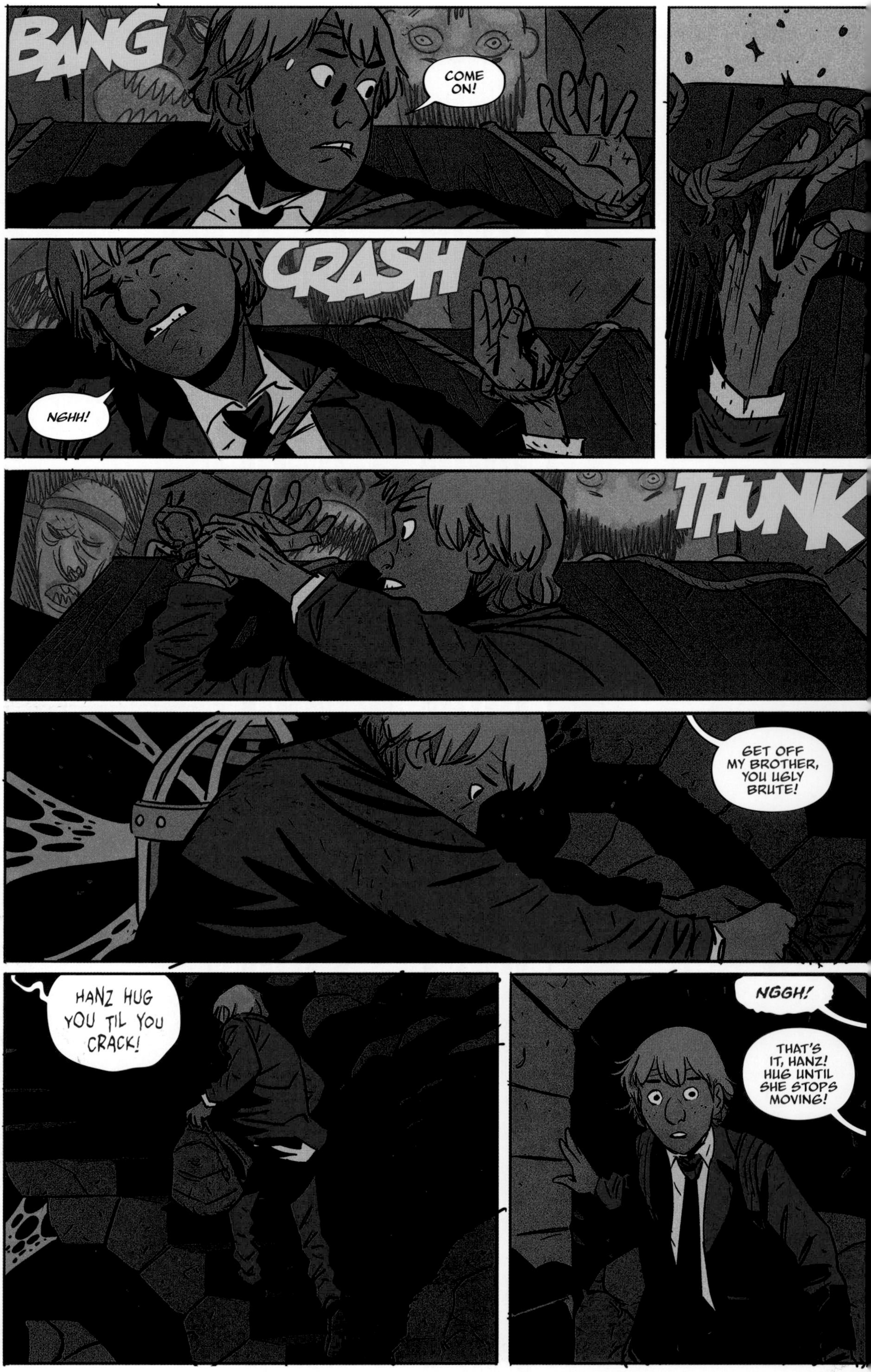
BANG
COME ON!
CRASH
NGHH!
THUNK
GET OFF MY BROTHER, YOU UGLY BRUTE!
HANZ HUG YOU TIL YOU CRACK!
NGGH!
THAT'S IT, HANZ! HUG UNTIL SHE STOPS MOVING!

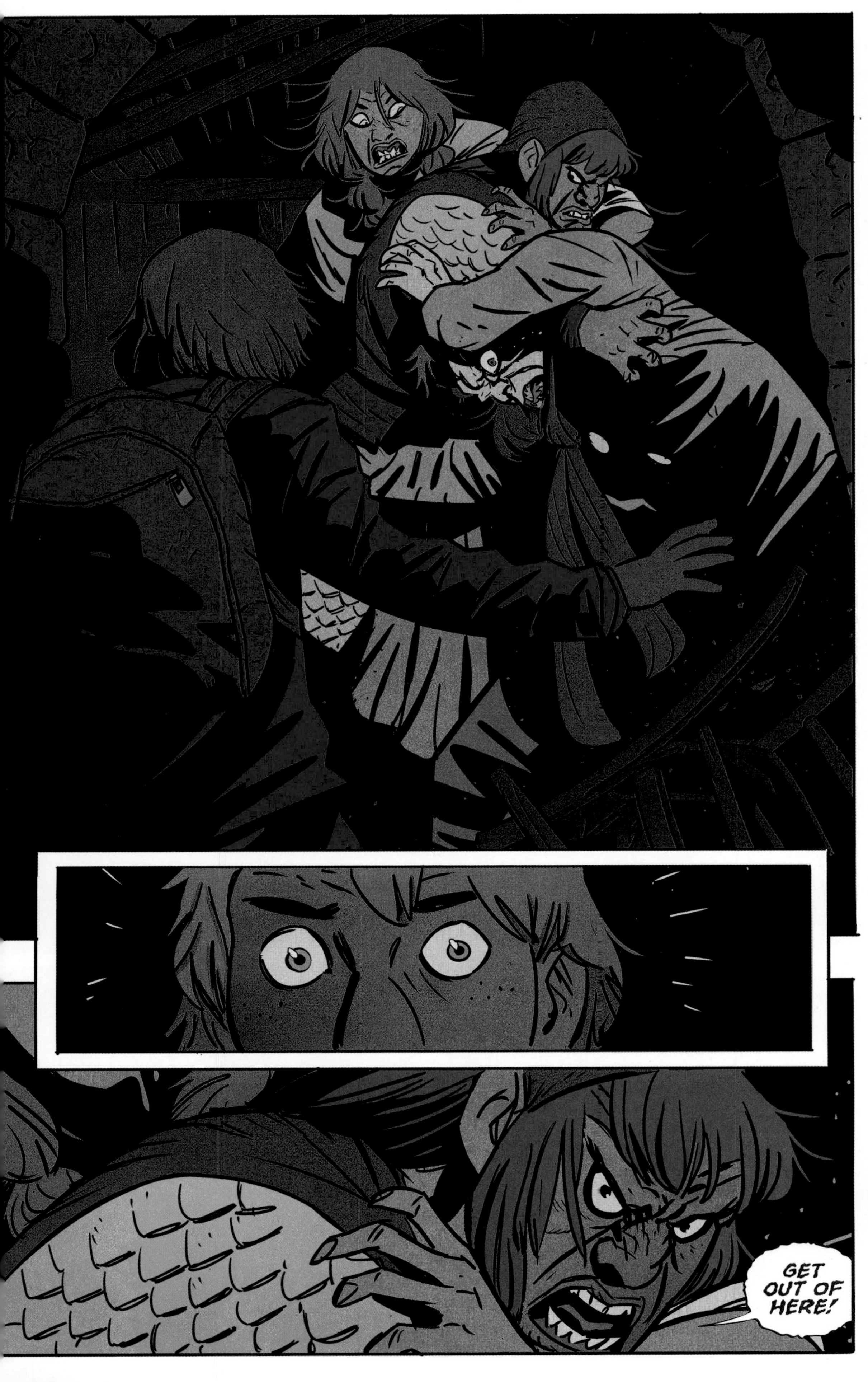
GET OUT OF HERE!

GAHH!

KRASH

UGLY! WE'LL KILL YOU!

KRAK

THEN WE'RE GONNA--

EEEATT... YOUUUu!

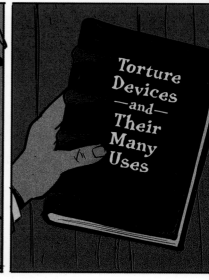

Torture
Devices
—and—
Their
Many
Uses

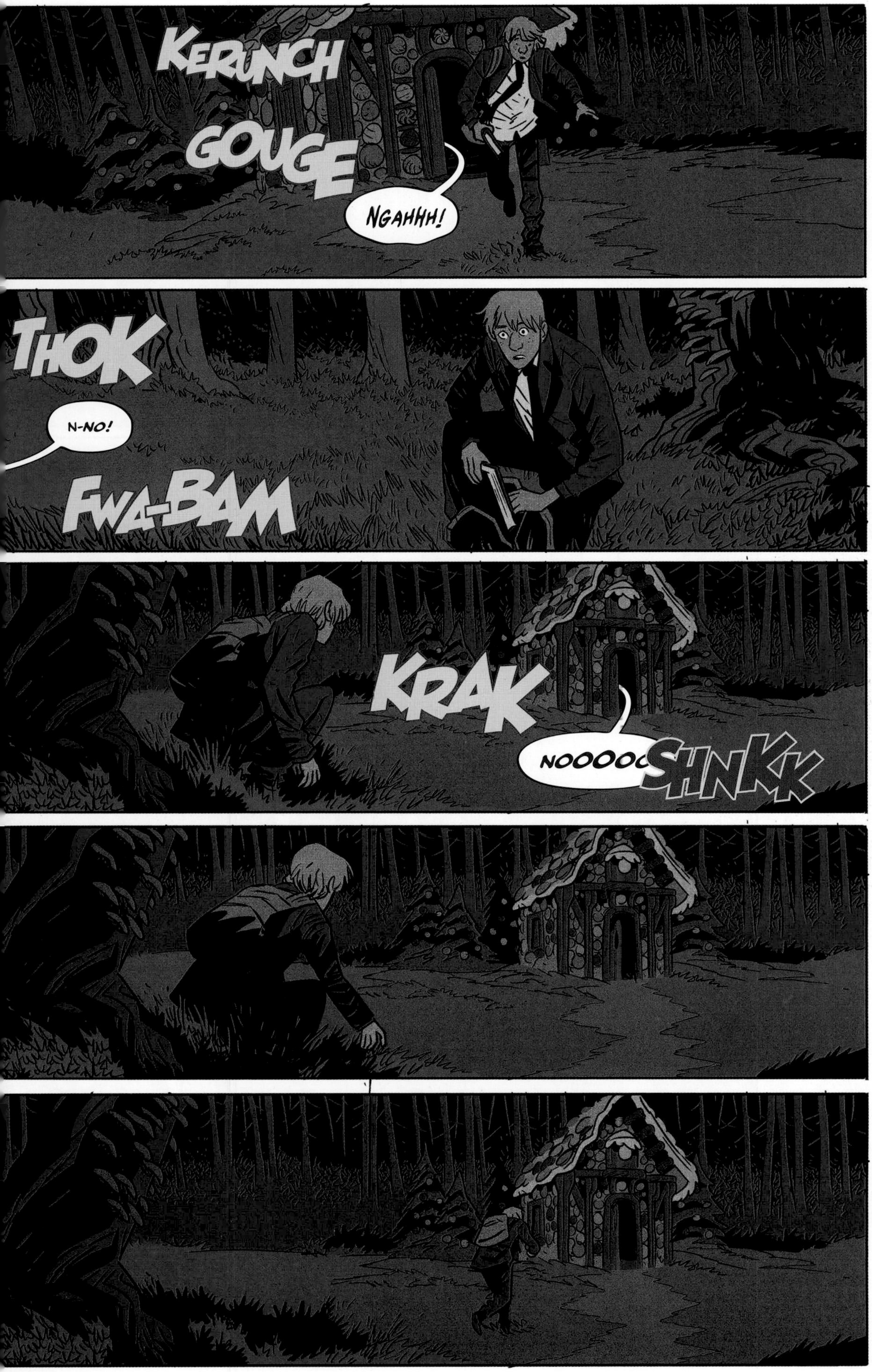
KERUNCH
GOUGE
NGAHHH!
THOK
N-NO!
FWA-BAM
KRAK
NOOOOO
SHNKK

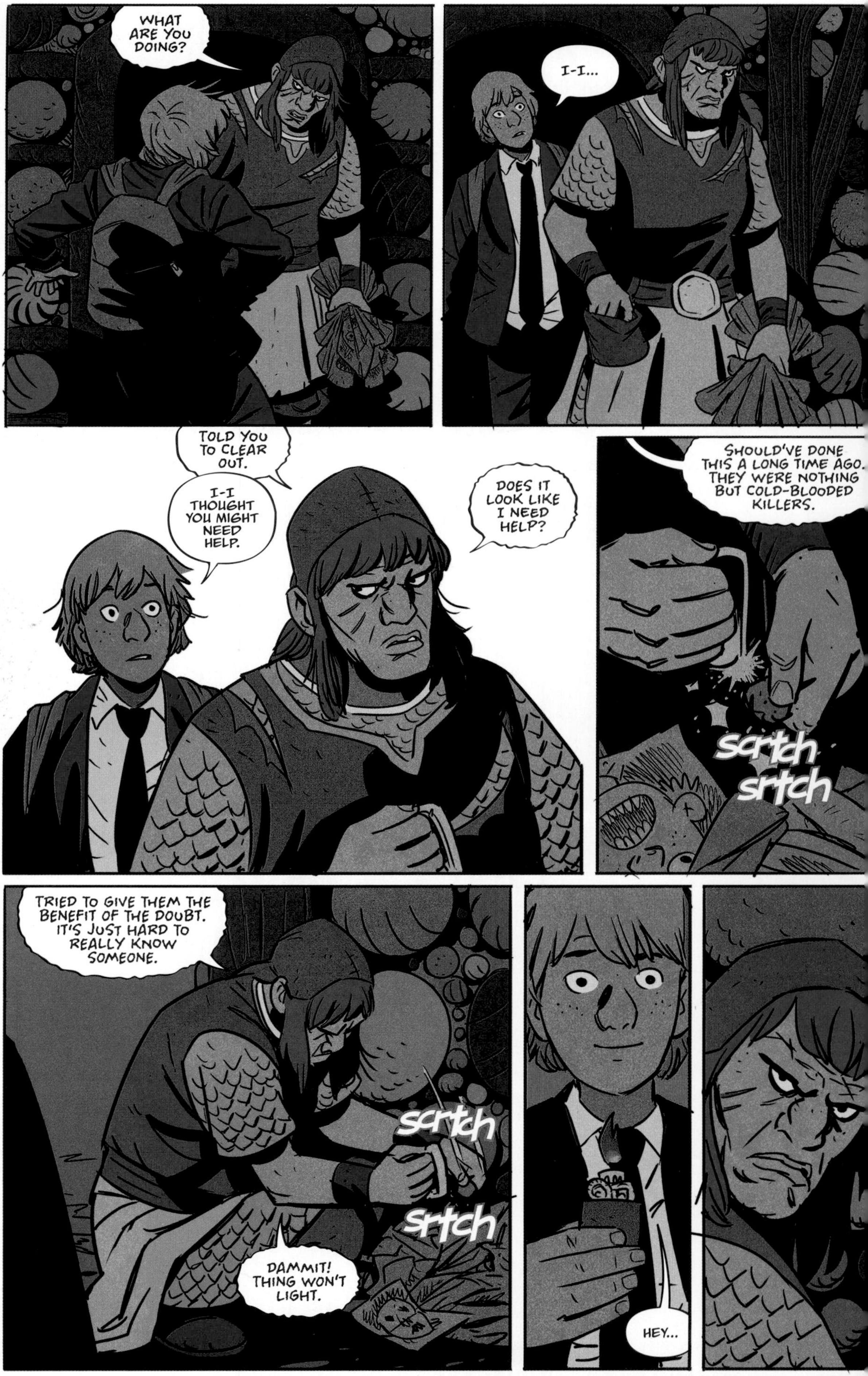
WHAT ARE YOU DOING?
I-I...
TOLD YOU TO CLEAR OUT.
I-I THOUGHT YOU MIGHT NEED HELP.
DOES IT LOOK LIKE I NEED HELP?
SHOULD'VE DONE THIS A LONG TIME AGO. THEY WERE NOTHING BUT COLD-BLOODED KILLERS.
SCRTCH
SRTCH
TRIED TO GIVE THEM THE BENEFIT OF THE DOUBT. IT'S JUST HARD TO REALLY KNOW SOMEONE.
SCRTCH
SRTCH
DAMMIT! THING WON'T LIGHT.
HEY...

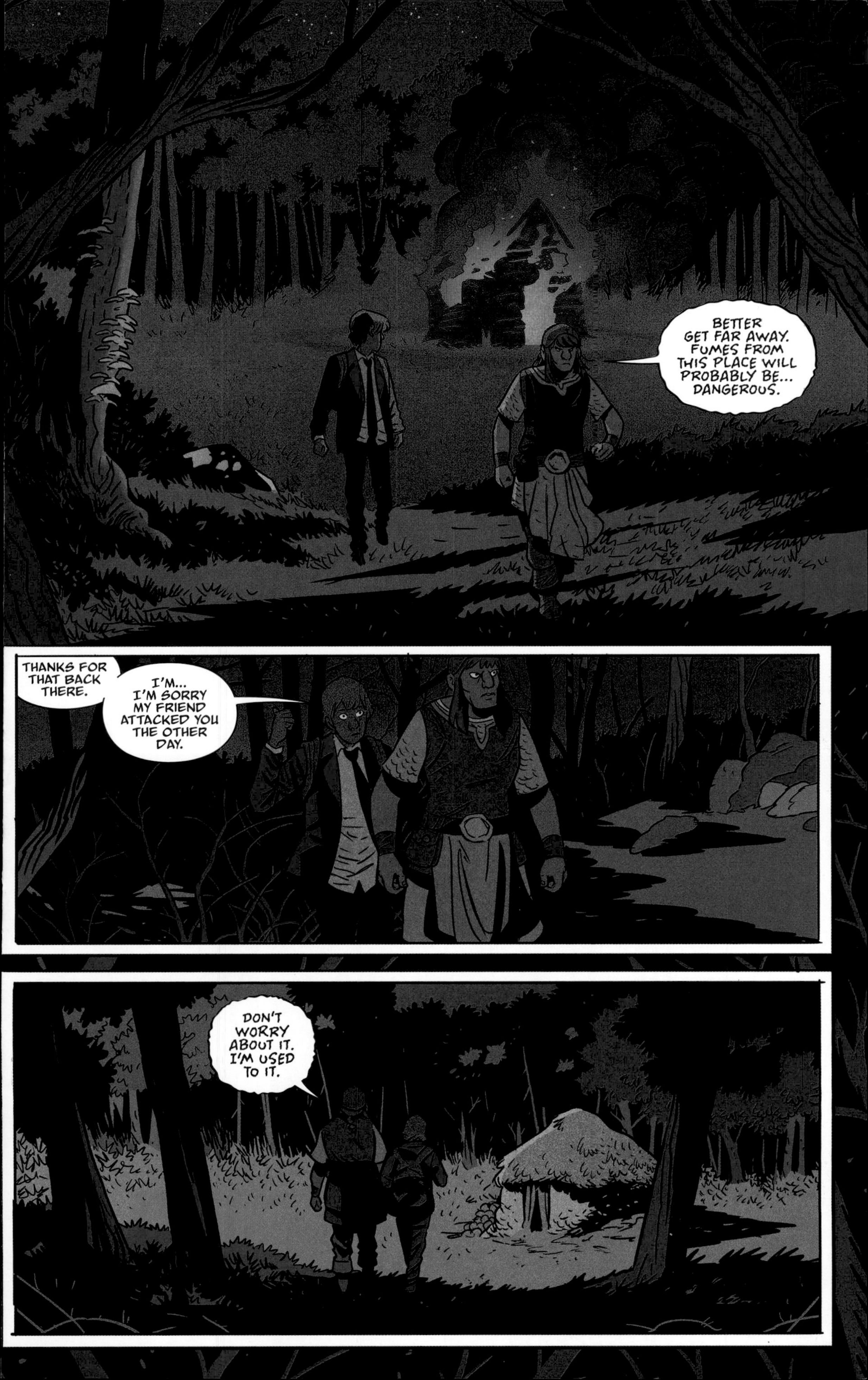
BETTER GET FAR AWAY. FUMES FROM THIS PLACE WILL PROBABLY BE... DANGEROUS.
THANKS FOR THAT BACK THERE.
I'M... I'M SORRY MY FRIEND ATTACKED YOU THE OTHER DAY.
DON'T WORRY ABOUT IT. I'M USED TO IT.

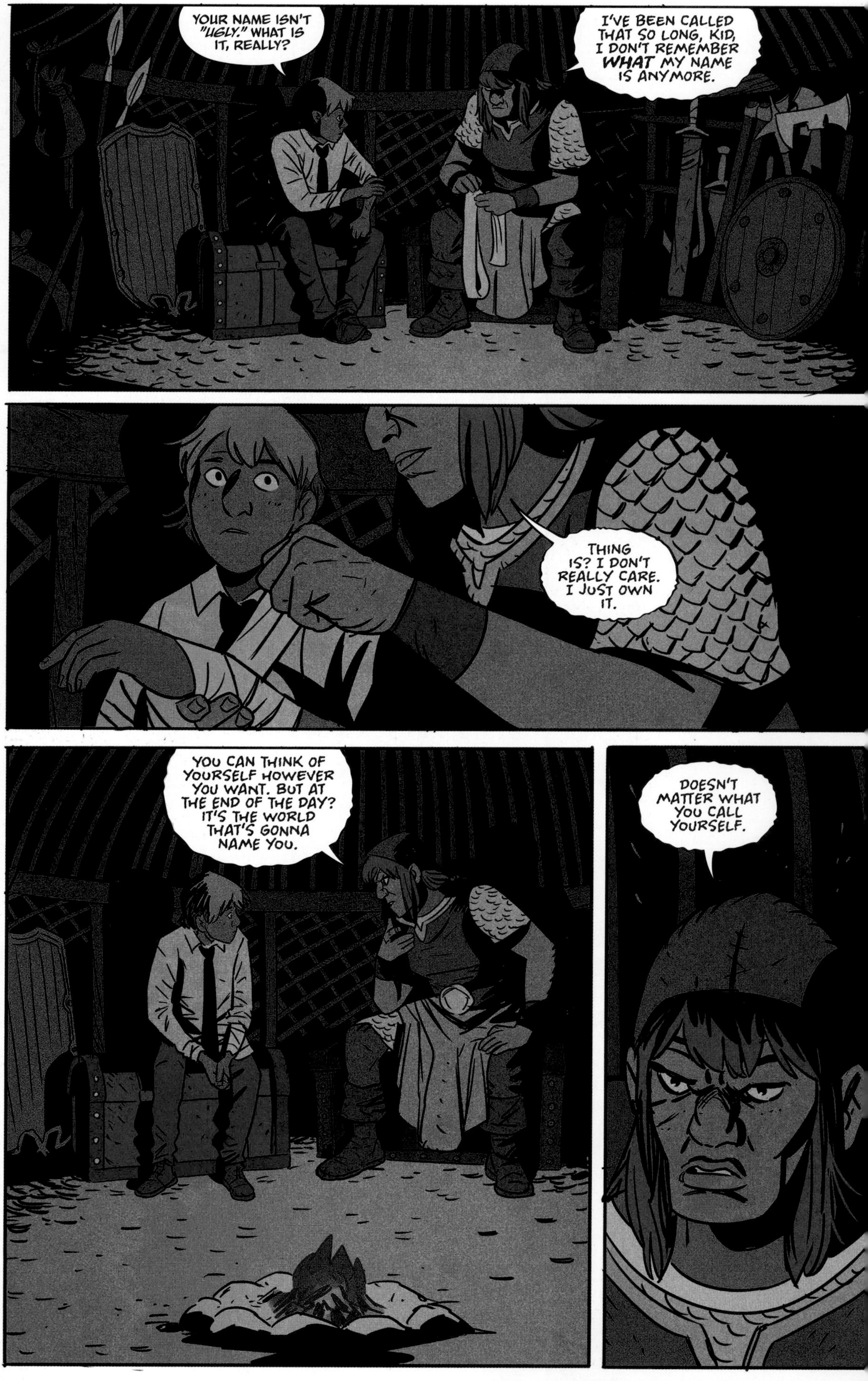
YOUR NAME ISN'T "UGLY." WHAT IS IT, REALLY?
I'VE BEEN CALLED THAT SO LONG, KID, I DON'T REMEMBER WHAT MY NAME IS ANYMORE.
THING IS? I DON'T REALLY CARE. I JUST OWN IT.
YOU CAN THINK OF YOURSELF HOWEVER YOU WANT. BUT AT THE END OF THE DAY? IT'S THE WORLD THAT'S GONNA NAME YOU.
DOESN'T MATTER WHAT YOU CALL YOURSELF.

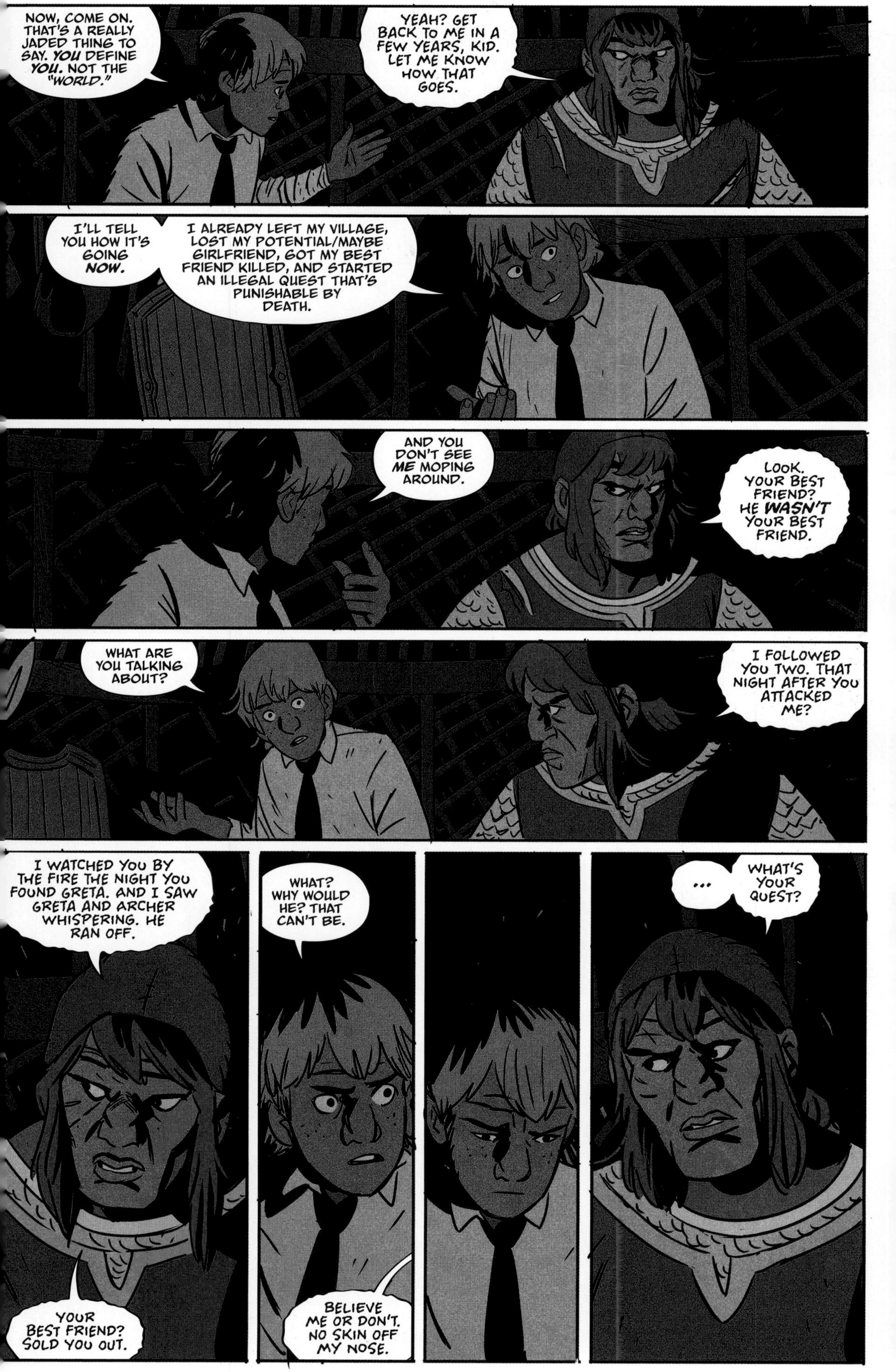
NOW, COME ON. THAT'S A REALLY JADED THING TO SAY. ***YOU*** DEFINE ***YOU***. NOT THE "*WORLD.*"
YEAH? GET BACK TO ME IN A FEW YEARS, KID. LET ME KNOW HOW THAT GOES.
I'LL TELL YOU HOW IT'S GOING ***NOW***.
I ALREADY LEFT MY VILLAGE, LOST MY POTENTIAL/MAYBE GIRLFRIEND, GOT MY BEST FRIEND KILLED, AND STARTED AN ILLEGAL QUEST THAT'S PUNISHABLE BY DEATH.
AND YOU DON'T SEE ***ME*** MOPING AROUND.
LOOK. YOUR BEST FRIEND? HE ***WASN'T*** YOUR BEST FRIEND.
WHAT ARE YOU TALKING ABOUT?
I FOLLOWED YOU TWO. THAT NIGHT AFTER YOU ATTACKED ME?
I WATCHED YOU BY THE FIRE THE NIGHT YOU FOUND GRETA. AND I SAW GRETA AND ARCHER WHISPERING. HE RAN OFF.
YOUR BEST FRIEND? SOLD YOU OUT.
WHAT? WHY WOULD HE? THAT CAN'T BE.
BELIEVE ME OR DON'T. NO SKIN OFF MY NOSE.
...
WHAT'S YOUR QUEST?

I'M TRYING TO FIND THE FOLKLORDS. AND AS IT HAPPENS? I FOUND THIS IN THE COTTAGE BACK THERE. LOOK!

THE FOLKLORDS? I THINK THEY'RE CONNECTED TO MY VISIONS.

"VISIONS"?

YEAH. LONG STORY.

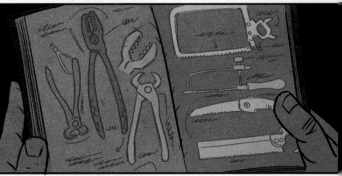

ANYWAY, MY VISIONS SHOW ME THESE SAME KINDS OF CRAZY CONTRAPTIONS. LIKE MY "FIRE LIGHTER." STUFF THAT DOESN'T EXIST. STUFF LIKE WHAT'S IN THIS BOOK!

WHOEVER MADE THIS? THEY WERE EITHER A FOLKLORD OR THEY HAD DIRECT KNOWLEDGE OF THEIR WORLD!

HUH.

"IF FOUND, PLEASE RETURN TO THE BRANCH LIBRARY OF BANNED BOOKS-- ON PENALTY OF DEATH."

WELL. IF THIS IS THE CLUE TO THE FOLKLORDS? THEN I KNOW WHERE YOU NEED TO GO.

THIS IS IT! THIS IS JUST THE BREADCRUMB WE NEED!

"WE"?

UGH. JUST, PLEASE. DON'T SAY "BREADCRUMB."

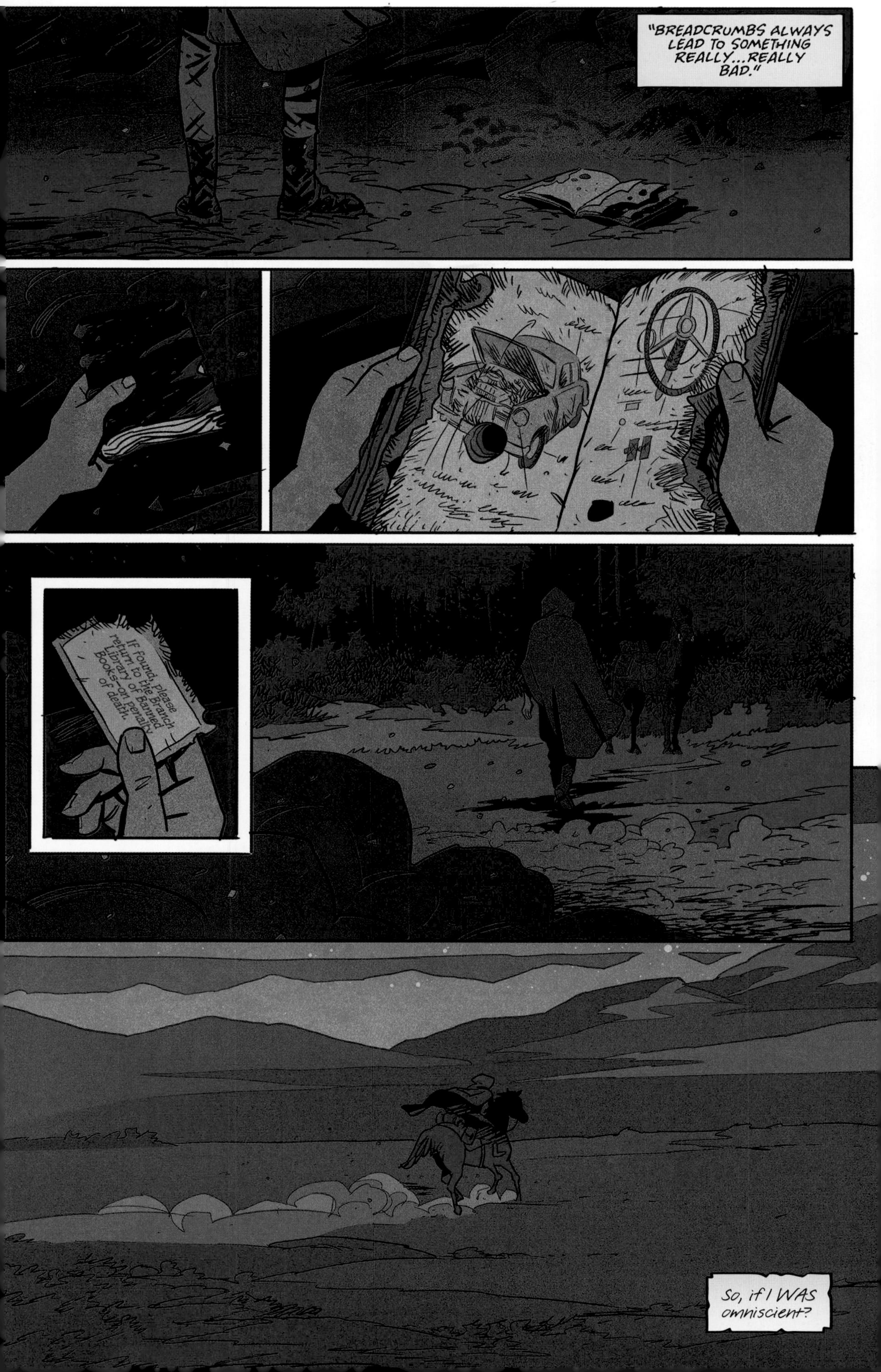
"BREADCRUMBS ALWAYS LEAD TO SOMETHING REALLY...REALLY BAD."
If found, please return to the Branch Library of Banned Books-on penalty of death.
So, if I WAS omniscient?

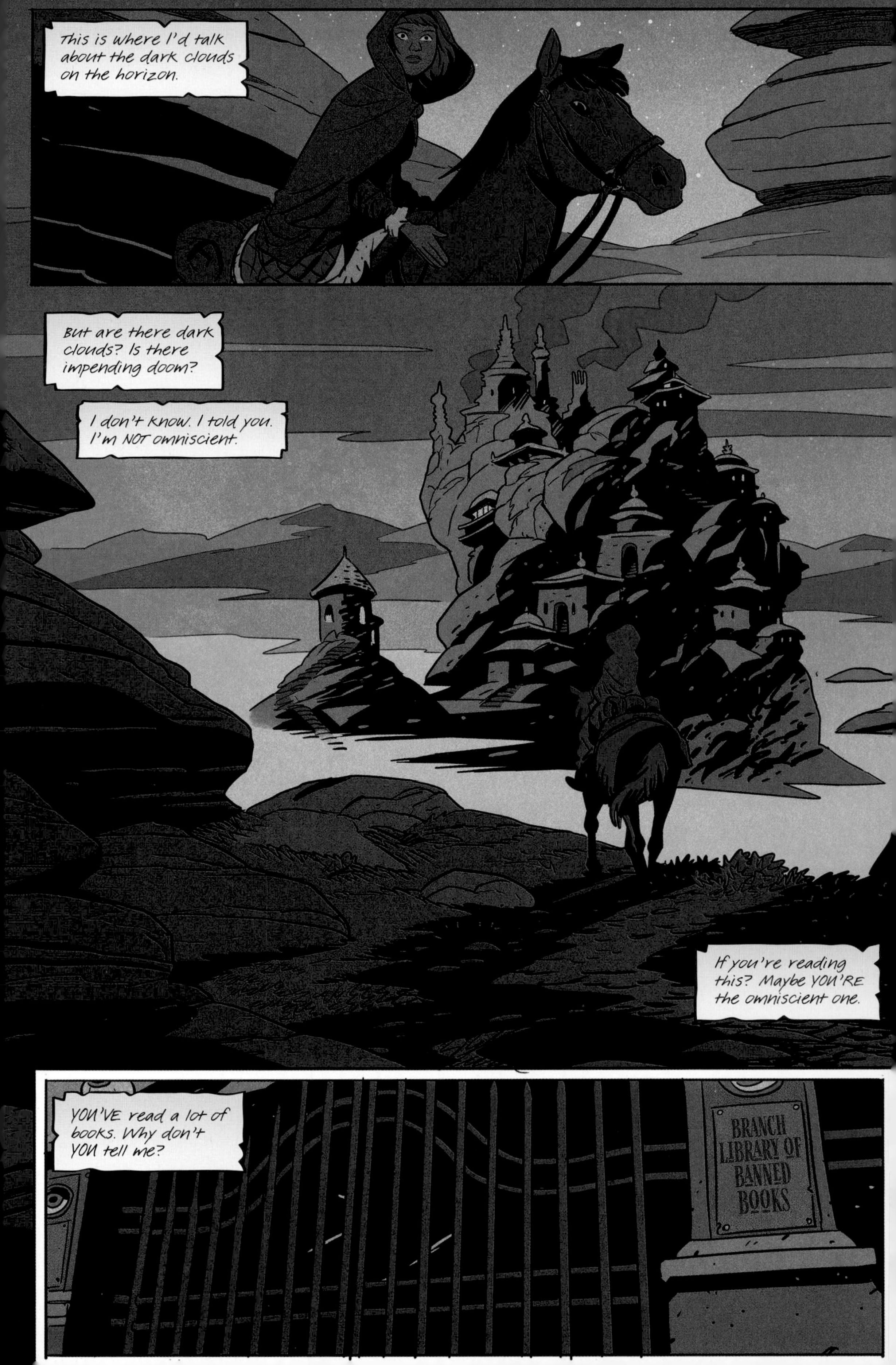
This is where I'd talk about the dark clouds on the horizon.
But are there dark clouds? Is there impending doom?
I don't know. I told you. I'm NOT omniscient.
If you're reading this? Maybe YOU'RE the omniscient one.
YOU'VE read a lot of books. Why don't YOU tell me?
BRANCH LIBRARY OF BANNED BOOKS

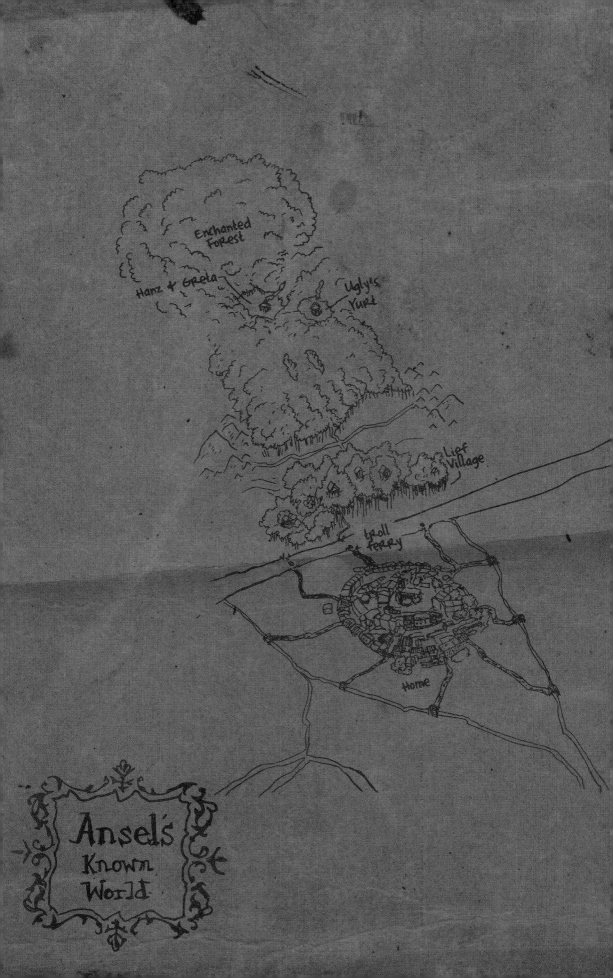

Enchanted
Forest

Hanz & Greta

Ugly's Yurt

Lief
Village

troll ferry

Home

Ansel's
Known
World

CHAPTER
FOUR

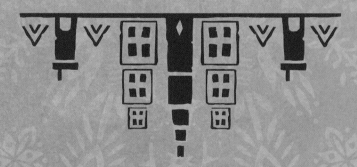

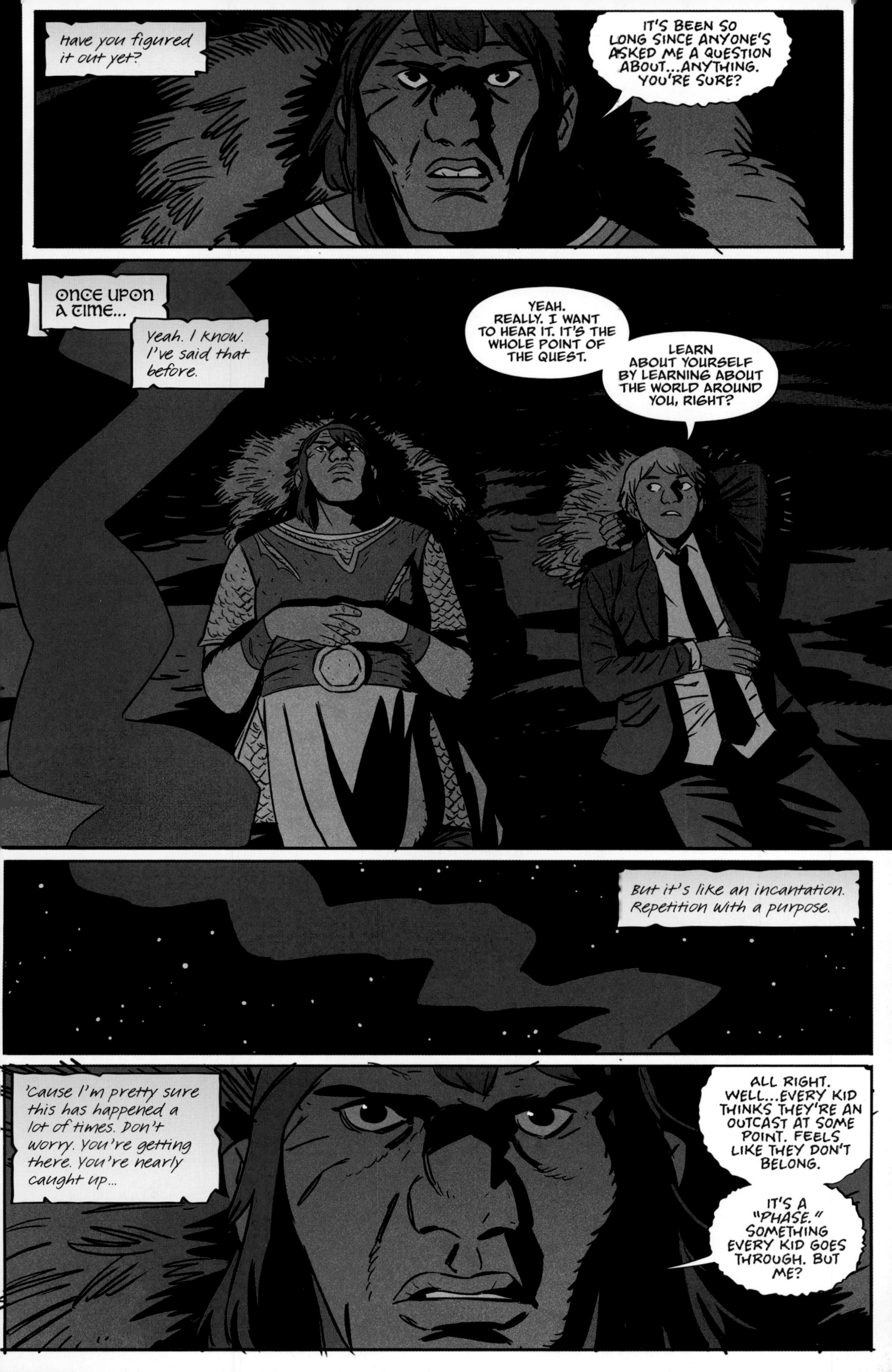
Have you figured it out yet?
IT'S BEEN SO LONG SINCE ANYONE'S ASKED ME A QUESTION ABOUT...ANYTHING. YOU'RE SURE?
ONCE UPON A TIME...
Yeah. I know. I've said that before.
YEAH. REALLY. I WANT TO HEAR IT. IT'S THE WHOLE POINT OF THE QUEST.
LEARN ABOUT YOURSELF BY LEARNING ABOUT THE WORLD AROUND YOU, RIGHT?
But it's like an incantation. Repetition with a purpose.
'Cause I'm pretty sure this has happened a lot of times. Don't worry. You're getting there. You're nearly caught up...
ALL RIGHT. WELL...EVERY KID THINKS THEY'RE AN OUTCAST AT SOME POINT. FEELS LIKE THEY DON'T BELONG.
IT'S A "PHASE." SOMETHING EVERY KID GOES THROUGH. BUT ME?

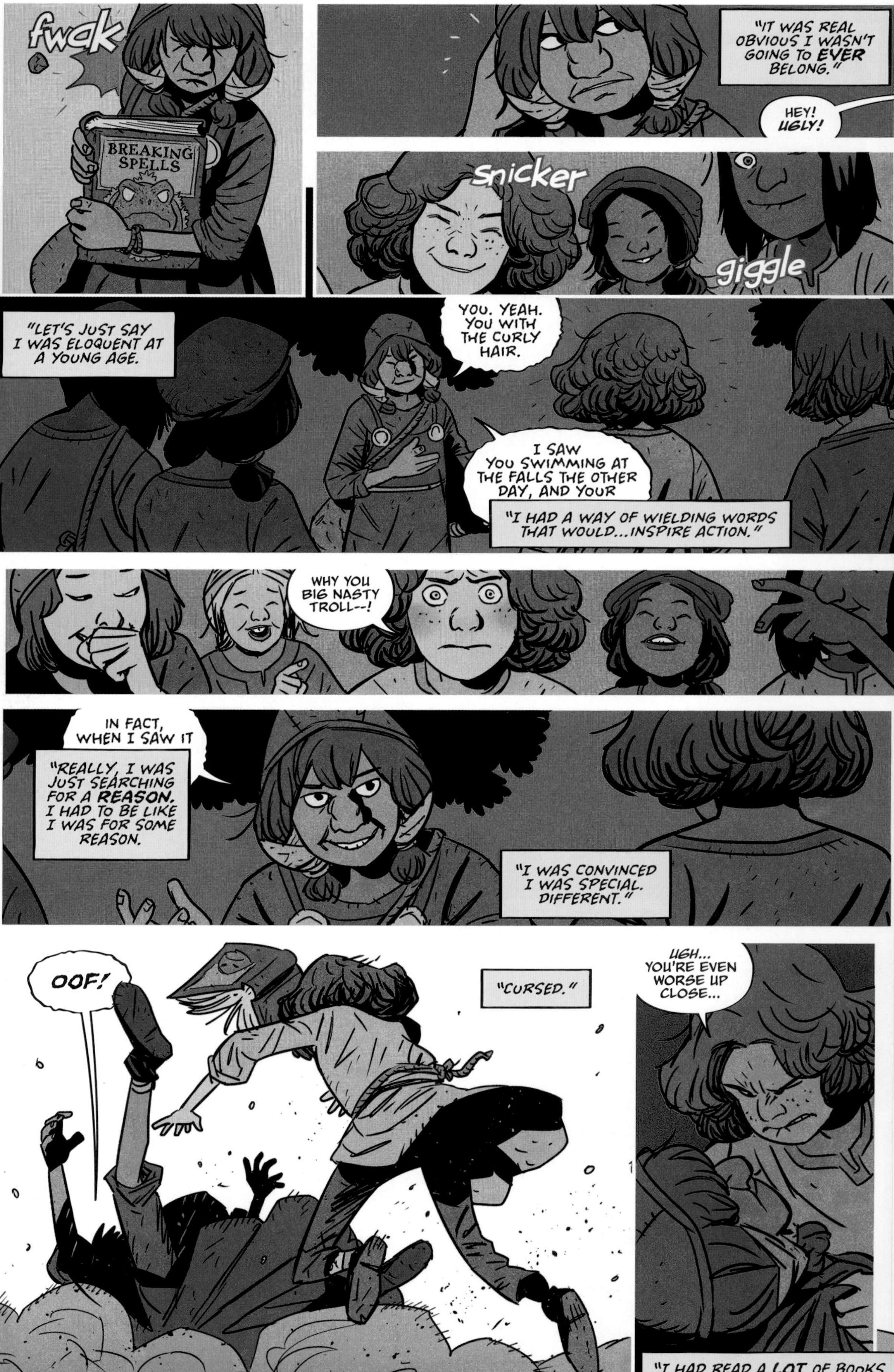
fwak
BREAKING SPELLS
"IT WAS REAL OBVIOUS I WASN'T GOING TO EVER BELONG."
HEY! UGLY!
snicker
giggle
"LET'S JUST SAY I WAS ELOQUENT AT A YOUNG AGE.
YOU. YEAH. YOU WITH THE CURLY HAIR.
I SAW YOU SWIMMING AT THE FALLS THE OTHER DAY, AND YOUR
"I HAD A WAY OF WIELDING WORDS THAT WOULD...INSPIRE ACTION."
WHY YOU BIG NASTY TROLL--!
IN FACT, WHEN I SAW IT
"REALLY, I WAS JUST SEARCHING FOR A REASON. I HAD TO BE LIKE I WAS FOR SOME REASON.
"I WAS CONVINCED I WAS SPECIAL. DIFFERENT."
OOF!
"CURSED."
UGH... YOU'RE EVEN WORSE UP CLOSE...
"I HAD READ A LOT OF BOOKS. I WAS ALSO CONVINCED I KNEW HOW TO LIFT THE CURSE."

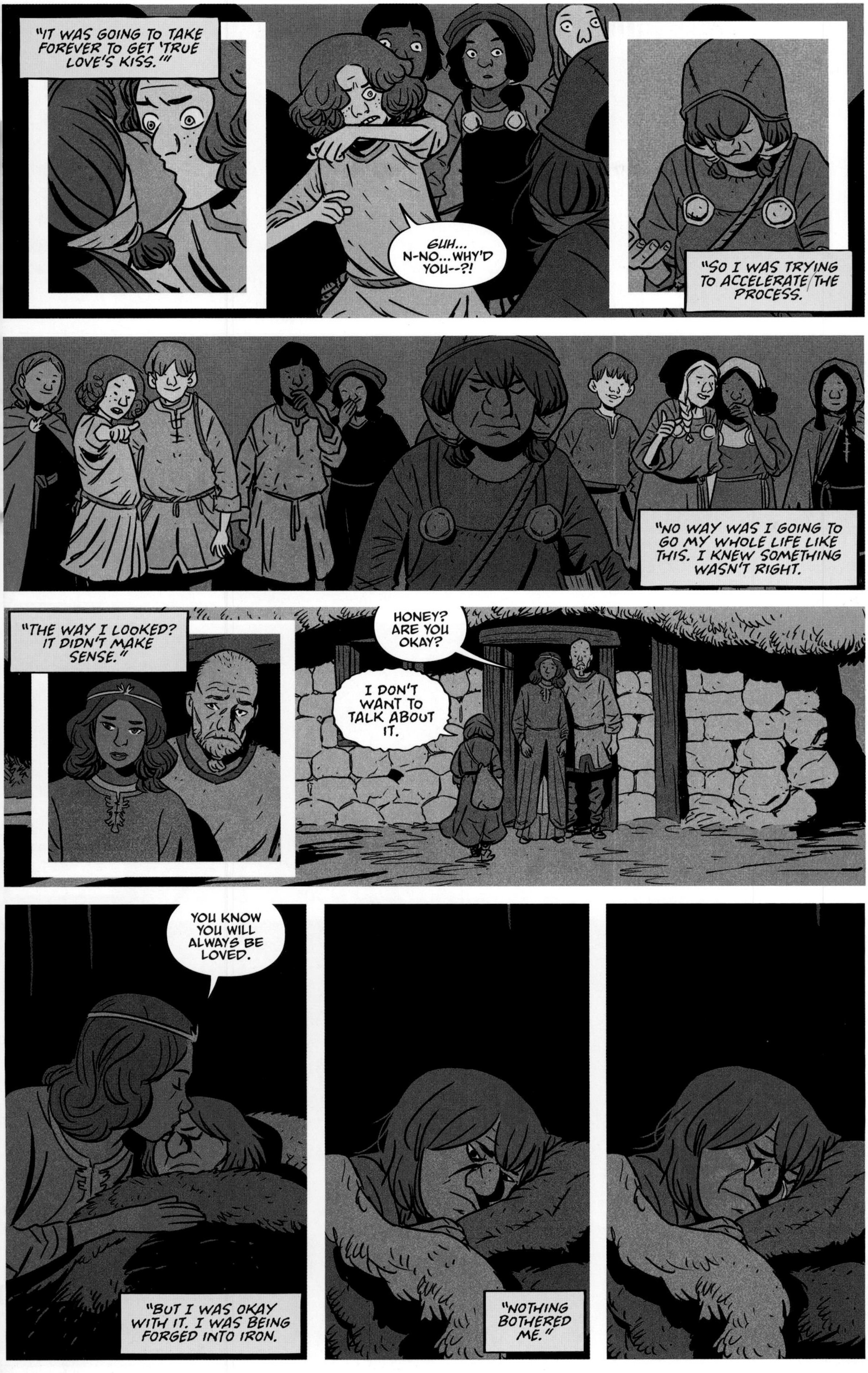
"IT WAS GOING TO TAKE FOREVER TO GET 'TRUE LOVE'S KISS.'"
GUH... N-NO...WHY'D YOU--?!
"SO I WAS TRYING TO ACCELERATE THE PROCESS.
"NO WAY WAS I GOING TO GO MY WHOLE LIFE LIKE THIS. I KNEW SOMETHING WASN'T RIGHT.
"THE WAY I LOOKED? IT DIDN'T MAKE SENSE."
HONEY? ARE YOU OKAY?
I DON'T WANT TO TALK ABOUT IT.
YOU KNOW YOU WILL ALWAYS BE LOVED.
"BUT I WAS OKAY WITH IT. I WAS BEING FORGED INTO IRON.
"NOTHING BOTHERED ME."

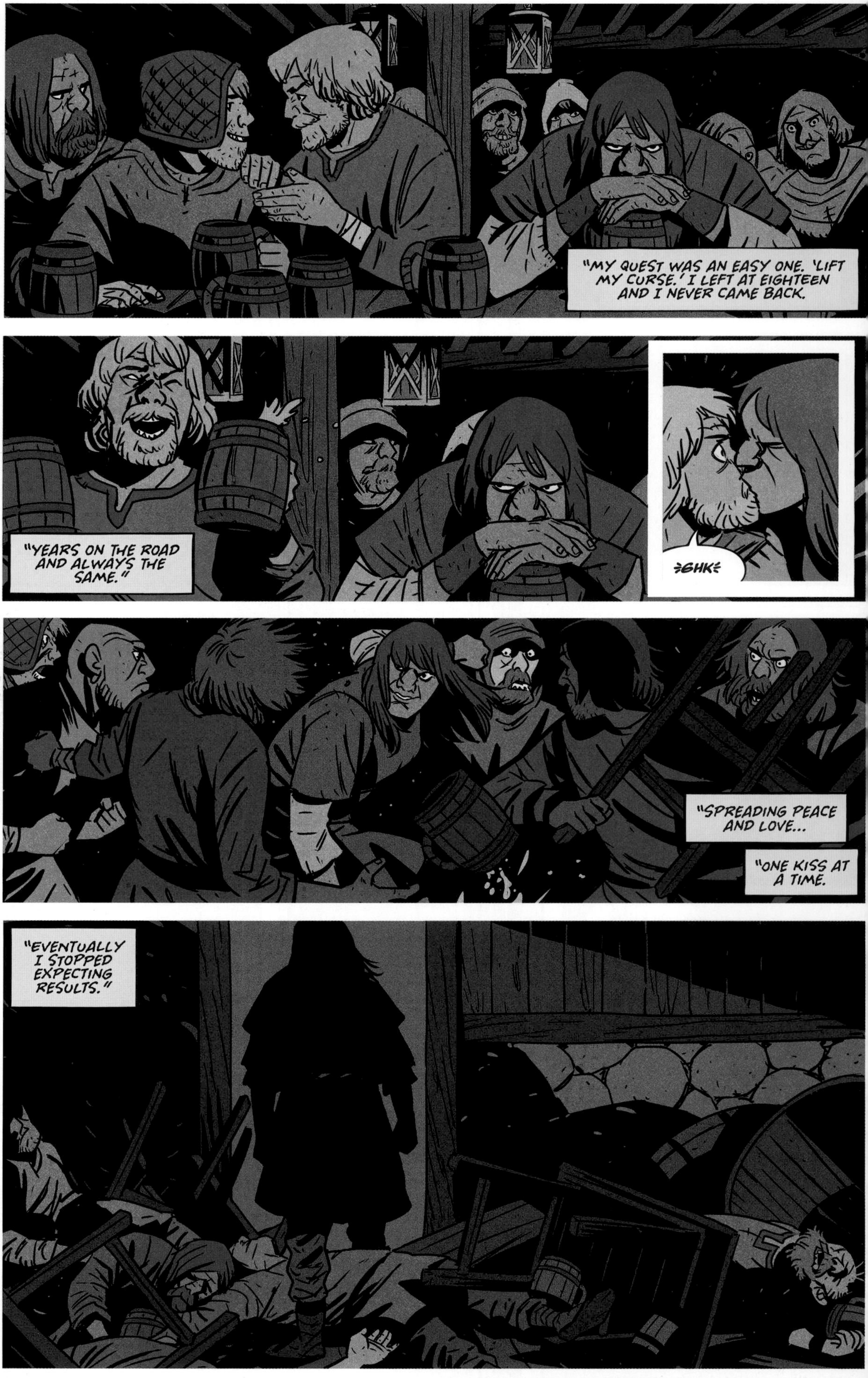
"MY QUEST WAS AN EASY ONE. 'LIFT MY CURSE.' I LEFT AT EIGHTEEN AND I NEVER CAME BACK.
"YEARS ON THE ROAD AND ALWAYS THE SAME."
GHK
"SPREADING PEACE AND LOVE...
"ONE KISS AT A TIME.
"EVENTUALLY I STOPPED EXPECTING RESULTS."

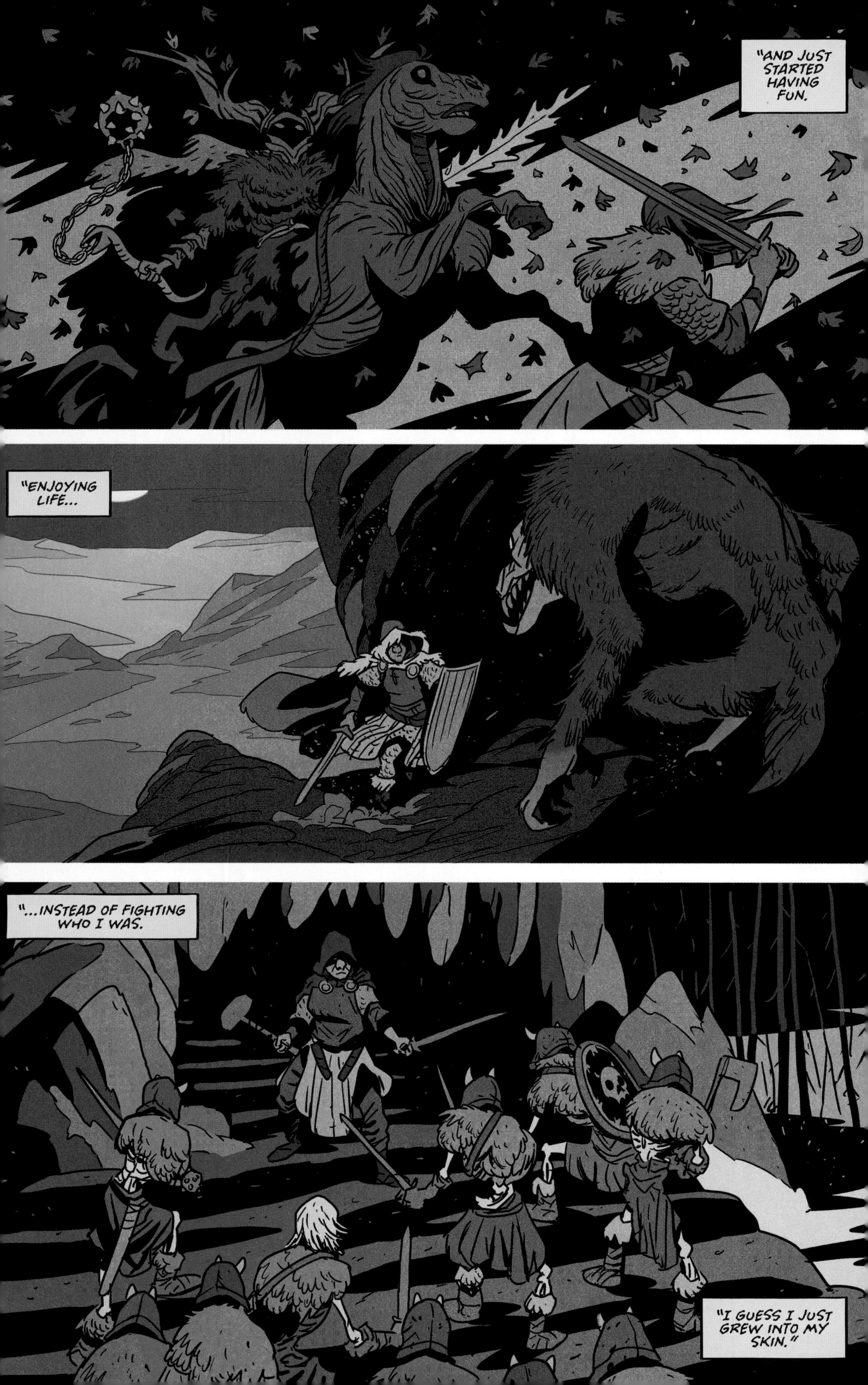
"AND JUST STARTED HAVING FUN.
"ENJOYING LIFE...
"...INSTEAD OF FIGHTING WHO I WAS.
"I GUESS I JUST GREW INTO MY SKIN."

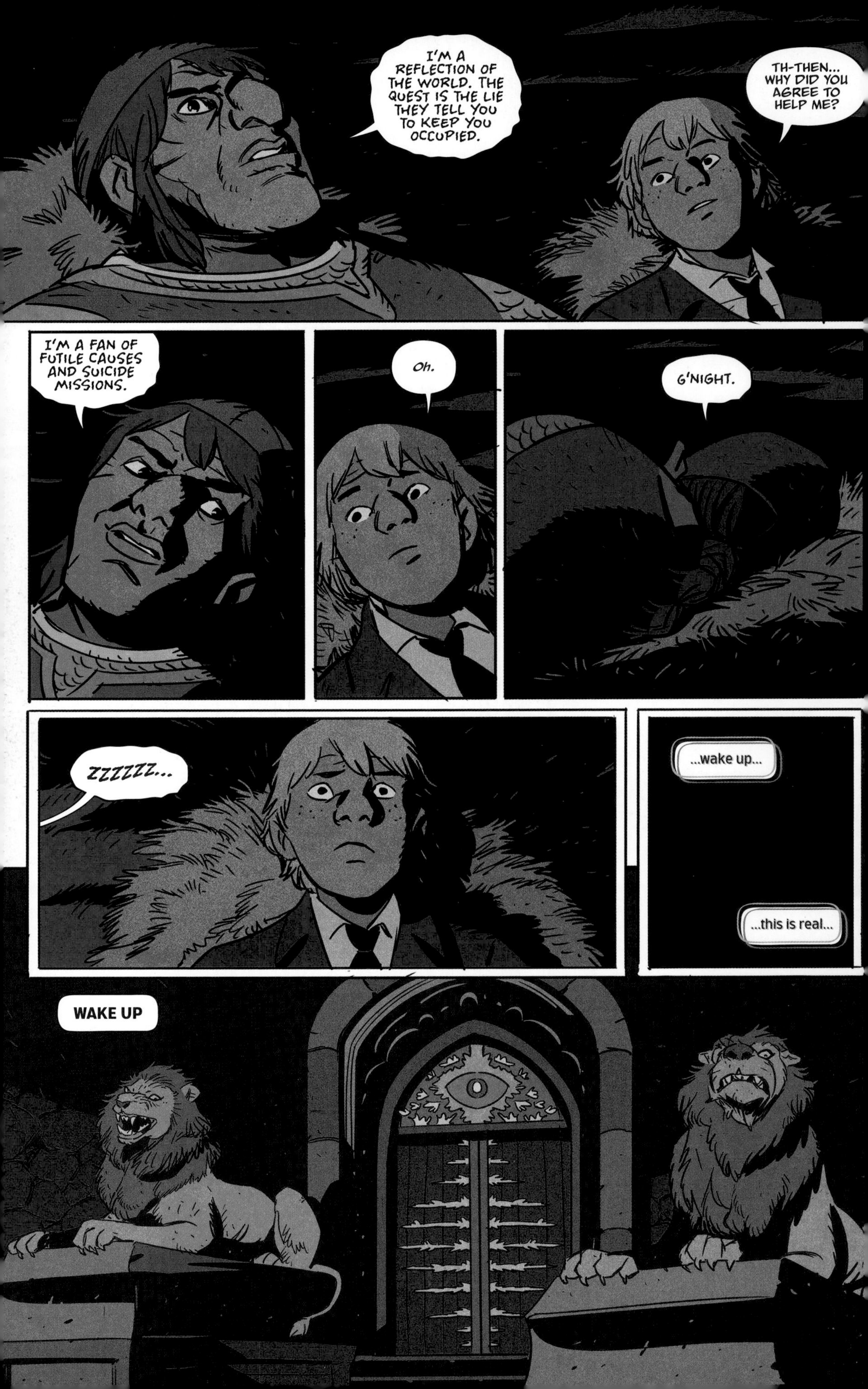
I'M A REFLECTION OF THE WORLD. THE QUEST IS THE LIE THEY TELL YOU TO KEEP YOU OCCUPIED.
TH-THEN... WHY DID YOU AGREE TO HELP ME?
I'M A FAN OF FUTILE CAUSES AND SUICIDE MISSIONS.
Oh.
G'NIGHT.
ZZZZZZ...
...wake up...
...this is real...
WAKE UP

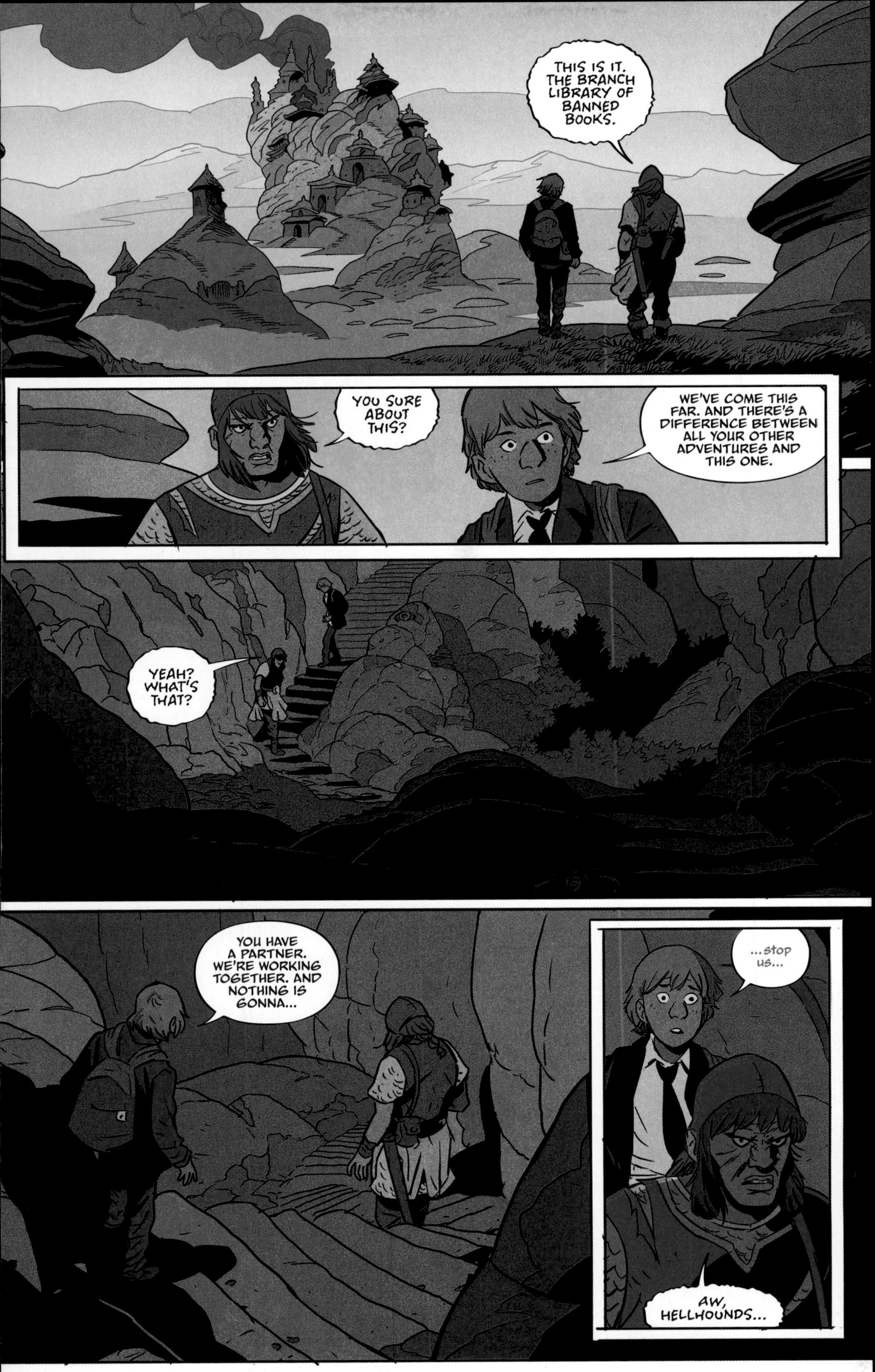
THIS IS IT. THE BRANCH LIBRARY OF BANNED BOOKS.
YOU SURE ABOUT THIS?
WE'VE COME THIS FAR. AND THERE'S A DIFFERENCE BETWEEN ALL YOUR OTHER ADVENTURES AND THIS ONE.
YEAH? WHAT'S THAT?
YOU HAVE A PARTNER. WE'RE WORKING TOGETHER. AND NOTHING IS GONNA...
...stop us...
AW, HELLHOUNDS...

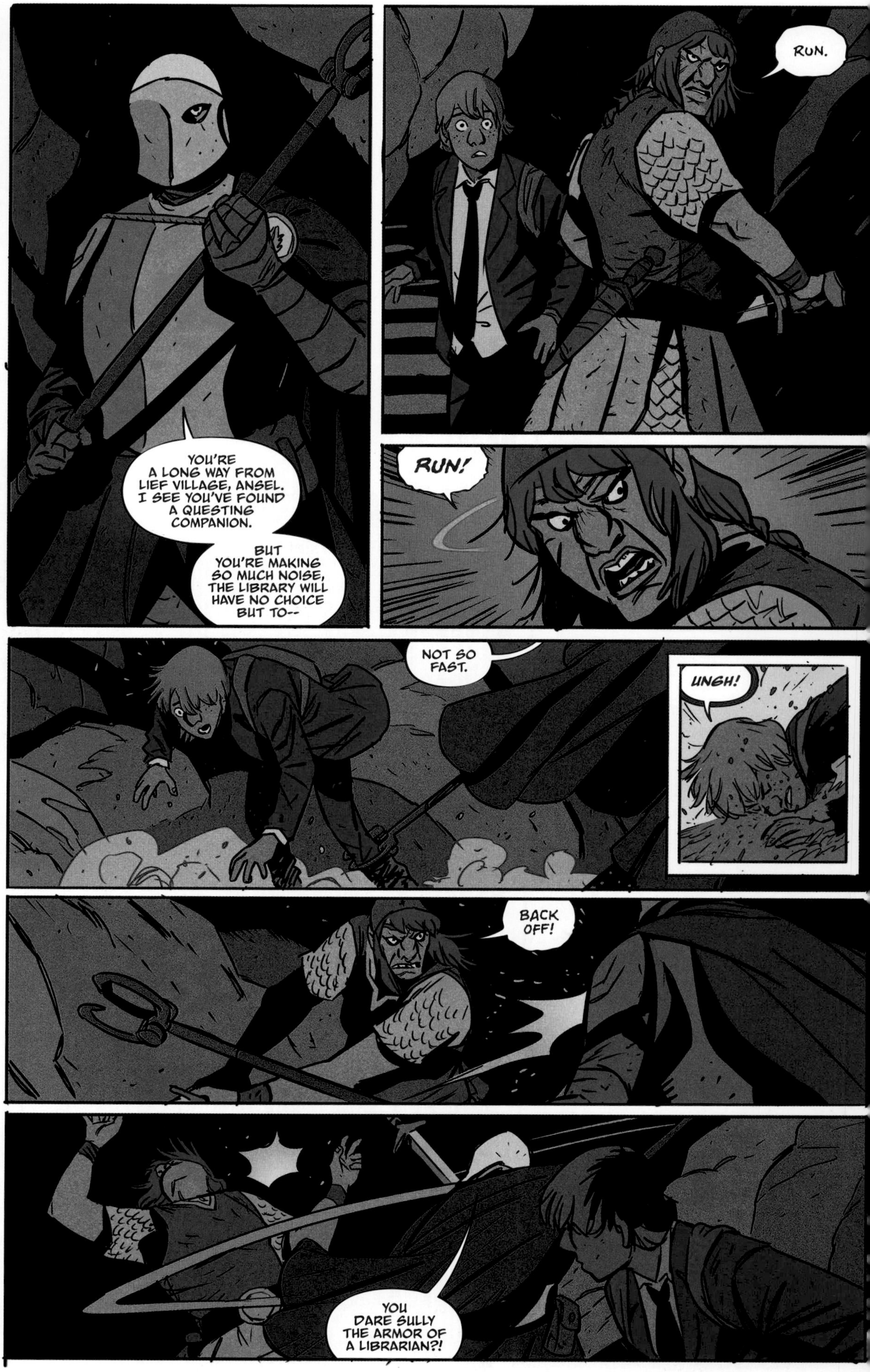
YOU'RE A LONG WAY FROM LIEF VILLAGE, ANSEL. I SEE YOU'VE FOUND A QUESTING COMPANION.
BUT YOU'RE MAKING SO MUCH NOISE, THE LIBRARY WILL HAVE NO CHOICE BUT TO--
RUN.
RUN!
NOT SO FAST.
UNGH!
BACK OFF!
YOU DARE SULLY THE ARMOR OF A LIBRARIAN?!

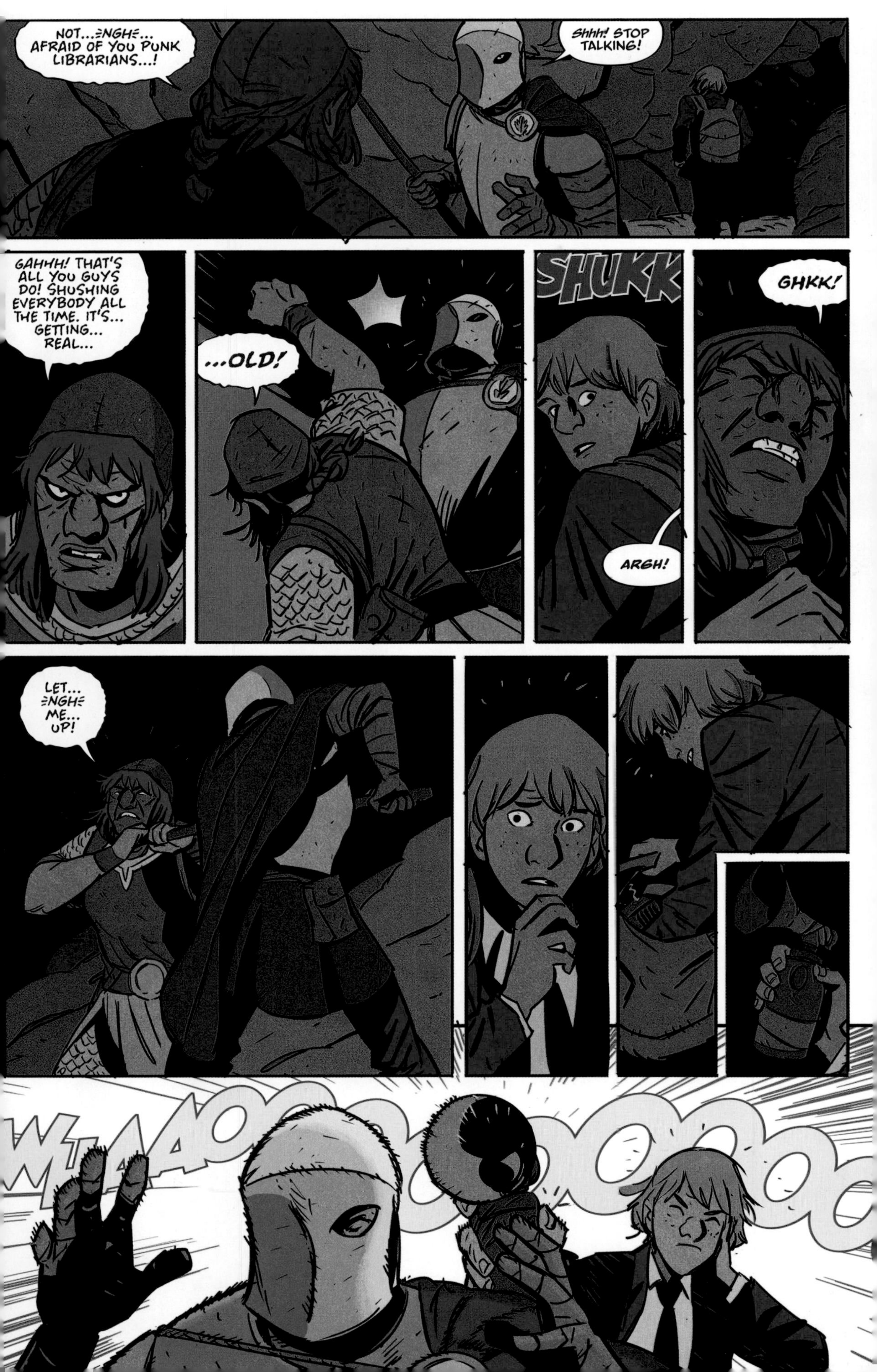
NOT... ≡NGH≡... AFRAID OF YOU PUNK LIBRARIANS...!
Shhh! STOP TALKING!
GAHHH! THAT'S ALL YOU GUYS DO! SHUSHING EVERYBODY ALL THE TIME. IT'S... GETTING... REAL...
...OLD!
SHUKK
ARGH!
GHKK!
LET... ≡NGH≡ ME... UP!

UNNGHH!

GAHHHH!

D-DON'T FIGHT! I KNOW YOU. NOT JUST FROM BEFORE...

...BUT FROM MY VISIONS. YOU'RE DIFFERENT FROM THE REST.

LISTEN. I'M HERE TO HELP...

WHAT?!

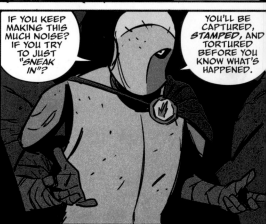

IF YOU KEEP MAKING THIS MUCH NOISE? IF YOU TRY TO JUST "SNEAK IN"?

YOU'LL BE CAPTURED, *STAMPED*, AND TORTURED BEFORE YOU KNOW WHAT'S HAPPENED.

FOLLOW ME IF YOU WANT TO SUCCEED.

YOU KNOW THIS GUY?

Uh...KIND OF? HE'S THE ONE LIBRARIAN THAT HASN'T BEEN HORRIBLE.

HE *SEEMS* PRETTY HORRIBLE...

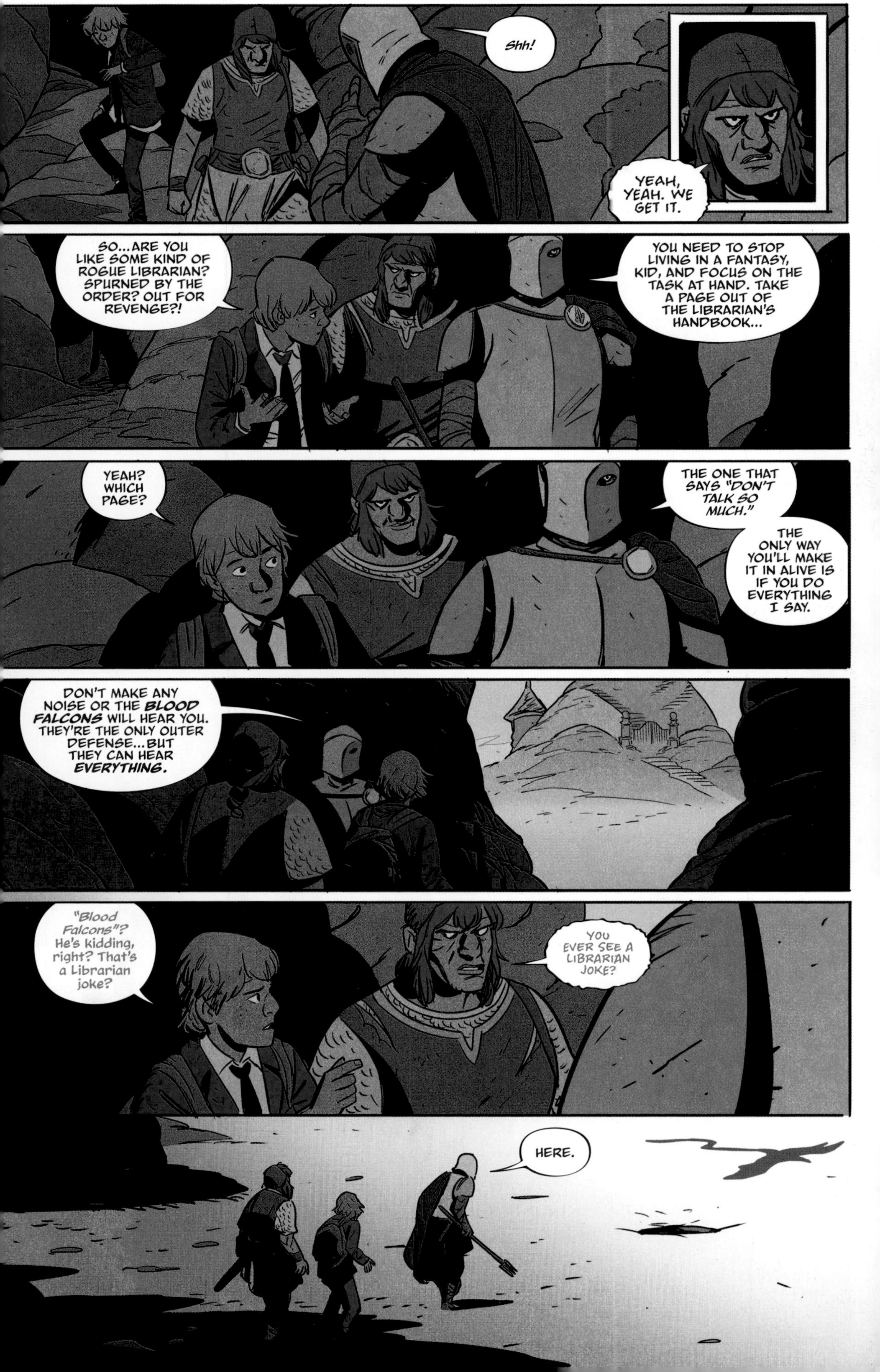
Shh!
YEAH, YEAH. WE GET IT.
SO...ARE YOU LIKE SOME KIND OF ROGUE LIBRARIAN? SPURNED BY THE ORDER? OUT FOR REVENGE?!
YOU NEED TO STOP LIVING IN A FANTASY, KID, AND FOCUS ON THE TASK AT HAND. TAKE A PAGE OUT OF THE LIBRARIAN'S HANDBOOK...
YEAH? WHICH PAGE?
THE ONE THAT SAYS "DON'T TALK SO MUCH."
THE ONLY WAY YOU'LL MAKE IT IN ALIVE IS IF YOU DO EVERYTHING I SAY.
DON'T MAKE ANY NOISE OR THE BLOOD FALCONS WILL HEAR YOU. THEY'RE THE ONLY OUTER DEFENSE...BUT THEY CAN HEAR EVERYTHING.
"Blood Falcons"? He's kidding, right? That's a Librarian joke?
YOU EVER SEE A LIBRARIAN JOKE?
HERE.

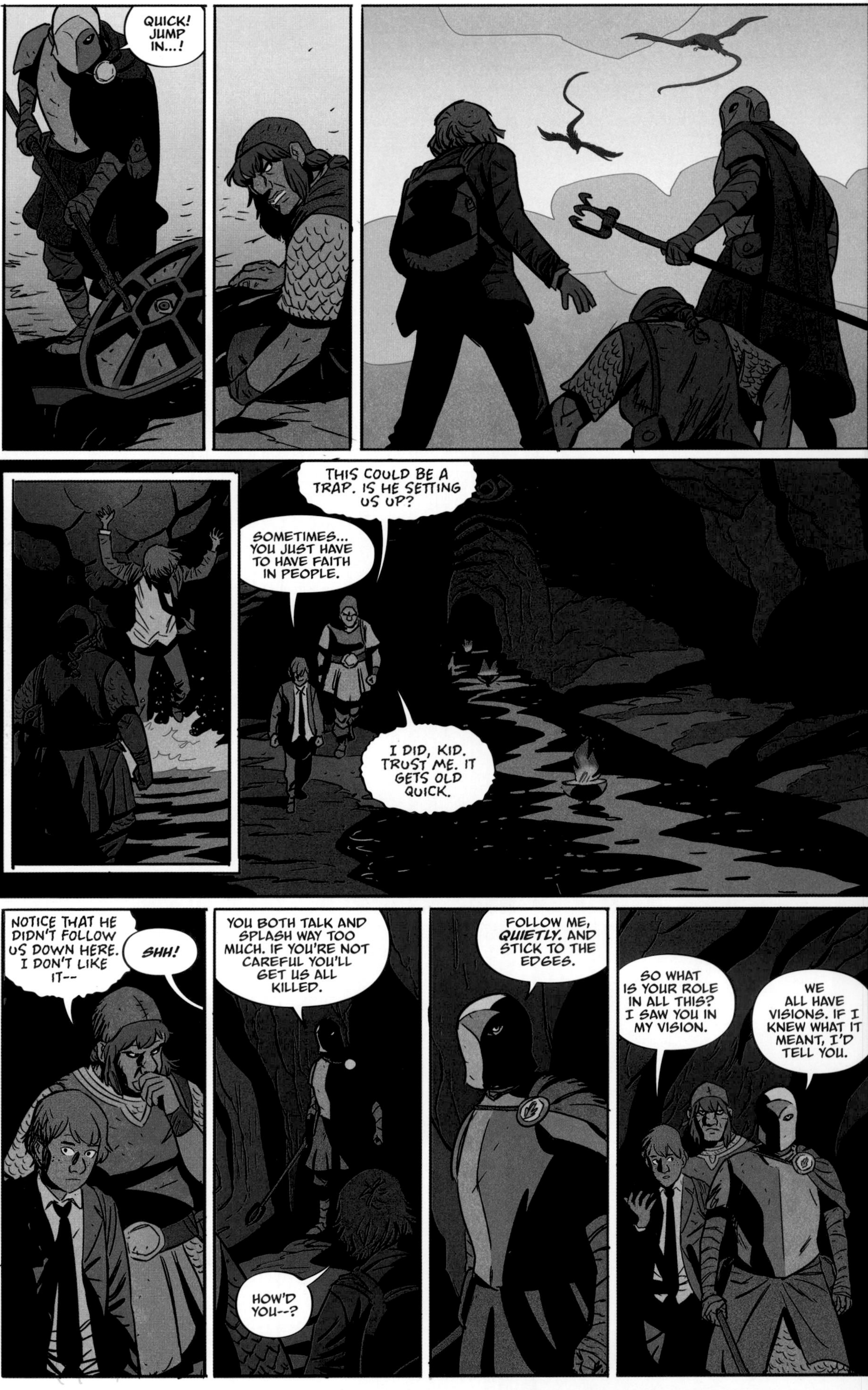
QUICK! JUMP IN...!
THIS COULD BE A TRAP. IS HE SETTING US UP?
SOMETIMES... YOU JUST HAVE TO HAVE FAITH IN PEOPLE.
I DID, KID. TRUST ME. IT GETS OLD QUICK.
NOTICE THAT HE DIDN'T FOLLOW US DOWN HERE. I DON'T LIKE IT--
SHH!
YOU BOTH TALK AND SPLASH WAY TOO MUCH. IF YOU'RE NOT CAREFUL YOU'LL GET US ALL KILLED.
HOW'D YOU--?
FOLLOW ME, QUIETLY. AND STICK TO THE EDGES.
SO WHAT IS YOUR ROLE IN ALL THIS? I SAW YOU IN MY VISION.
WE ALL HAVE VISIONS. IF I KNEW WHAT IT MEANT, I'D TELL YOU.

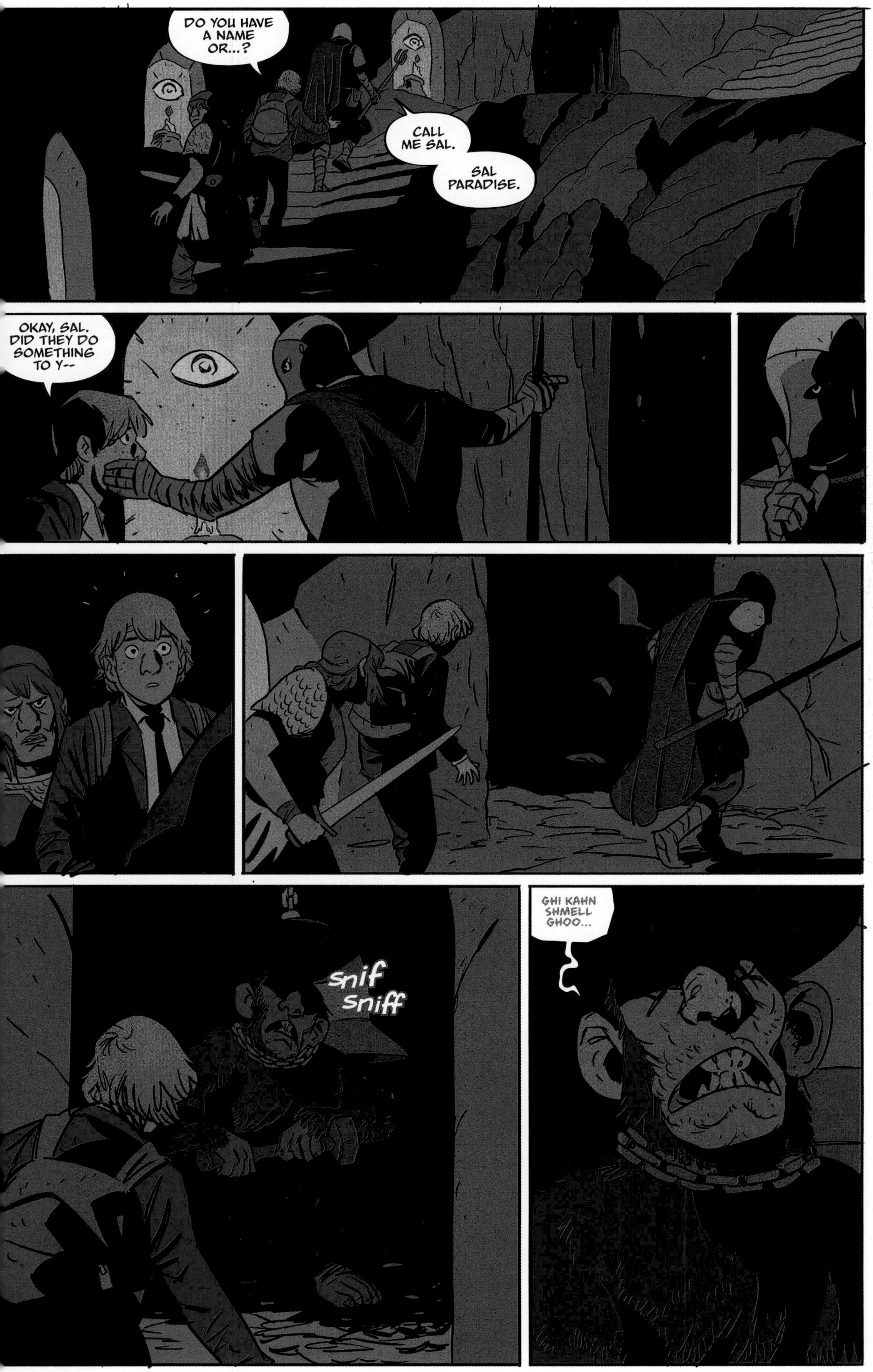
DO YOU HAVE A NAME OR...?
CALL ME SAL.
SAL PARADISE.
OKAY, SAL. DID THEY DO SOMETHING TO Y--
snif sniff
GHI KAHN SHMELL GHOO...

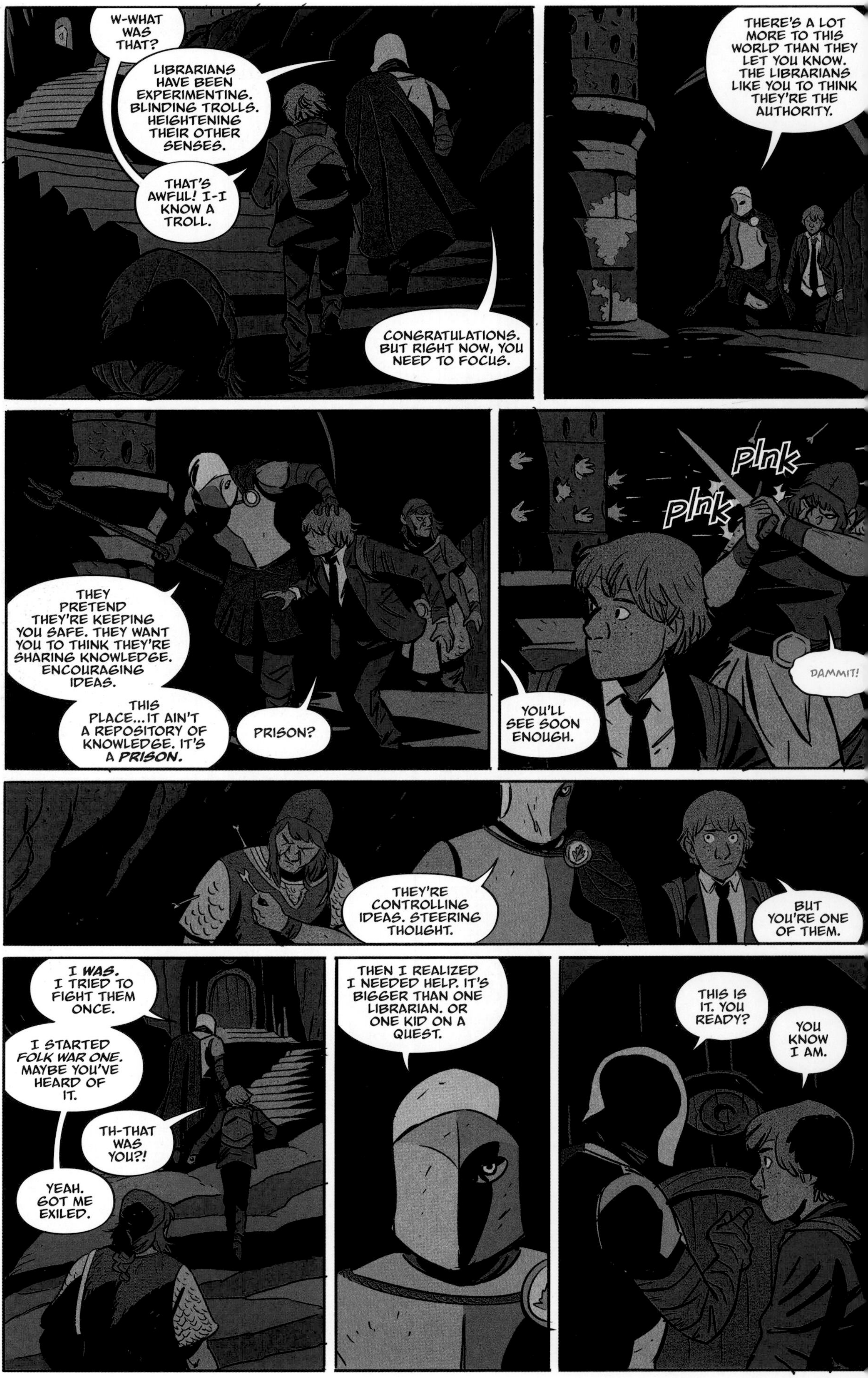

W-WHAT WAS THAT?
LIBRARIANS HAVE BEEN EXPERIMENTING. BLINDING TROLLS. HEIGHTENING THEIR OTHER SENSES.
THAT'S AWFUL! I-I KNOW A TROLL.
CONGRATULATIONS. BUT RIGHT NOW, YOU NEED TO FOCUS.
THERE'S A LOT MORE TO THIS WORLD THAN THEY LET YOU KNOW. THE LIBRARIANS LIKE YOU TO THINK THEY'RE THE AUTHORITY.
THEY PRETEND THEY'RE KEEPING YOU SAFE. THEY WANT YOU TO THINK THEY'RE SHARING KNOWLEDGE. ENCOURAGING IDEAS.
THIS PLACE...IT AIN'T A REPOSITORY OF KNOWLEDGE. IT'S A *PRISON*.
PRISON?
PLNK
PLNK
DAMMIT!
YOU'LL SEE SOON ENOUGH.
THEY'RE CONTROLLING IDEAS. STEERING THOUGHT.
BUT YOU'RE ONE OF THEM.
I *WAS*. I TRIED TO FIGHT THEM ONCE.
I STARTED *FOLK WAR ONE*. MAYBE YOU'VE HEARD OF IT.
TH-THAT WAS YOU?!
YEAH. GOT ME EXILED.
THEN I REALIZED I NEEDED HELP. IT'S BIGGER THAN ONE LIBRARIAN. OR ONE KID ON A QUEST.
THIS IS IT. YOU READY?
YOU KNOW I AM.

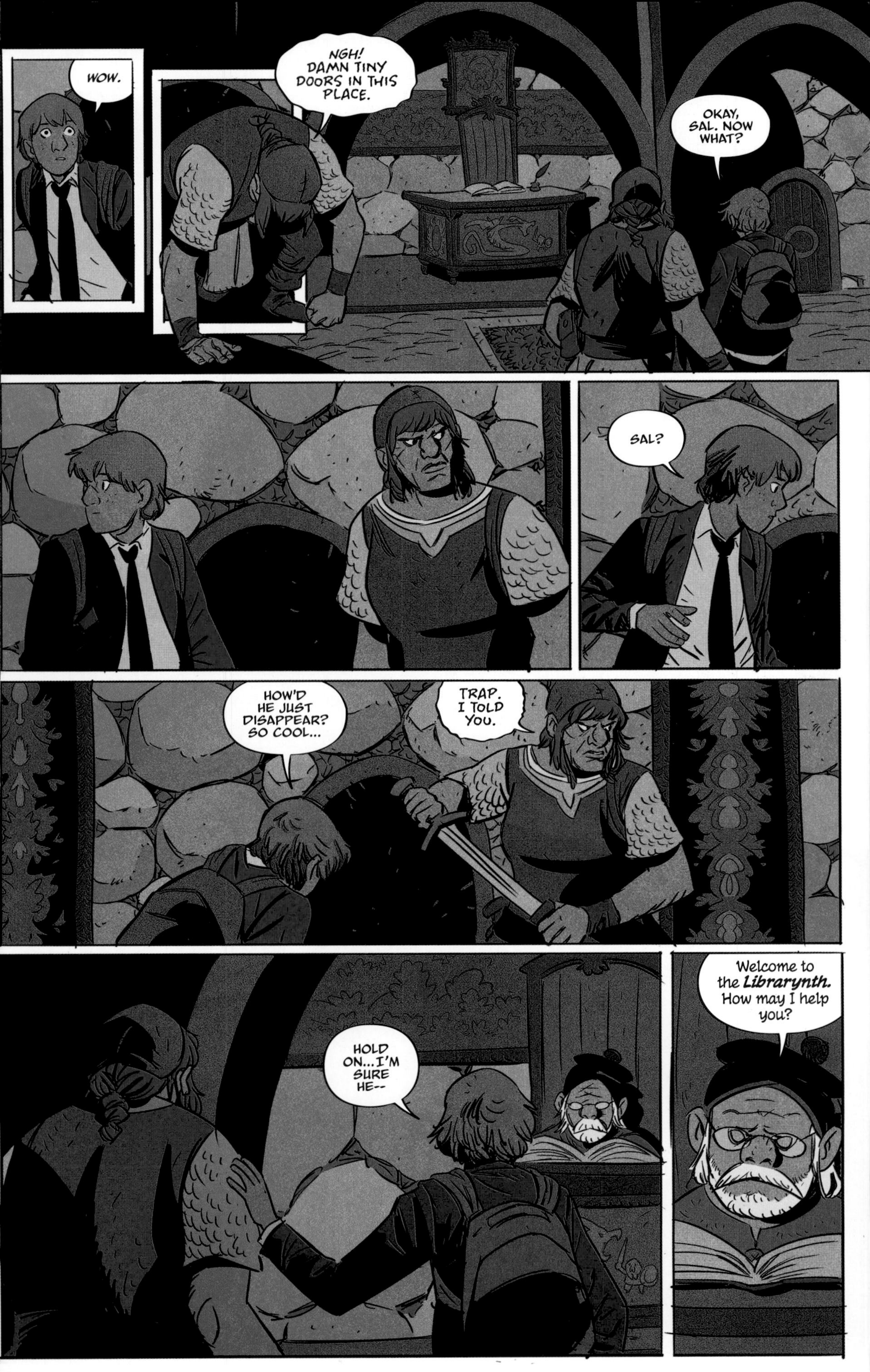
WOW.
NGH! DAMN TINY DOORS IN THIS PLACE.
OKAY, SAL. NOW WHAT?
SAL?
HOW'D HE JUST DISAPPEAR? SO COOL...
TRAP. I TOLD YOU.
HOLD ON...I'M SURE HE--
Welcome to the *Librarynth.* How may I help you?

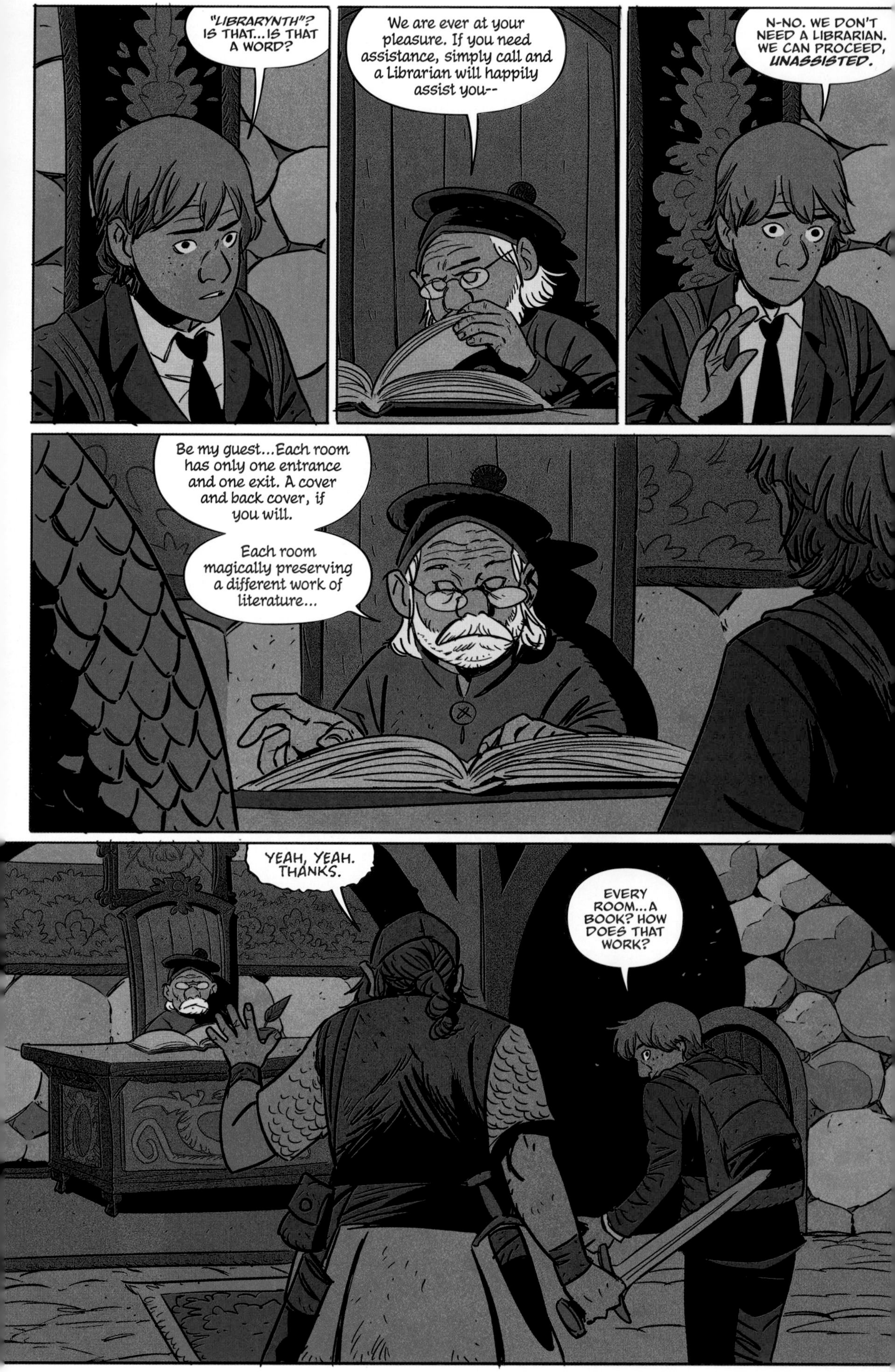
"LIBRARYNTH"? IS THAT...IS THAT A WORD?
We are ever at your pleasure. If you need assistance, simply call and a Librarian will happily assist you--
N-NO. WE DON'T NEED A LIBRARIAN. WE CAN PROCEED, UNASSISTED.
Be my guest...Each room has only one entrance and one exit. A cover and back cover, if you will.
Each room magically preserving a different work of literature...
YEAH, YEAH. THANKS.
EVERY ROOM...A BOOK? HOW DOES THAT WORK?

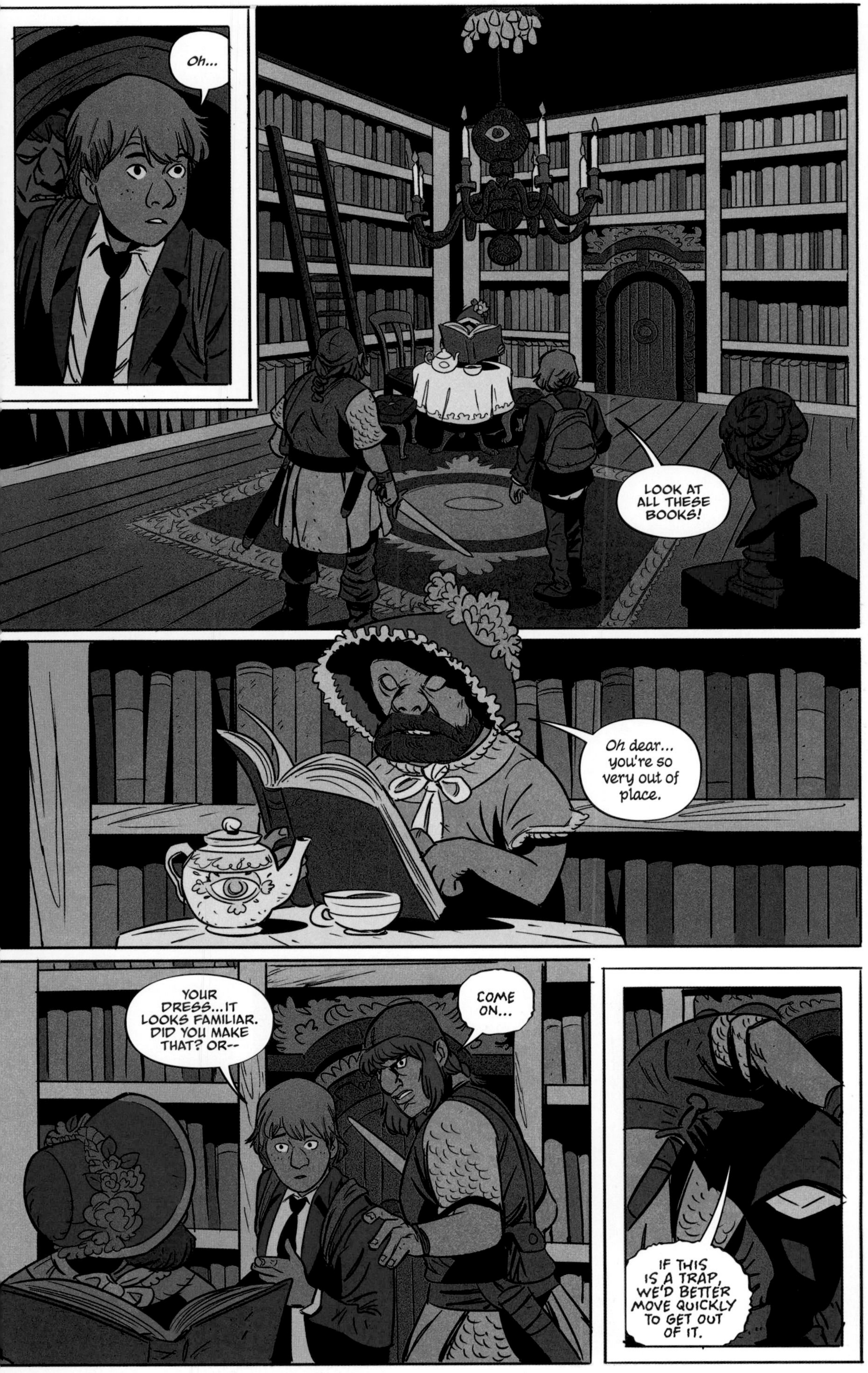
Oh...
LOOK AT ALL THESE BOOKS!
Oh dear... you're so very out of place.
YOUR DRESS...IT LOOKS FAMILIAR. DID YOU MAKE THAT? OR--
COME ON...
IF THIS IS A TRAP, WE'D BETTER MOVE QUICKLY TO GET OUT OF IT.

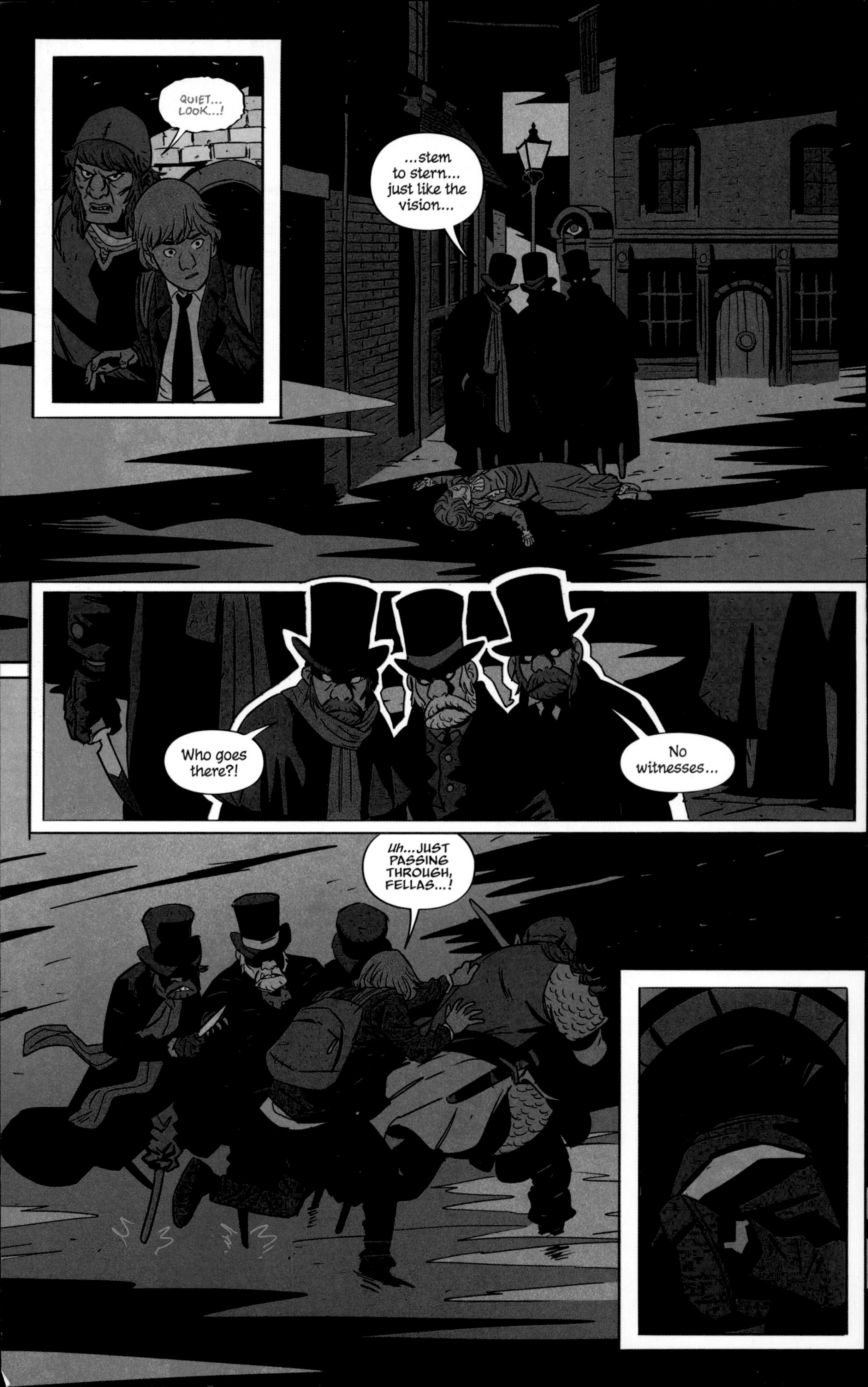
QUIET... LOOK...!
...stem to stern... just like the vision...
Who goes there?!
No witnesses...
Uh... JUST PASSING THROUGH, FELLAS...!

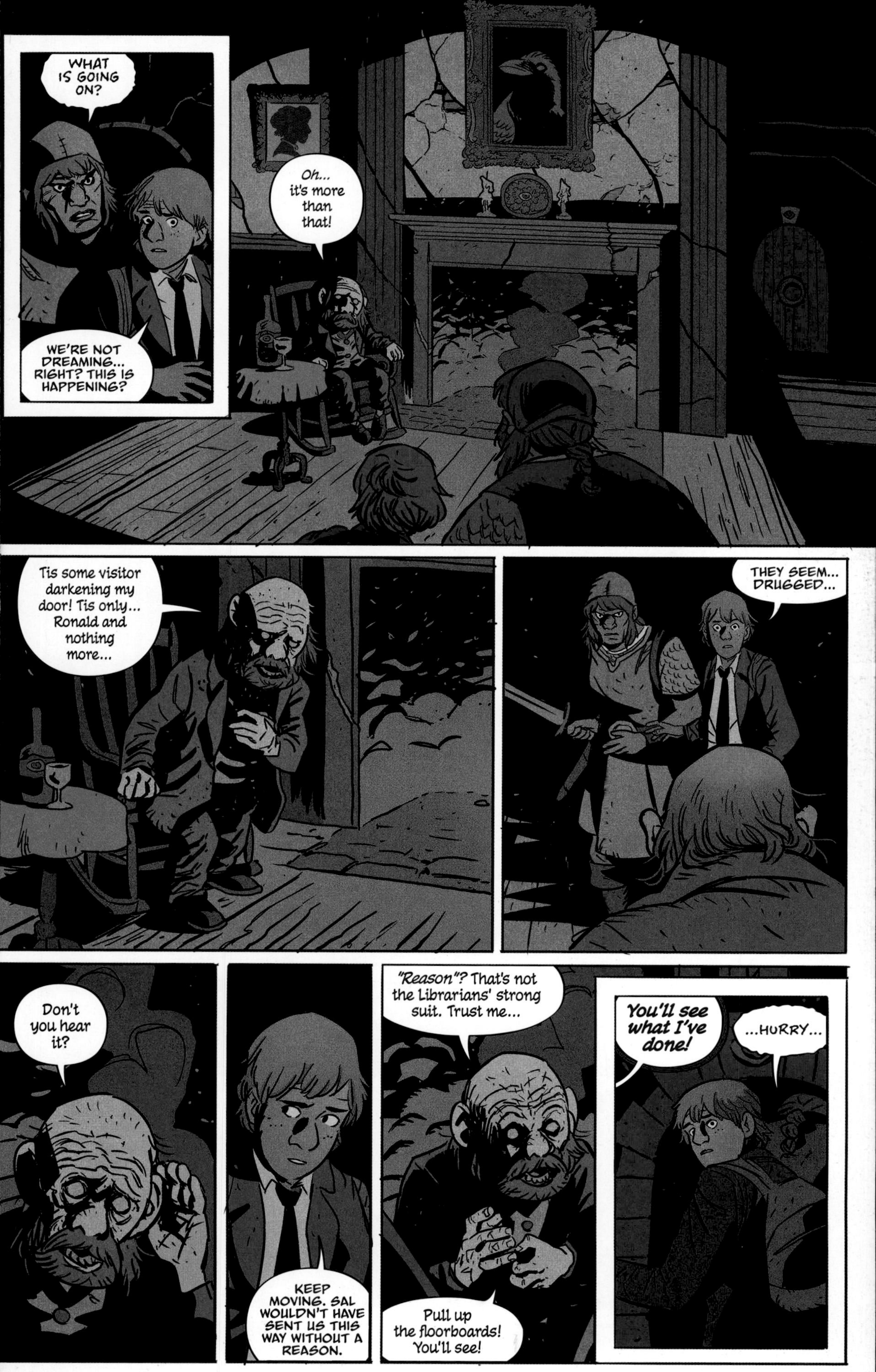
WHAT IS GOING ON?
WE'RE NOT DREAMING... RIGHT? THIS IS HAPPENING?
Oh... it's more than that!
Tis some visitor darkening my door! Tis only... Ronald and nothing more...
THEY SEEM... DRUGGED...
Don't you hear it?
KEEP MOVING. SAL WOULDN'T HAVE SENT US THIS WAY WITHOUT A REASON.
"Reason"? That's not the Librarians' strong suit. Trust me...
Pull up the floorboards! You'll see!
You'll see what I've done!
...HURRY...

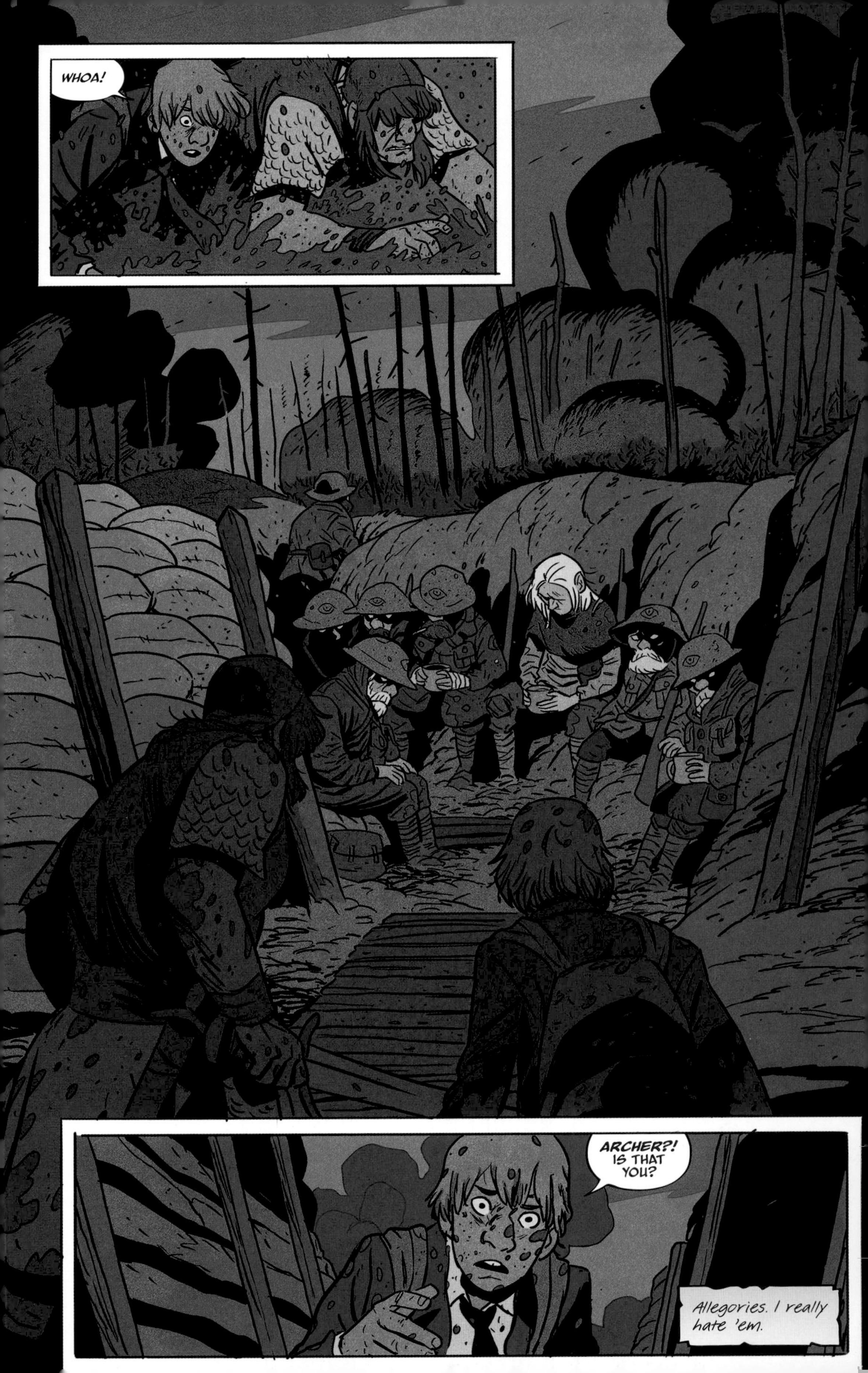
WHOA!
ARCHER?! IS THAT YOU?
Allegories. I really hate 'em.

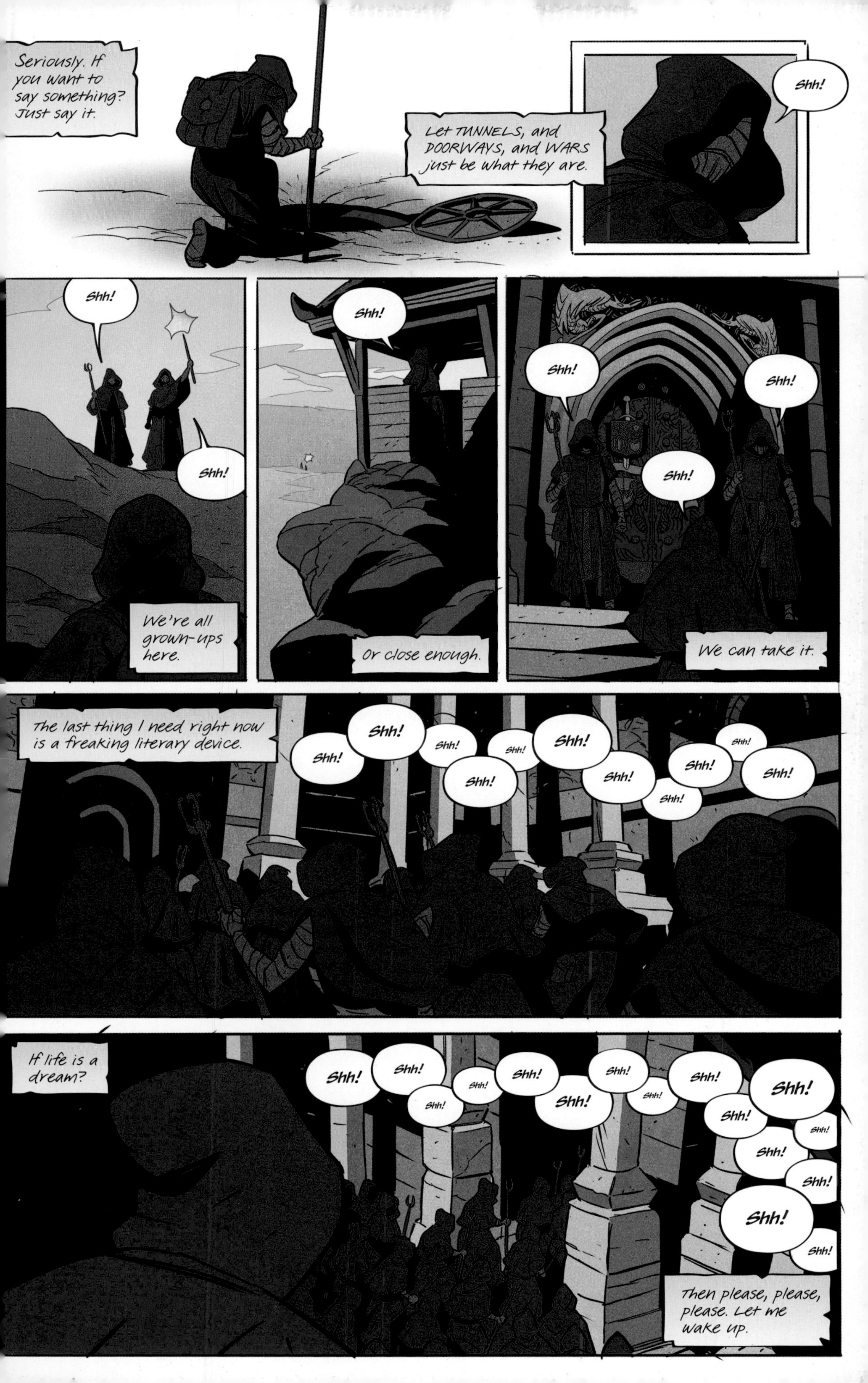

Seriously. If you want to say something? Just say it.
Let TUNNELS, and DOORWAYS, and WARS just be what they are.
Shh!
Shh!
Shh!
We're all grown-ups here.
Shh!
Or close enough.
Shh!
Shh!
Shh!
We can take it.
The last thing I need right now is a freaking literary device.
Shh!
Shh!
Shh!
Shh!
Shh!
Shh!
Shh!
Shh!
Shh!
Shh!
Shh!
If life is a dream?
Shh!
Shh!
Shh!
Shh!
Shh!
Shh!
Shh!
Shh!
Shh!
Shh!
Shh!
Shh!
Shh!
Shh!
Shh!
Shh!
Shh!
Then please, please, please. Let me wake up.

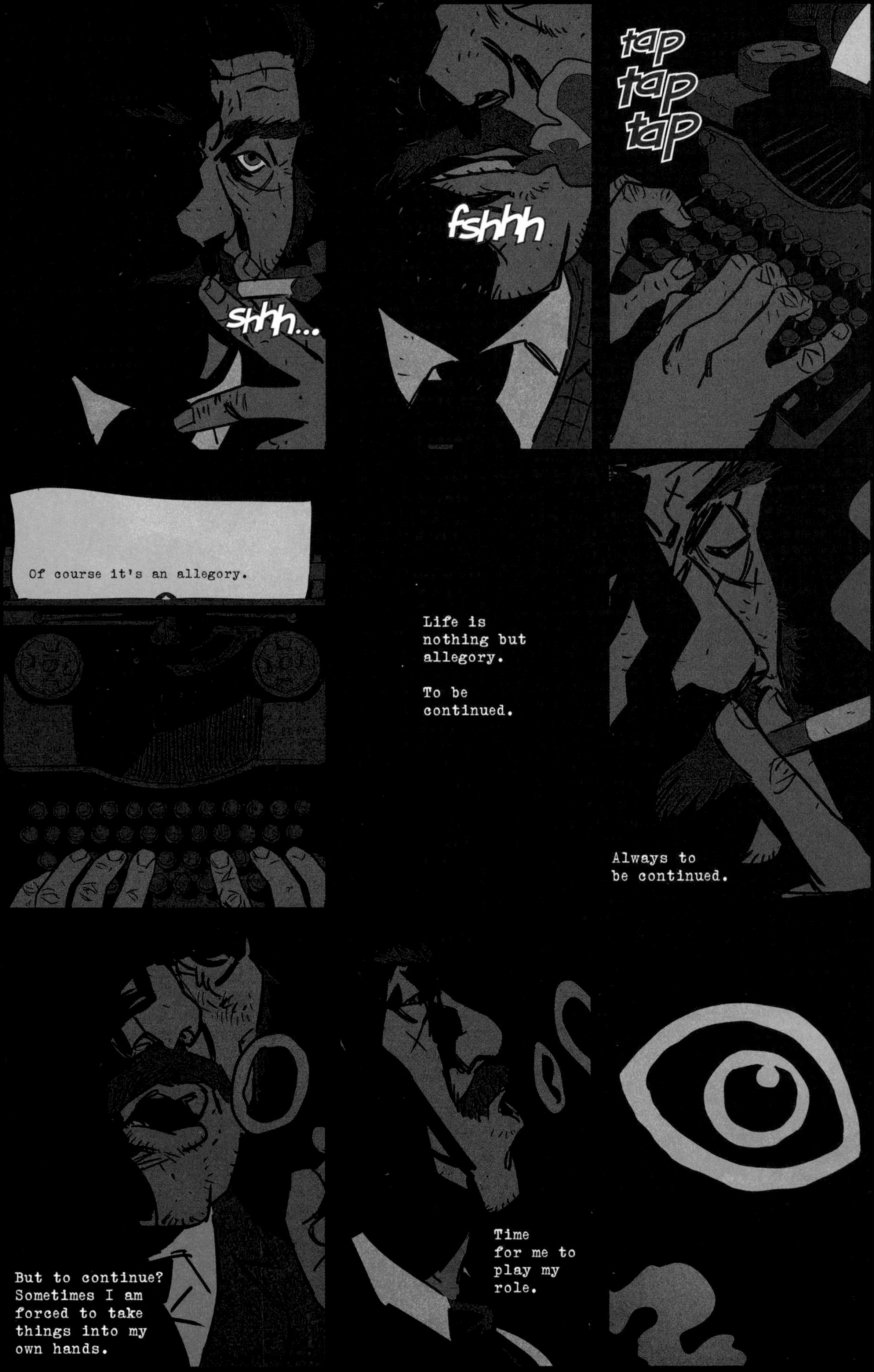
shhh...
fshhh
tap
tap
tap
Of course it's an allegory.
Life is nothing but allegory.
To be continued.
Always to be continued.
But to continue? Sometimes I am forced to take things into my own hands.
Time for me to play my role.

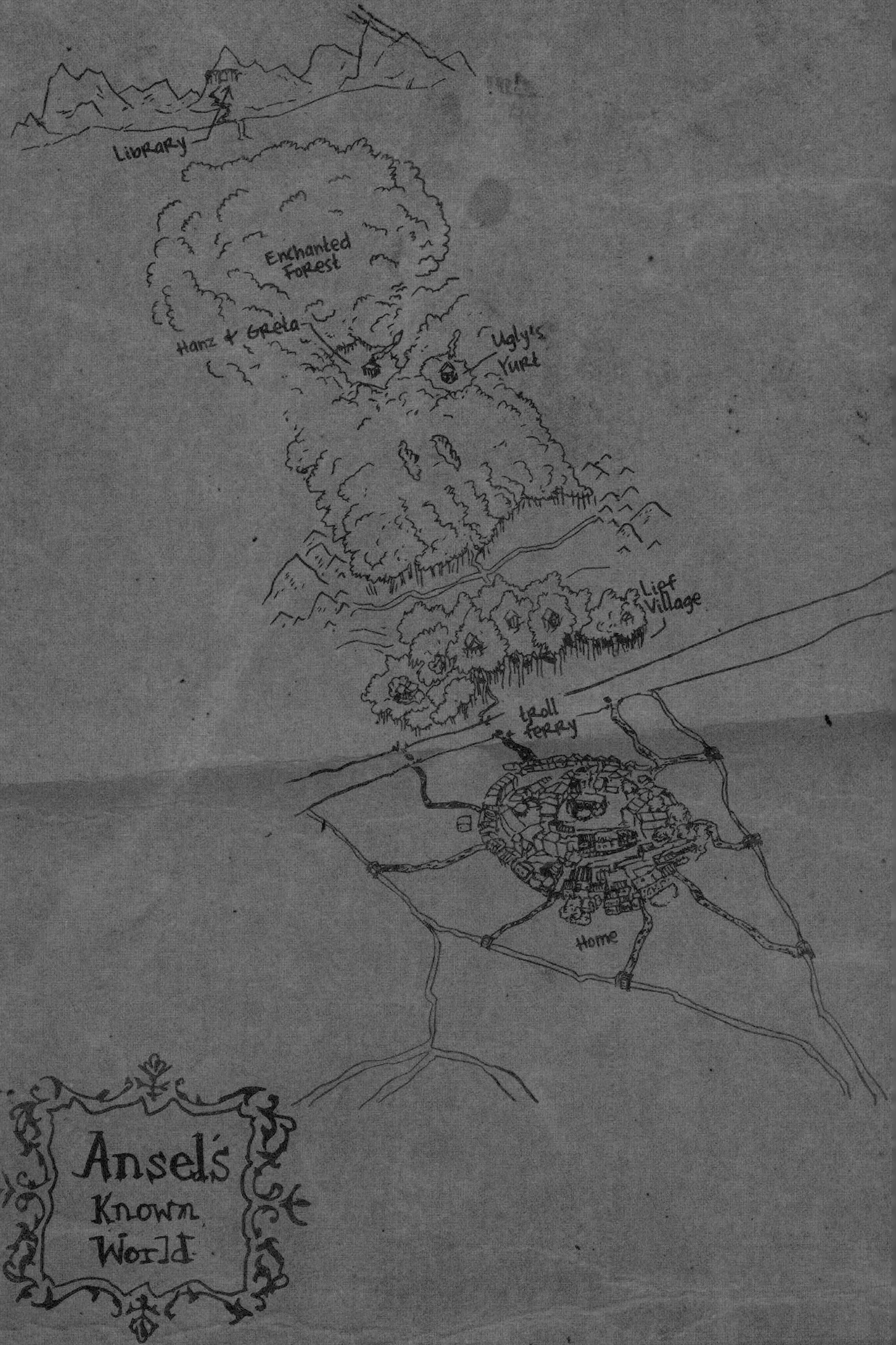
Library
Enchanted Forest
Hanz & Greta
Ugly's Yurt
Lief Village
troll ferry
Home
Ansel's Known World

CHAPTER

FIVE

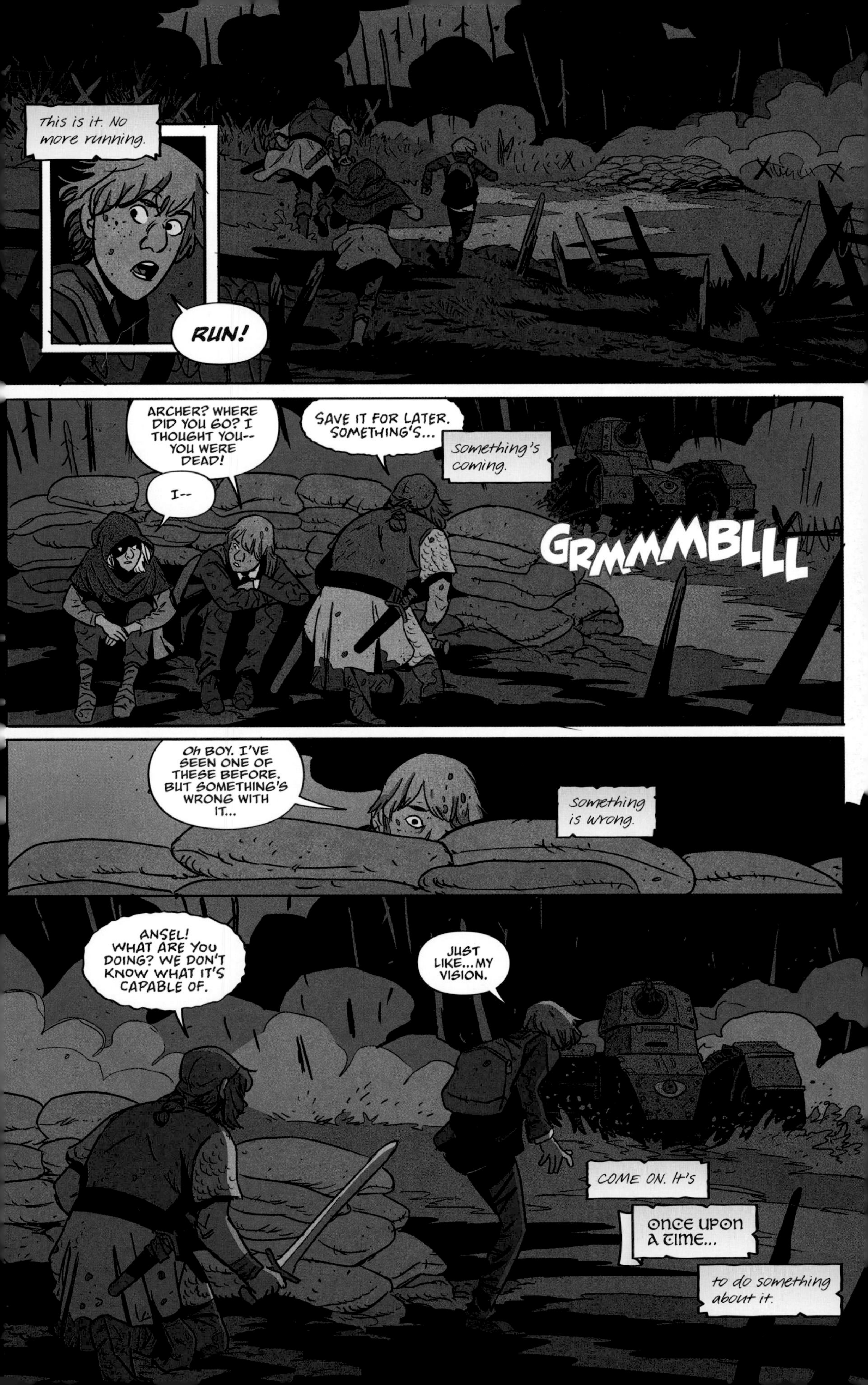
This is it. No more running.
RUN!
ARCHER? WHERE DID YOU GO? I THOUGHT YOU-- YOU WERE DEAD!
I--
SAVE IT FOR LATER. SOMETHING'S...
something's coming.
GRMMMBLLL
Oh BOY. I'VE SEEN ONE OF THESE BEFORE. BUT SOMETHING'S WRONG WITH IT...
something is wrong.
ANSEL! WHAT ARE YOU DOING? WE DON'T KNOW WHAT IT'S CAPABLE OF.
JUST LIKE...MY VISION.
COME ON. It's
ONCE UPON A TIME...
to do something about it.

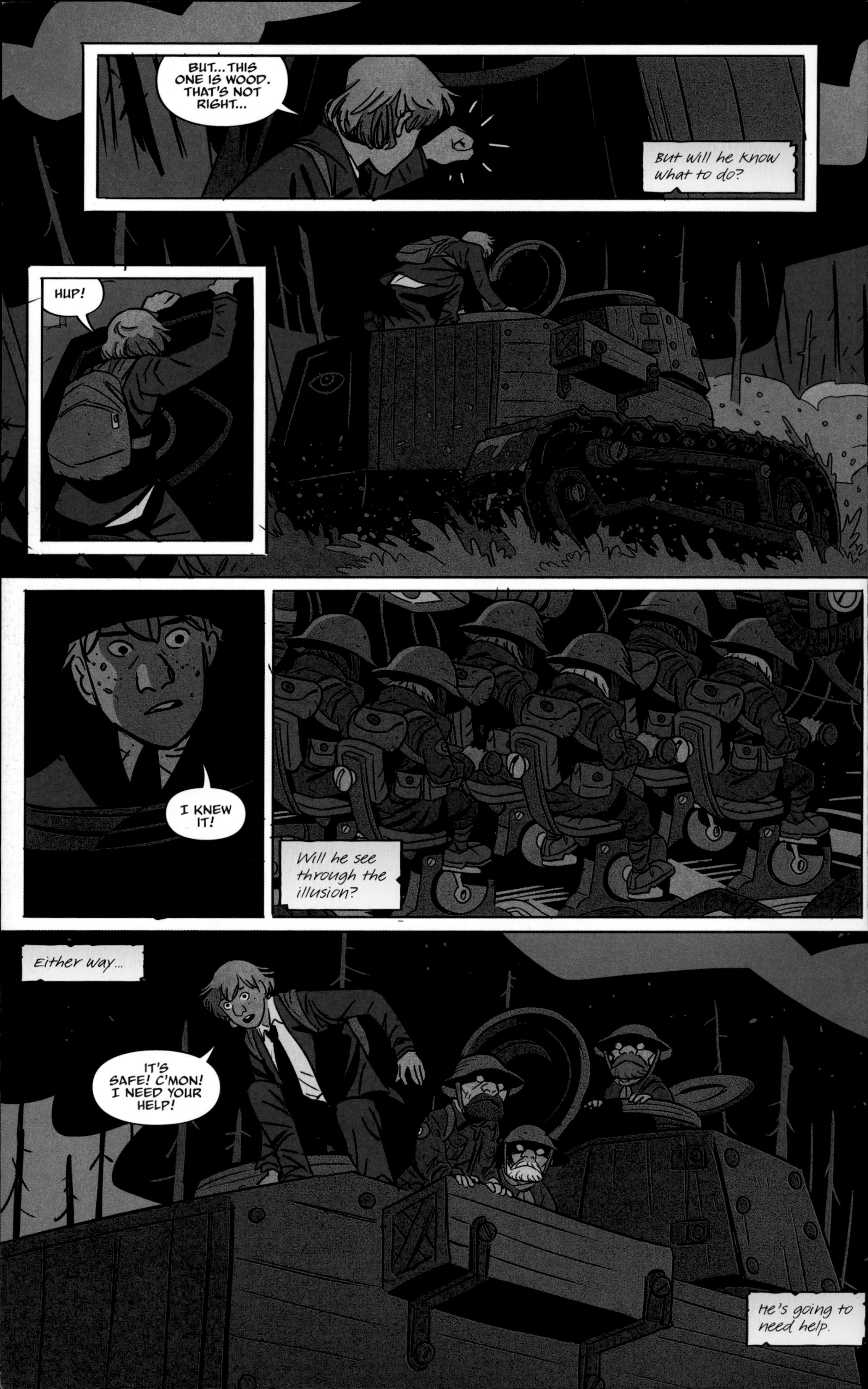
BUT... THIS ONE IS WOOD. THAT'S NOT RIGHT...
But will he know what to do?
HUP!
I KNEW IT!
Will he see through the illusion?
Either way...
IT'S SAFE! C'MON! I NEED YOUR HELP!
He's going to need help.

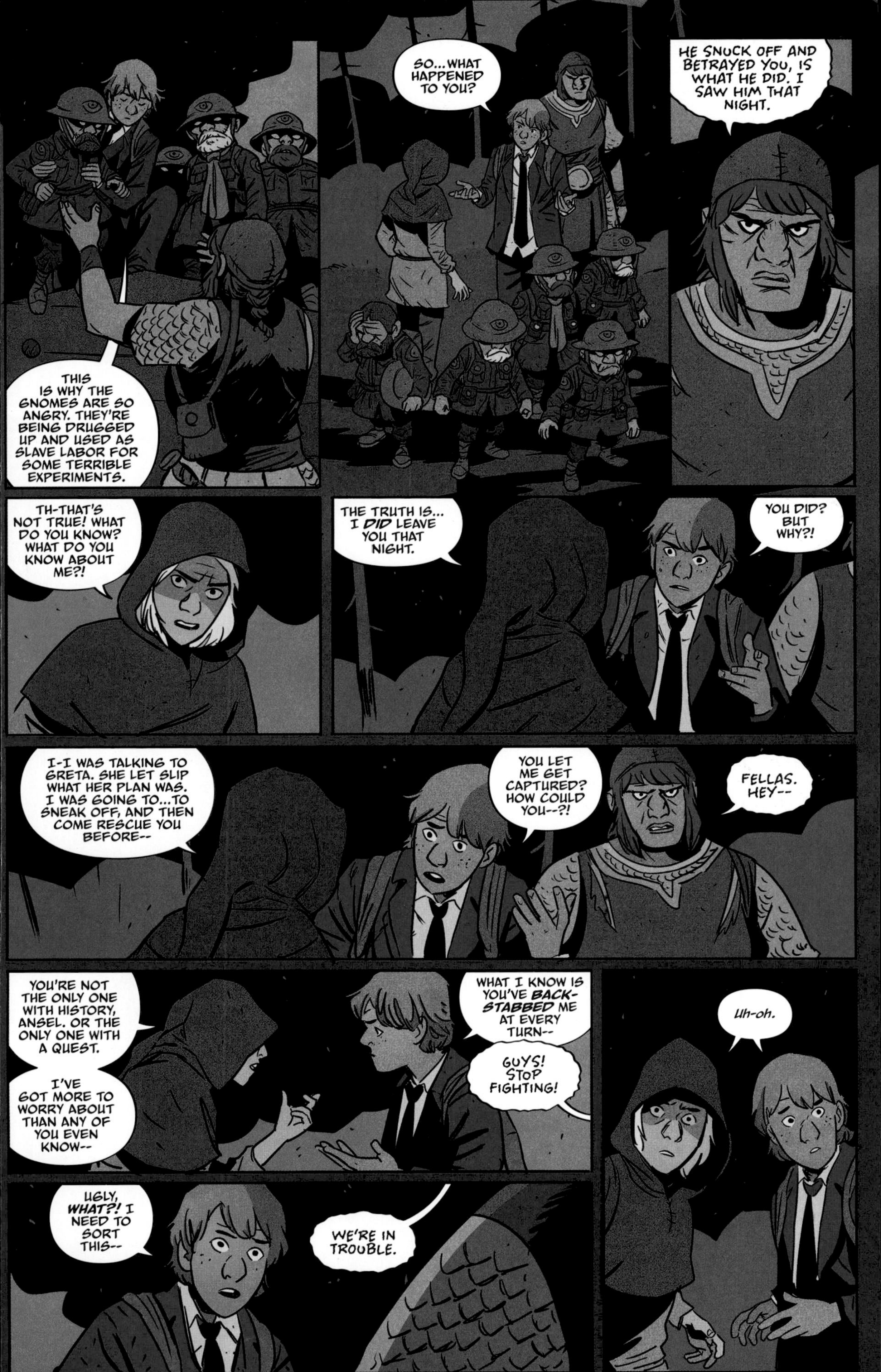
THIS IS WHY THE GNOMES ARE SO ANGRY. THEY'RE BEING DRUGGED UP AND USED AS SLAVE LABOR FOR SOME TERRIBLE EXPERIMENTS.
SO...WHAT HAPPENED TO YOU?
HE SNUCK OFF AND BETRAYED YOU, IS WHAT HE DID. I SAW HIM THAT NIGHT.
TH-THAT'S NOT TRUE! WHAT DO YOU KNOW? WHAT DO YOU KNOW ABOUT ME?!
THE TRUTH IS... I DID LEAVE YOU THAT NIGHT.
YOU DID? BUT WHY?!
I-I WAS TALKING TO GRETA. SHE LET SLIP WHAT HER PLAN WAS. I WAS GOING TO...TO SNEAK OFF, AND THEN COME RESCUE YOU BEFORE--
YOU LET ME GET CAPTURED? HOW COULD YOU--?!
FELLAS. HEY--
YOU'RE NOT THE ONLY ONE WITH HISTORY, ANSEL. OR THE ONLY ONE WITH A QUEST.
I'VE GOT MORE TO WORRY ABOUT THAN ANY OF YOU EVEN KNOW--
WHAT I KNOW IS YOU'VE BACK-STABBED ME AT EVERY TURN--
GUYS! STOP FIGHTING!
UGLY, WHAT?! I NEED TO SORT THIS--
WE'RE IN TROUBLE.
Uh-oh.

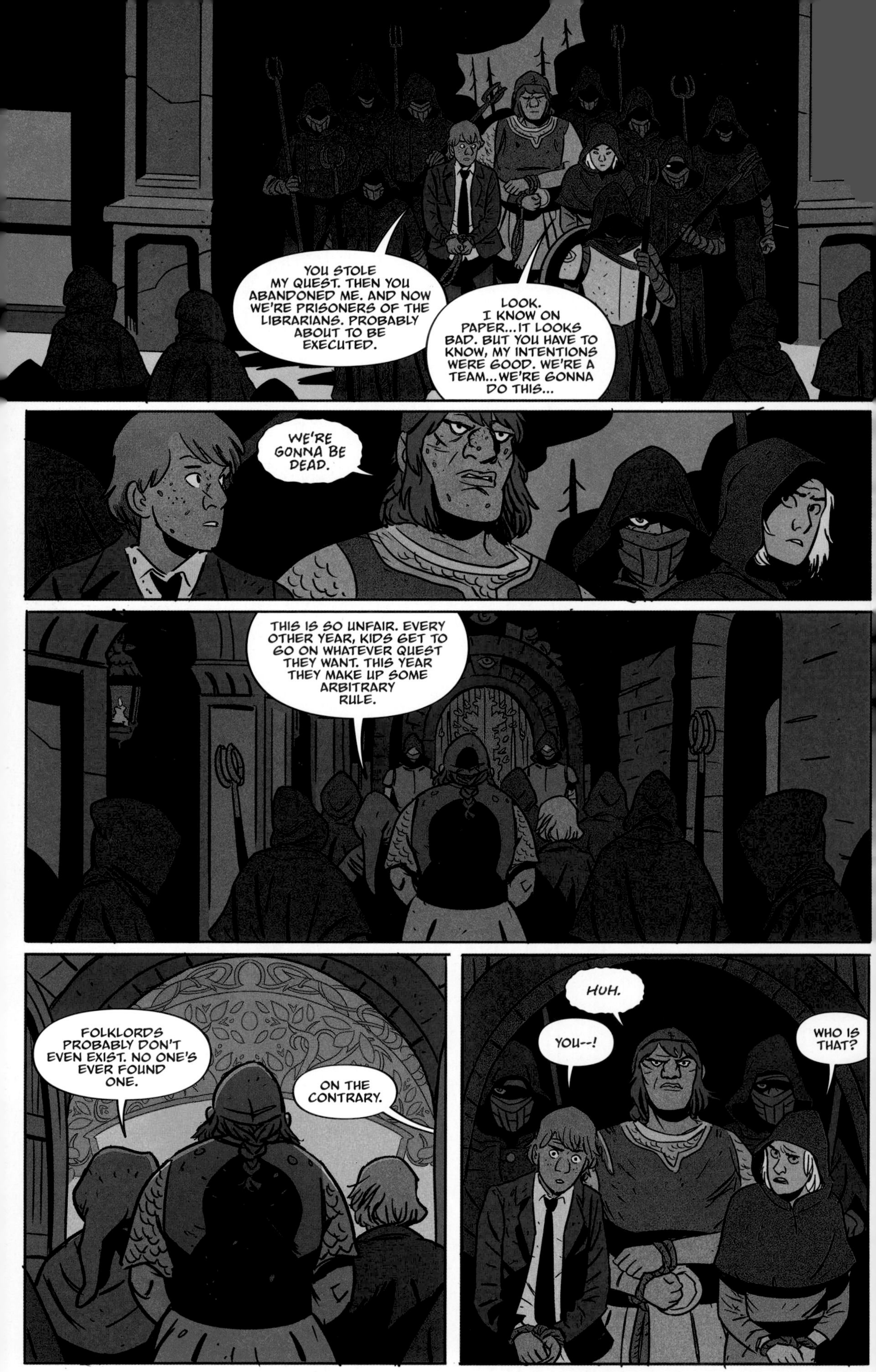
YOU STOLE MY QUEST. THEN YOU ABANDONED ME. AND NOW WE'RE PRISONERS OF THE LIBRARIANS. PROBABLY ABOUT TO BE EXECUTED.
LOOK. I KNOW ON PAPER...IT LOOKS BAD. BUT YOU HAVE TO KNOW, MY INTENTIONS WERE GOOD. WE'RE A TEAM...WE'RE GONNA DO THIS...
WE'RE GONNA BE DEAD.
THIS IS SO UNFAIR. EVERY OTHER YEAR, KIDS GET TO GO ON WHATEVER QUEST THEY WANT. THIS YEAR THEY MAKE UP SOME ARBITRARY RULE.
FOLKLORDS PROBABLY DON'T EVEN EXIST. NO ONE'S EVER FOUND ONE.
ON THE CONTRARY.
HUH.
YOU--!
WHO IS THAT?

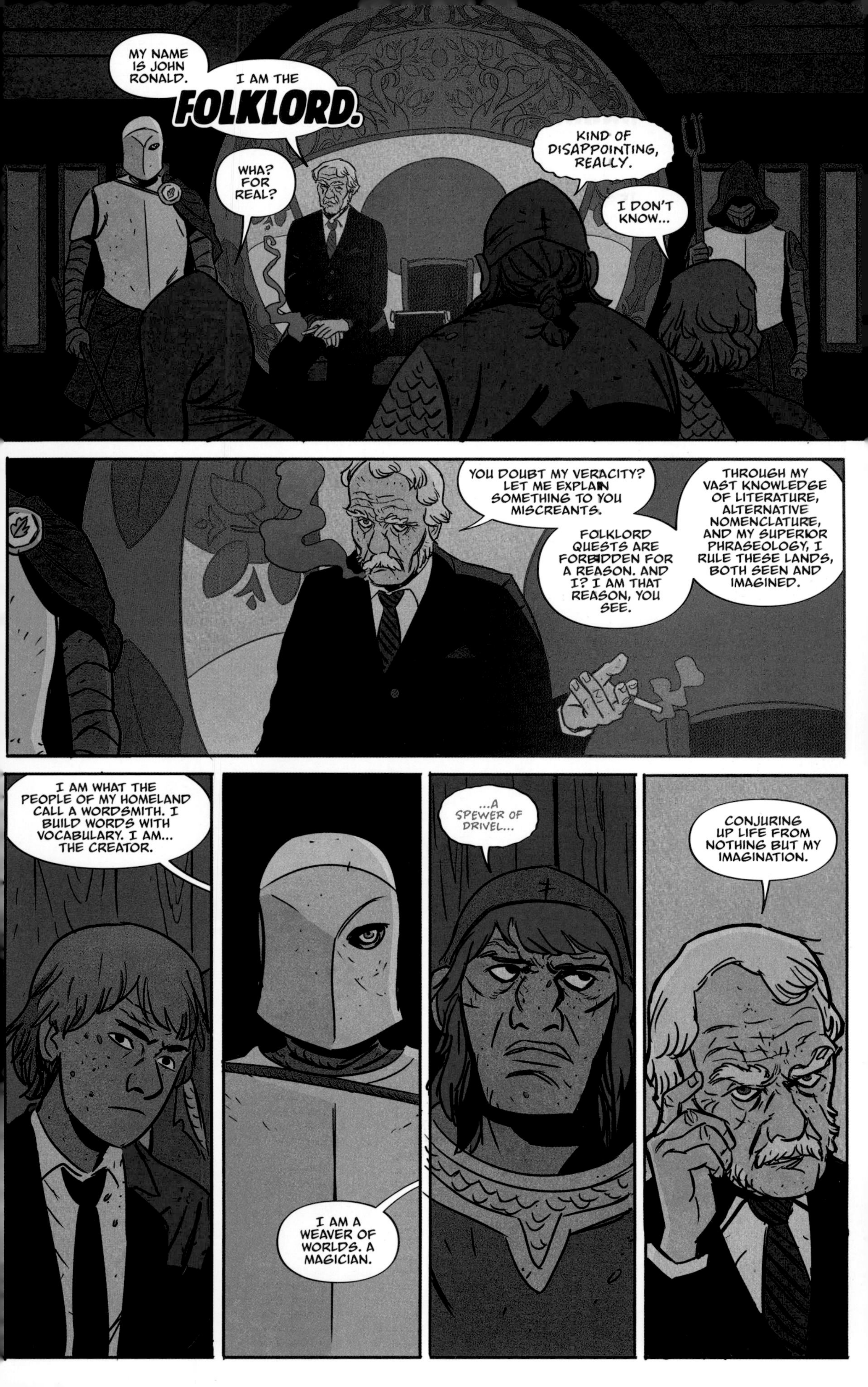
MY NAME IS JOHN RONALD.
I AM THE FOLKLORD.
WHA? FOR REAL?
KIND OF DISAPPOINTING, REALLY.
I DON'T KNOW...
YOU DOUBT MY VERACITY? LET ME EXPLAIN SOMETHING TO YOU MISCREANTS.
FOLKLORD QUESTS ARE FORBIDDEN FOR A REASON. AND I? I AM THAT REASON, YOU SEE.
THROUGH MY VAST KNOWLEDGE OF LITERATURE, ALTERNATIVE NOMENCLATURE, AND MY SUPERIOR PHRASEOLOGY, I RULE THESE LANDS, BOTH SEEN AND IMAGINED.
I AM WHAT THE PEOPLE OF MY HOMELAND CALL A WORDSMITH. I BUILD WORDS WITH VOCABULARY. I AM... THE CREATOR.
I AM A WEAVER OF WORLDS. A MAGICIAN.
...A SPEWER OF DRIVEL...
CONJURING UP LIFE FROM NOTHING BUT MY IMAGINATION.

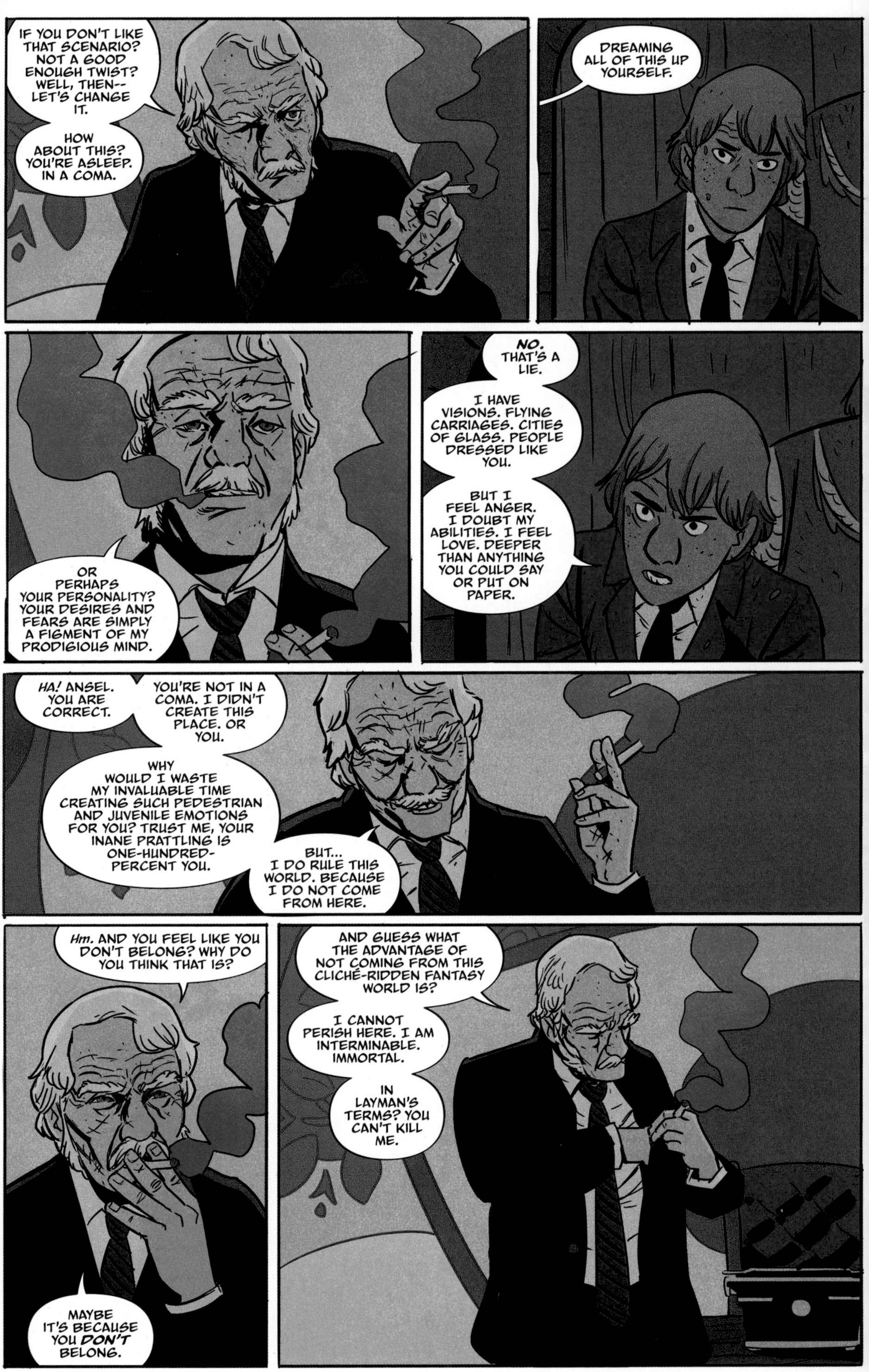
IF YOU DON'T LIKE THAT SCENARIO? NOT A GOOD ENOUGH TWIST? WELL, THEN-- LET'S CHANGE IT.
HOW ABOUT THIS? YOU'RE ASLEEP. IN A COMA.
DREAMING ALL OF THIS UP YOURSELF.
OR PERHAPS YOUR PERSONALITY? YOUR DESIRES AND FEARS ARE SIMPLY A FIGMENT OF MY PRODIGIOUS MIND.
NO. THAT'S A LIE.
I HAVE VISIONS. FLYING CARRIAGES. CITIES OF GLASS. PEOPLE DRESSED LIKE YOU.
BUT I FEEL ANGER. I DOUBT MY ABILITIES. I FEEL LOVE. DEEPER THAN ANYTHING YOU COULD SAY OR PUT ON PAPER.
HA! ANSEL. YOU ARE CORRECT.
YOU'RE NOT IN A COMA. I DIDN'T CREATE THIS PLACE. OR YOU.
WHY WOULD I WASTE MY INVALUABLE TIME CREATING SUCH PEDESTRIAN AND JUVENILE EMOTIONS FOR YOU? TRUST ME, YOUR INANE PRATTLING IS ONE-HUNDRED-PERCENT YOU.
BUT... I DO RULE THIS WORLD. BECAUSE I DO NOT COME FROM HERE.
Hm. AND YOU FEEL LIKE YOU DON'T BELONG? WHY DO YOU THINK THAT IS?
MAYBE IT'S BECAUSE YOU *DON'T* BELONG.
AND GUESS WHAT THE ADVANTAGE OF NOT COMING FROM THIS CLICHÉ-RIDDEN FANTASY WORLD IS?
I CANNOT PERISH HERE. I AM INTERMINABLE. IMMORTAL.
IN LAYMAN'S TERMS? YOU CAN'T KILL ME.

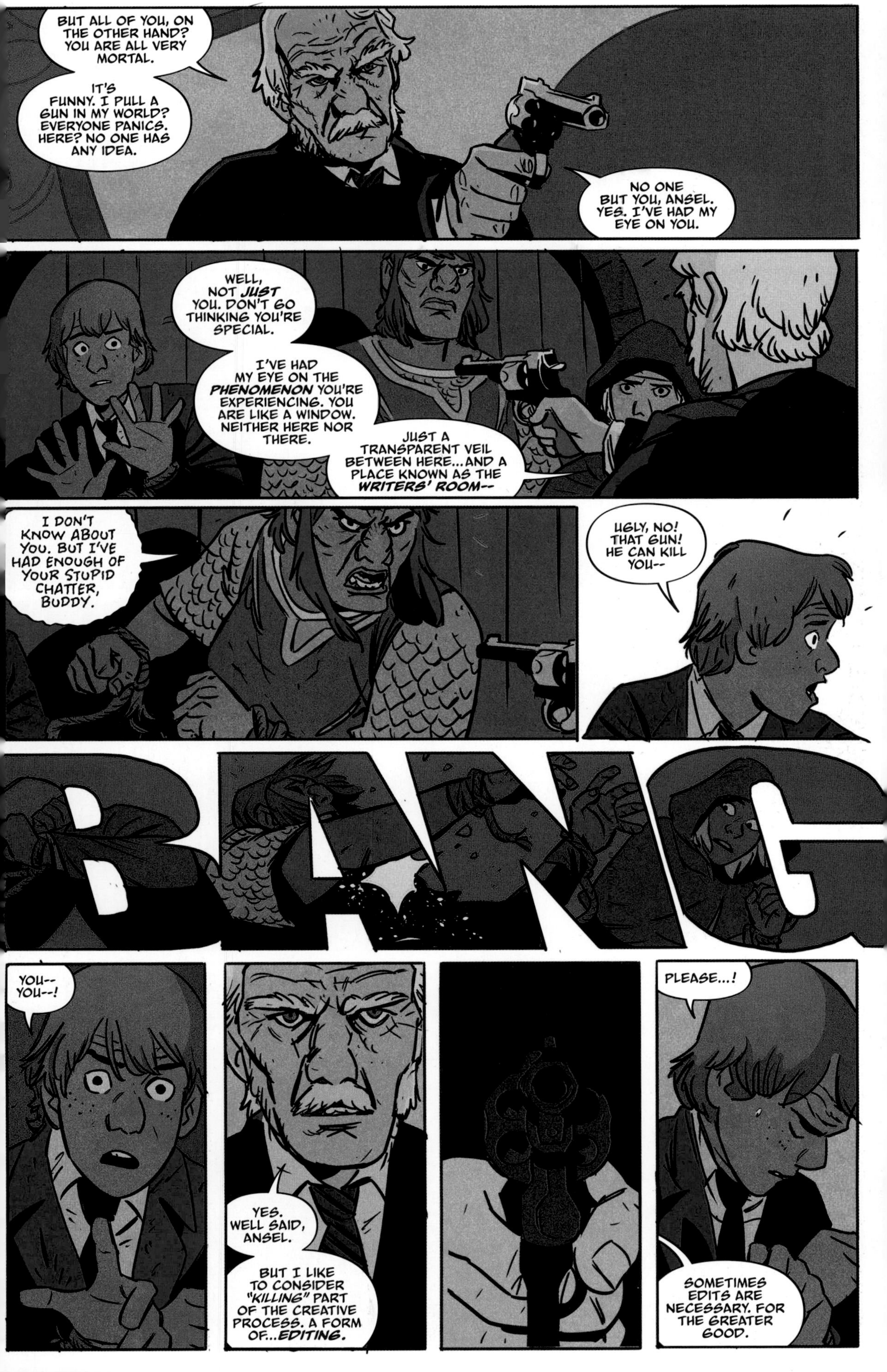
BUT ALL OF YOU, ON THE OTHER HAND? YOU ARE ALL VERY MORTAL.
IT'S FUNNY. I PULL A GUN IN MY WORLD? EVERYONE PANICS. HERE? NO ONE HAS ANY IDEA.
NO ONE BUT YOU, ANSEL. YES. I'VE HAD MY EYE ON YOU.
WELL, NOT JUST YOU. DON'T GO THINKING YOU'RE SPECIAL.
I'VE HAD MY EYE ON THE PHENOMENON YOU'RE EXPERIENCING. YOU ARE LIKE A WINDOW. NEITHER HERE NOR THERE.
JUST A TRANSPARENT VEIL BETWEEN HERE...AND A PLACE KNOWN AS THE WRITERS' ROOM--
I DON'T KNOW ABOUT YOU. BUT I'VE HAD ENOUGH OF YOUR STUPID CHATTER, BUDDY.
UGLY, NO! THAT GUN! HE CAN KILL YOU--
BANG
YOU-- YOU--!
YES. WELL SAID, ANSEL.
BUT I LIKE TO CONSIDER "KILLING" PART OF THE CREATIVE PROCESS. A FORM OF...EDITING.
PLEASE...!
SOMETIMES EDITS ARE NECESSARY. FOR THE GREATER GOOD.

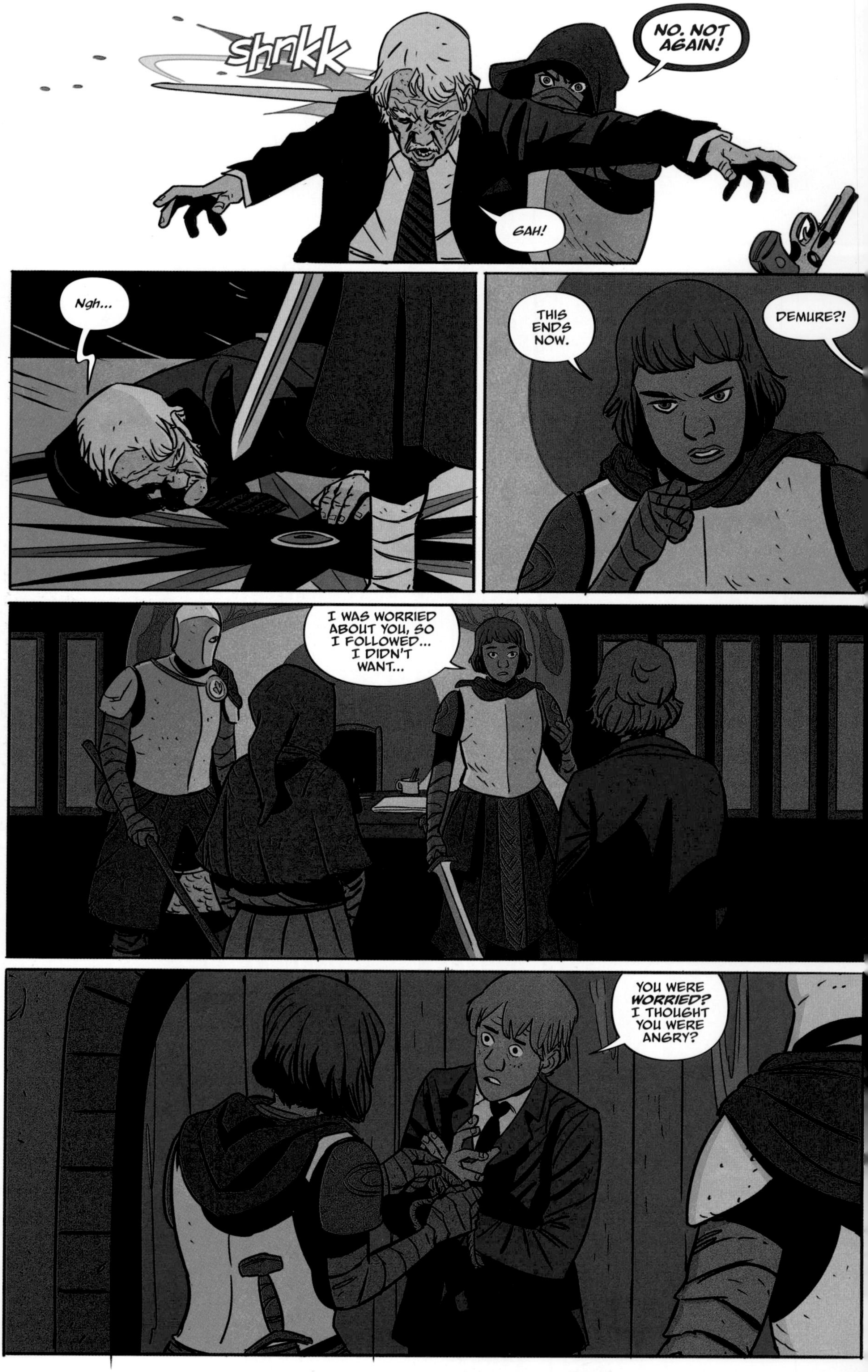
shrkk
NO. NOT AGAIN!
GAH!
Ngh...
THIS ENDS NOW.
DEMURE?!
I WAS WORRIED ABOUT YOU, SO I FOLLOWED... I DIDN'T WANT...
YOU WERE *WORRIED?* I THOUGHT YOU WERE ANGRY?

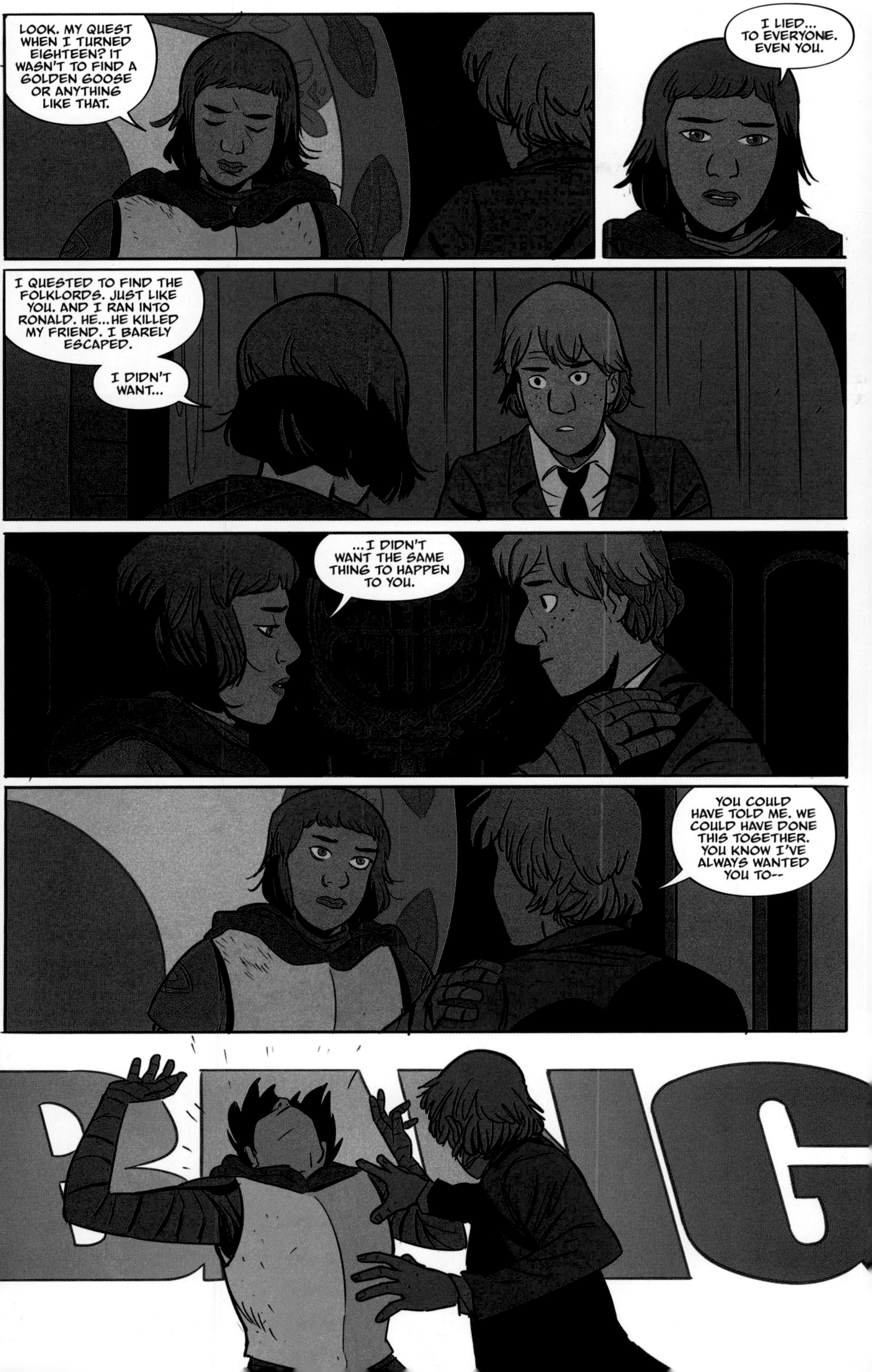
LOOK. MY QUEST WHEN I TURNED EIGHTEEN? IT WASN'T TO FIND A GOLDEN GOOSE OR ANYTHING LIKE THAT.
I LIED... TO EVERYONE. EVEN YOU.
I QUESTED TO FIND THE FOLKLORDS. JUST LIKE YOU. AND I RAN INTO RONALD. HE...HE KILLED MY FRIEND. I BARELY ESCAPED.
I DIDN'T WANT...
...I DIDN'T WANT THE SAME THING TO HAPPEN TO YOU.
YOU COULD HAVE TOLD ME. WE COULD HAVE DONE THIS TOGETHER. YOU KNOW I'VE ALWAYS WANTED YOU TO--

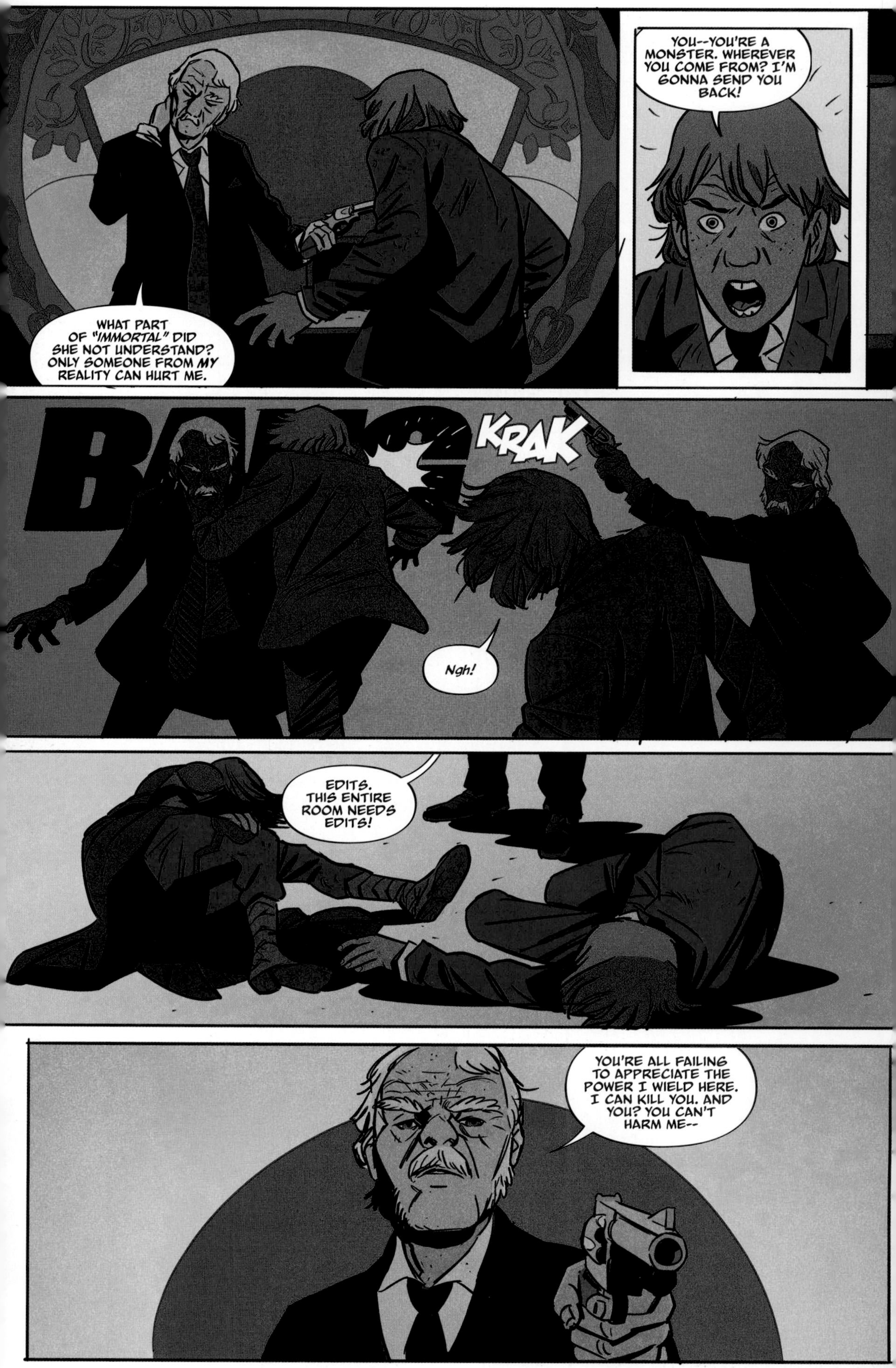
WHAT PART OF "IMMORTAL" DID SHE NOT UNDERSTAND? ONLY SOMEONE FROM MY REALITY CAN HURT ME.
YOU--YOU'RE A MONSTER. WHEREVER YOU COME FROM? I'M GONNA SEND YOU BACK!
KRAK
Ngh!
EDITS. THIS ENTIRE ROOM NEEDS EDITS!
YOU'RE ALL FAILING TO APPRECIATE THE POWER I WIELD HERE. I CAN KILL YOU. AND YOU? YOU CAN'T HARM ME--

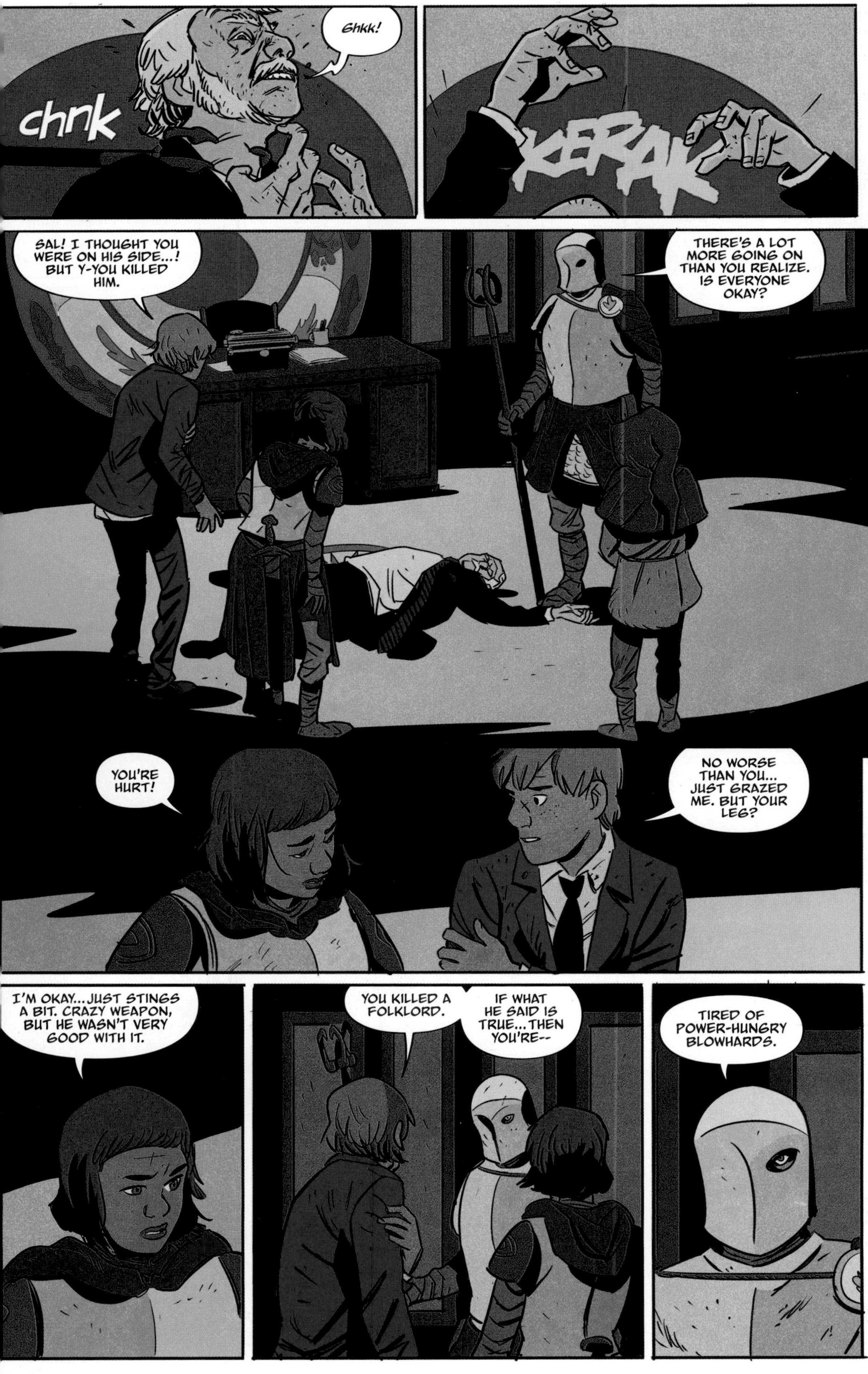
Ghkk!
chnk
KERAK
SAL! I THOUGHT YOU WERE ON HIS SIDE...! BUT Y-YOU KILLED HIM.
THERE'S A LOT MORE GOING ON THAN YOU REALIZE. IS EVERYONE OKAY?
YOU'RE HURT!
NO WORSE THAN YOU... JUST GRAZED ME. BUT YOUR LEG?
I'M OKAY...JUST STINGS A BIT. CRAZY WEAPON, BUT HE WASN'T VERY GOOD WITH IT.
YOU KILLED A FOLKLORD.
IF WHAT HE SAID IS TRUE...THEN YOU'RE--
TIRED OF POWER-HUNGRY BLOWHARDS.

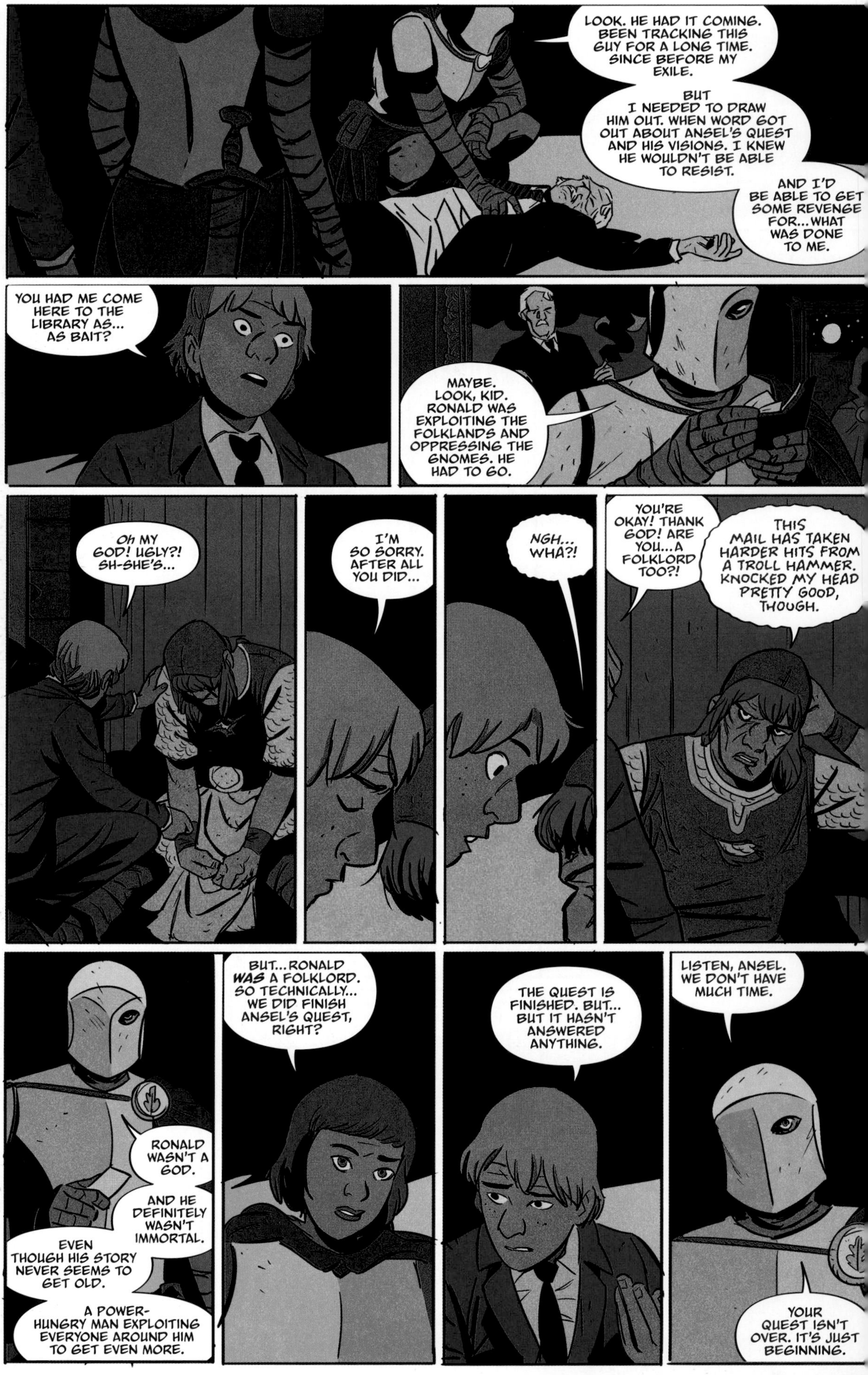
LOOK. HE HAD IT COMING. BEEN TRACKING THIS GUY FOR A LONG TIME. SINCE BEFORE MY EXILE.
BUT I NEEDED TO DRAW HIM OUT. WHEN WORD GOT OUT ABOUT ANSEL'S QUEST AND HIS VISIONS, I KNEW HE WOULDN'T BE ABLE TO RESIST.
AND I'D BE ABLE TO GET SOME REVENGE FOR...WHAT WAS DONE TO ME.
YOU HAD ME COME HERE TO THE LIBRARY AS... AS BAIT?
MAYBE. LOOK, KID. RONALD WAS EXPLOITING THE FOLKLANDS AND OPPRESSING THE GNOMES. HE HAD TO GO.
Oh MY GOD! UGLY?! SH-SHE'S...
I'M SO SORRY. AFTER ALL YOU DID...
NGH... WHA?!
YOU'RE OKAY! THANK GOD! ARE YOU...A FOLKLORD TOO?!
THIS MAIL HAS TAKEN HARDER HITS FROM A TROLL HAMMER. KNOCKED MY HEAD PRETTY GOOD, THOUGH.
RONALD WASN'T A GOD.
AND HE DEFINITELY WASN'T IMMORTAL.
EVEN THOUGH HIS STORY NEVER SEEMS TO GET OLD.
A POWER-HUNGRY MAN EXPLOITING EVERYONE AROUND HIM TO GET EVEN MORE.
BUT...RONALD WAS A FOLKLORD. SO TECHNICALLY... WE DID FINISH ANSEL'S QUEST, RIGHT?
THE QUEST IS FINISHED. BUT... BUT IT HASN'T ANSWERED ANYTHING.
LISTEN, ANSEL. WE DON'T HAVE MUCH TIME.
YOUR QUEST ISN'T OVER. IT'S JUST BEGINNING.

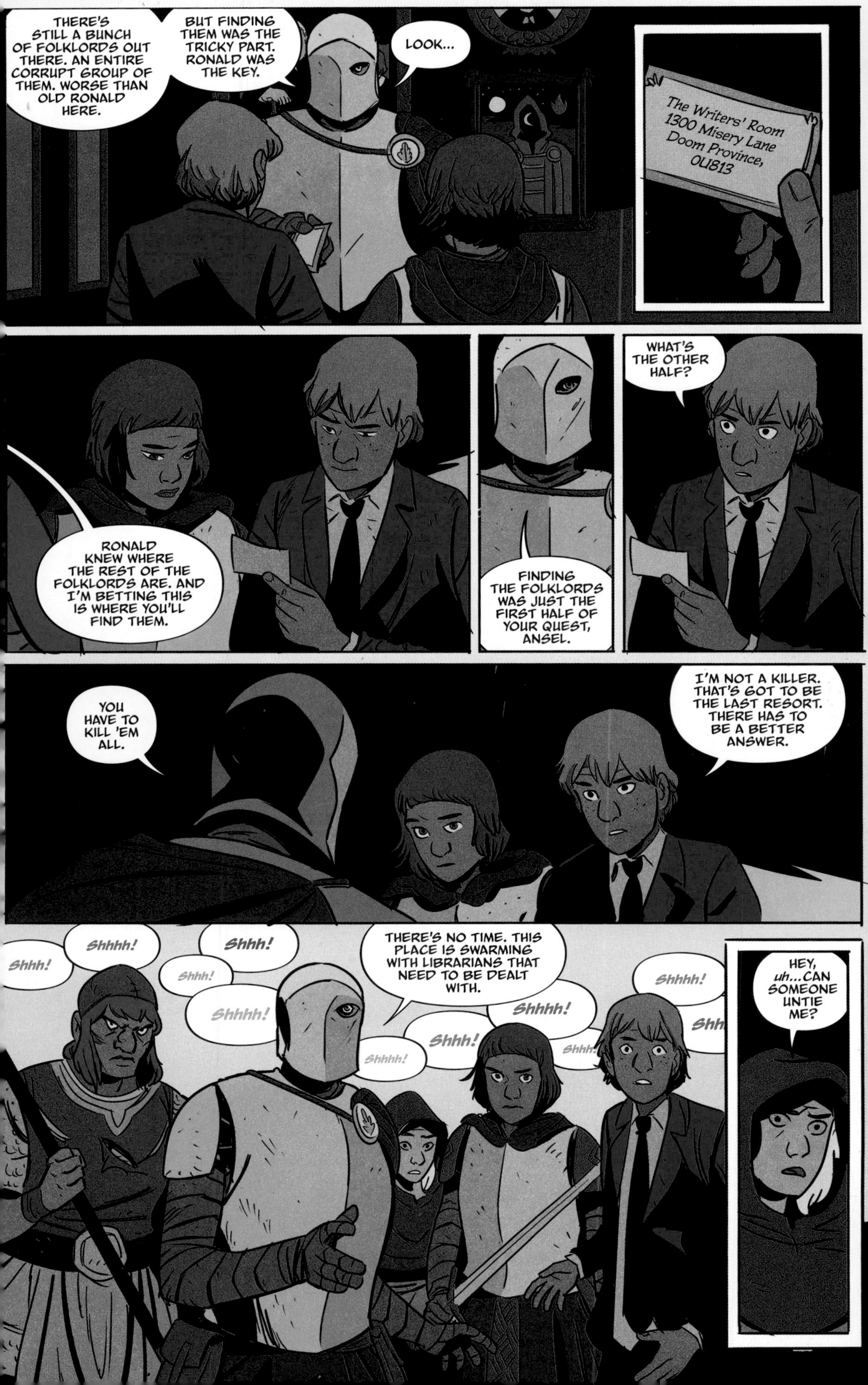
THERE'S STILL A BUNCH OF FOLKLORDS OUT THERE. AN ENTIRE CORRUPT GROUP OF THEM. WORSE THAN OLD RONALD HERE.
BUT FINDING THEM WAS THE TRICKY PART. RONALD WAS THE KEY.
LOOK...
The Writers' Room
1300 Misery Lane
Doom Province,
OU813
RONALD KNEW WHERE THE REST OF THE FOLKLORDS ARE. AND I'M BETTING THIS IS WHERE YOU'LL FIND THEM.
FINDING THE FOLKLORDS WAS JUST THE FIRST HALF OF YOUR QUEST, ANSEL.
WHAT'S THE OTHER HALF?
YOU HAVE TO KILL 'EM ALL.
I'M NOT A KILLER. THAT'S GOT TO BE THE LAST RESORT. THERE HAS TO BE A BETTER ANSWER.
Shhh!
Shhhh!
Shhh!
Shhh!
Shhhh!
THERE'S NO TIME. THIS PLACE IS SWARMING WITH LIBRARIANS THAT NEED TO BE DEALT WITH.
Shhhh!
Shhh!
Shhhh!
Shhhh!
Shhhh!
HEY, UH...CAN SOMEONE UNTIE ME?

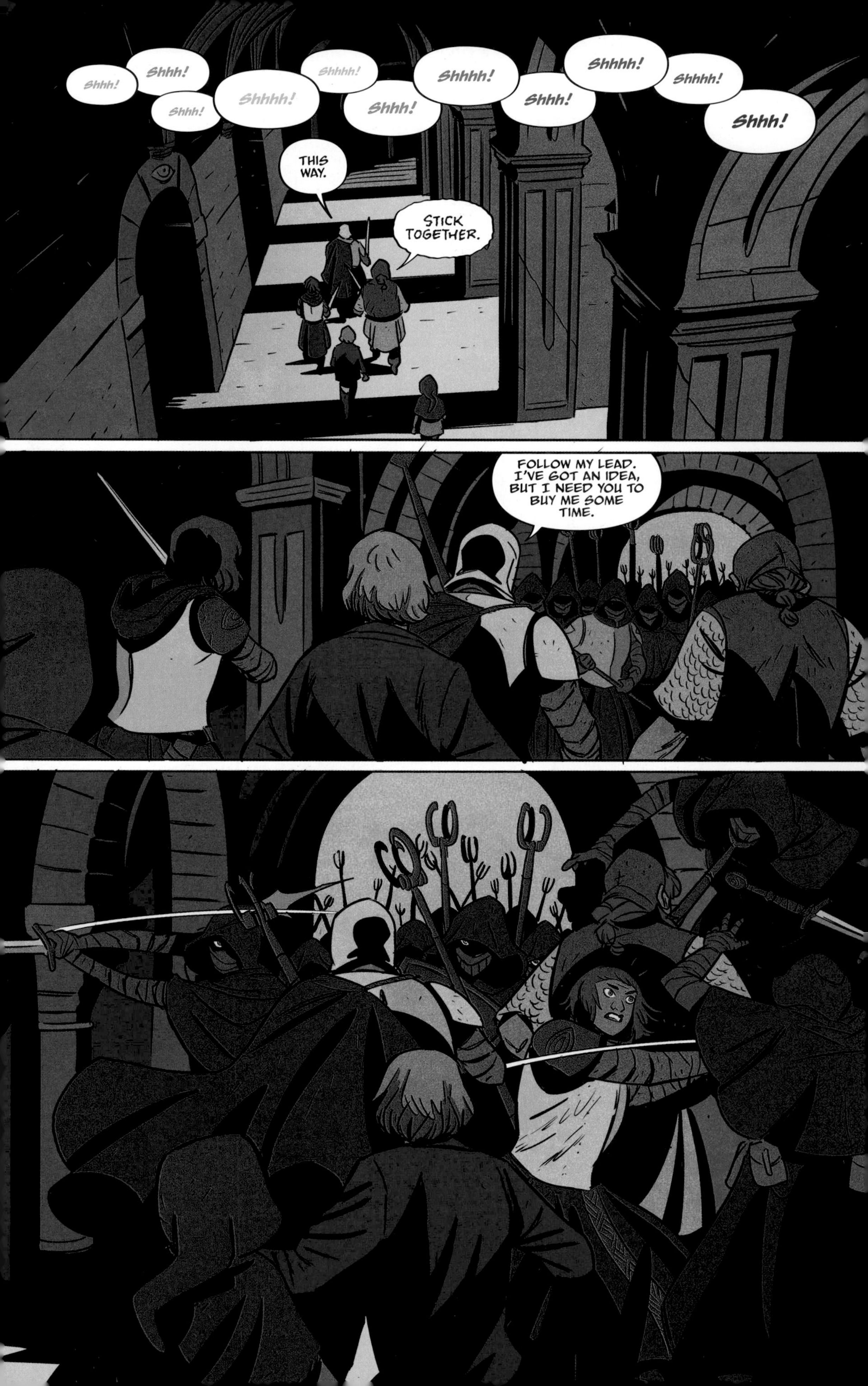
Shhh!
Shhh!
Shhh!
Shhhh!
Shhhh!
Shhh!
Shhhh!
Shhh!
Shhhh!
Shhhh!
Shhh!
THIS WAY.
STICK TOGETHER.
FOLLOW MY LEAD. I'VE GOT AN IDEA, BUT I NEED YOU TO BUY ME SOME TIME.

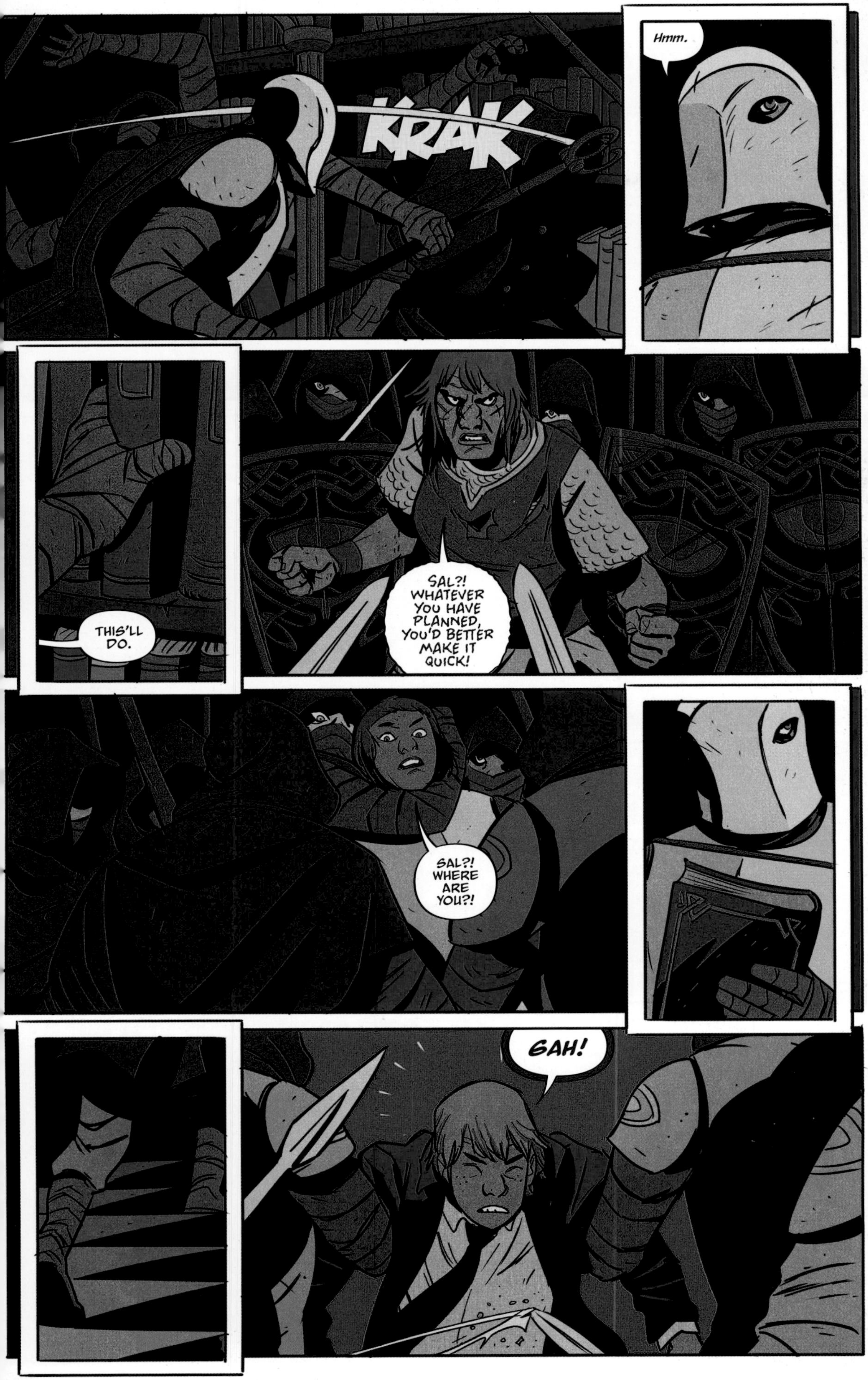
KRAK
Hmm.
THIS'LL DO.
SAL?! WHATEVER YOU HAVE PLANNED, YOU'D BETTER MAKE IT QUICK!
SAL?! WHERE ARE YOU?!
GAH!

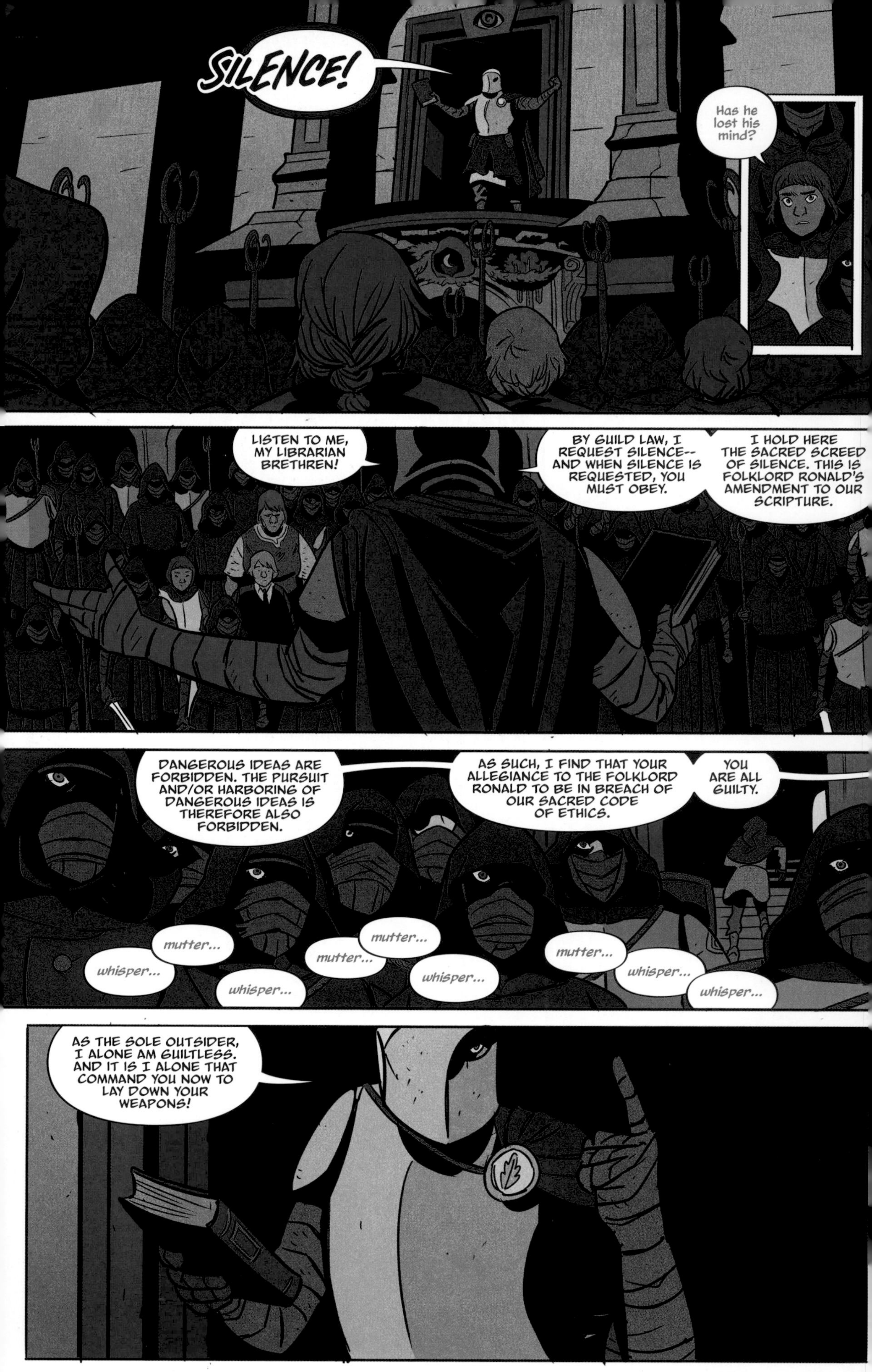
SILENCE!
Has he lost his mind?
LISTEN TO ME, MY LIBRARIAN BRETHREN!
BY GUILD LAW, I REQUEST SILENCE-- AND WHEN SILENCE IS REQUESTED, YOU MUST OBEY.
I HOLD HERE THE SACRED SCREED OF SILENCE. THIS IS FOLKLORD RONALD'S AMENDMENT TO OUR SCRIPTURE.
DANGEROUS IDEAS ARE FORBIDDEN. THE PURSUIT AND/OR HARBORING OF DANGEROUS IDEAS IS THEREFORE ALSO FORBIDDEN.
AS SUCH, I FIND THAT YOUR ALLEGIANCE TO THE FOLKLORD RONALD TO BE IN BREACH OF OUR SACRED CODE OF ETHICS.
YOU ARE ALL GUILTY.
mutter...
whisper...
whisper...
mutter...
mutter...
whisper...
mutter...
whisper...
whisper...
AS THE SOLE OUTSIDER, I ALONE AM GUILTLESS. AND IT IS I ALONE THAT COMMAND YOU NOW TO LAY DOWN YOUR WEAPONS!

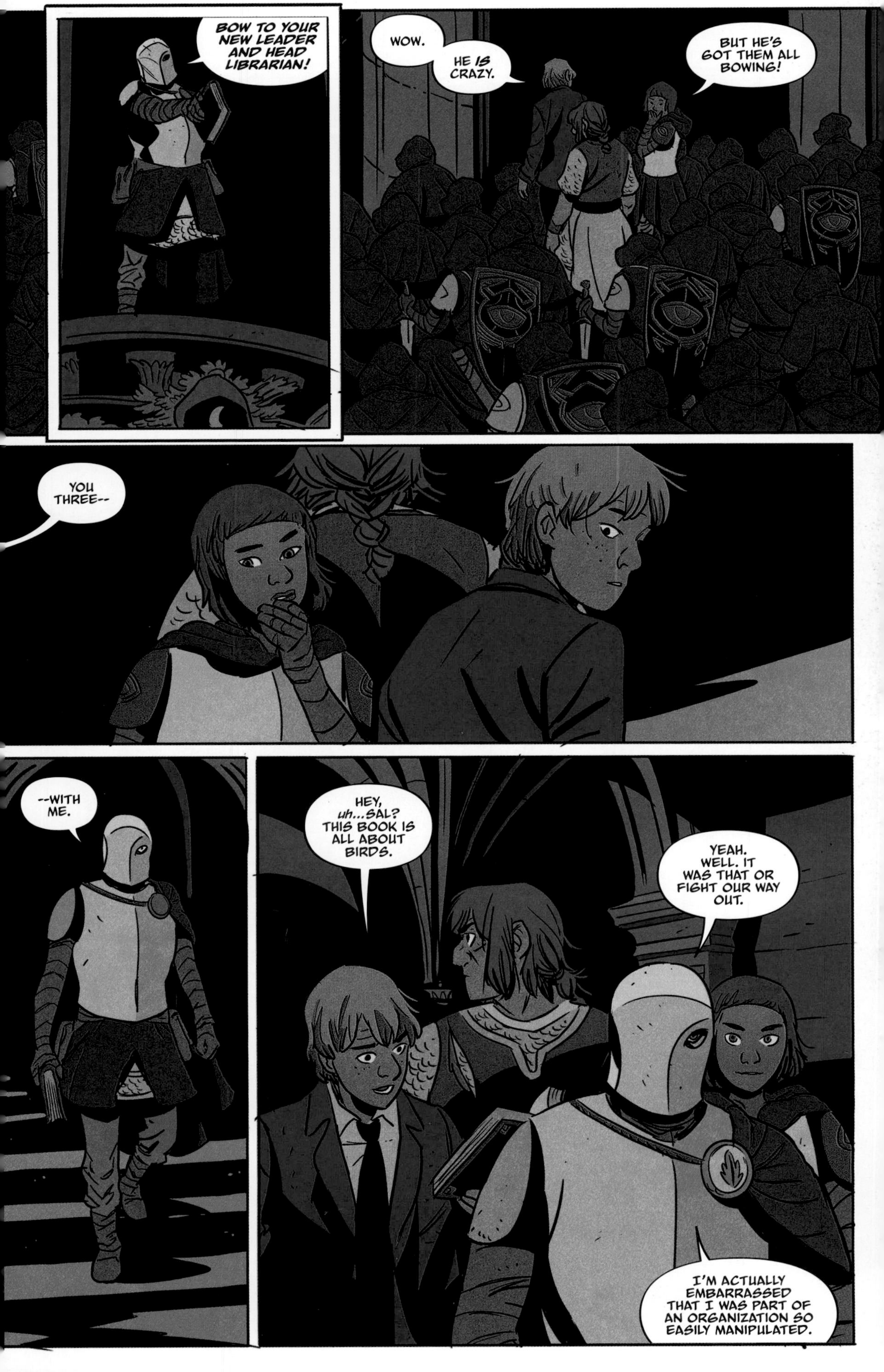
BOW TO YOUR NEW LEADER AND HEAD LIBRARIAN!
WOW.
HE IS CRAZY.
BUT HE'S GOT THEM ALL BOWING!
YOU THREE--
--WITH ME.
HEY, uh...SAL? THIS BOOK IS ALL ABOUT BIRDS.
YEAH. WELL. IT WAS THAT OR FIGHT OUR WAY OUT.
I'M ACTUALLY EMBARRASSED THAT I WAS PART OF AN ORGANIZATION SO EASILY MANIPULATED.

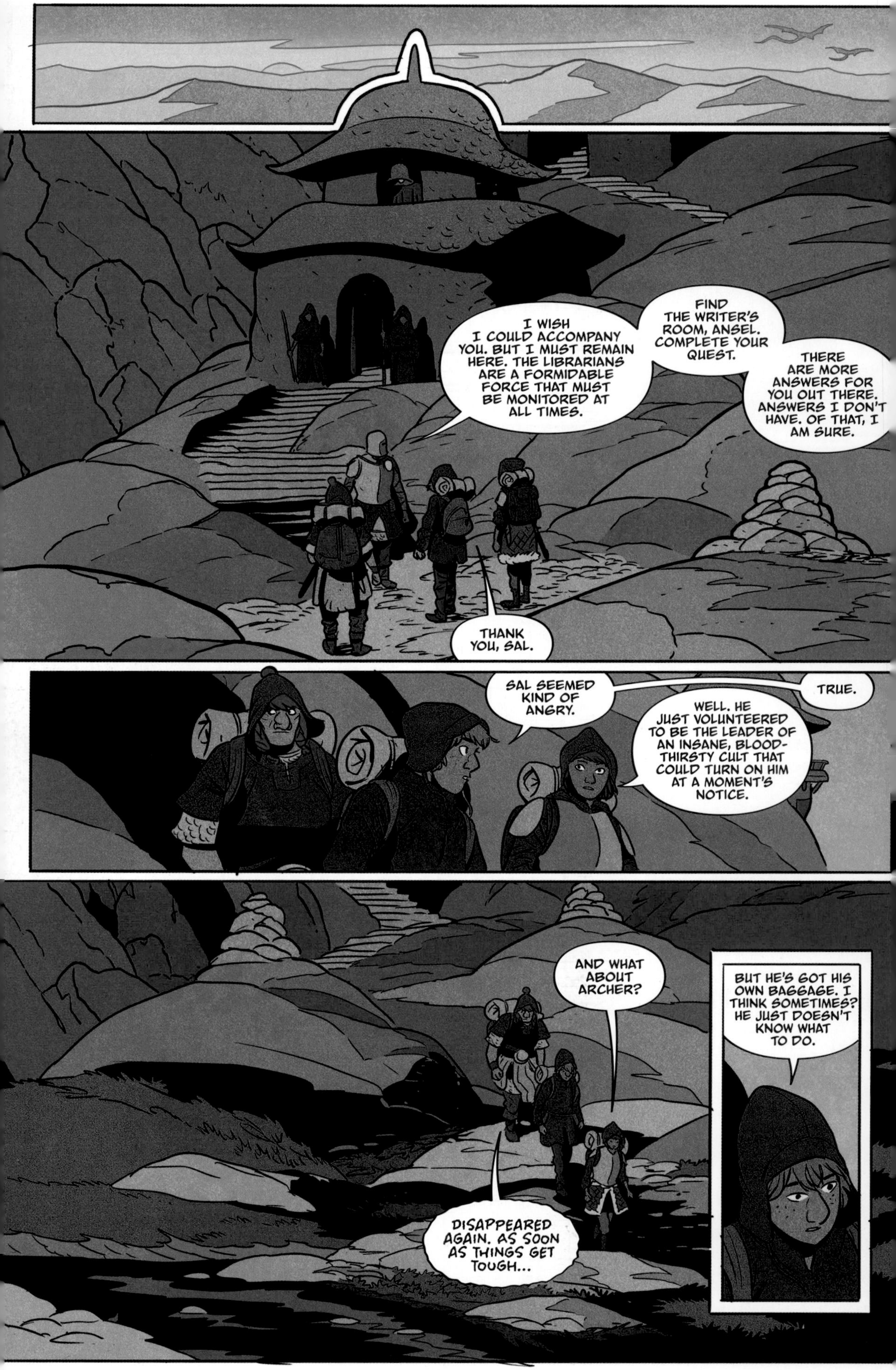
I WISH I COULD ACCOMPANY YOU. BUT I MUST REMAIN HERE. THE LIBRARIANS ARE A FORMIDABLE FORCE THAT MUST BE MONITORED AT ALL TIMES.
FIND THE WRITER'S ROOM, ANSEL. COMPLETE YOUR QUEST.
THERE ARE MORE ANSWERS FOR YOU OUT THERE. ANSWERS I DON'T HAVE. OF THAT, I AM SURE.
THANK YOU, SAL.
SAL SEEMED KIND OF ANGRY.
TRUE.
WELL. HE JUST VOLUNTEERED TO BE THE LEADER OF AN INSANE, BLOOD-THIRSTY CULT THAT COULD TURN ON HIM AT A MOMENT'S NOTICE.
AND WHAT ABOUT ARCHER?
DISAPPEARED AGAIN. AS SOON AS THINGS GET TOUGH...
BUT HE'S GOT HIS OWN BAGGAGE. I THINK SOMETIMES? HE JUST DOESN'T KNOW WHAT TO DO.

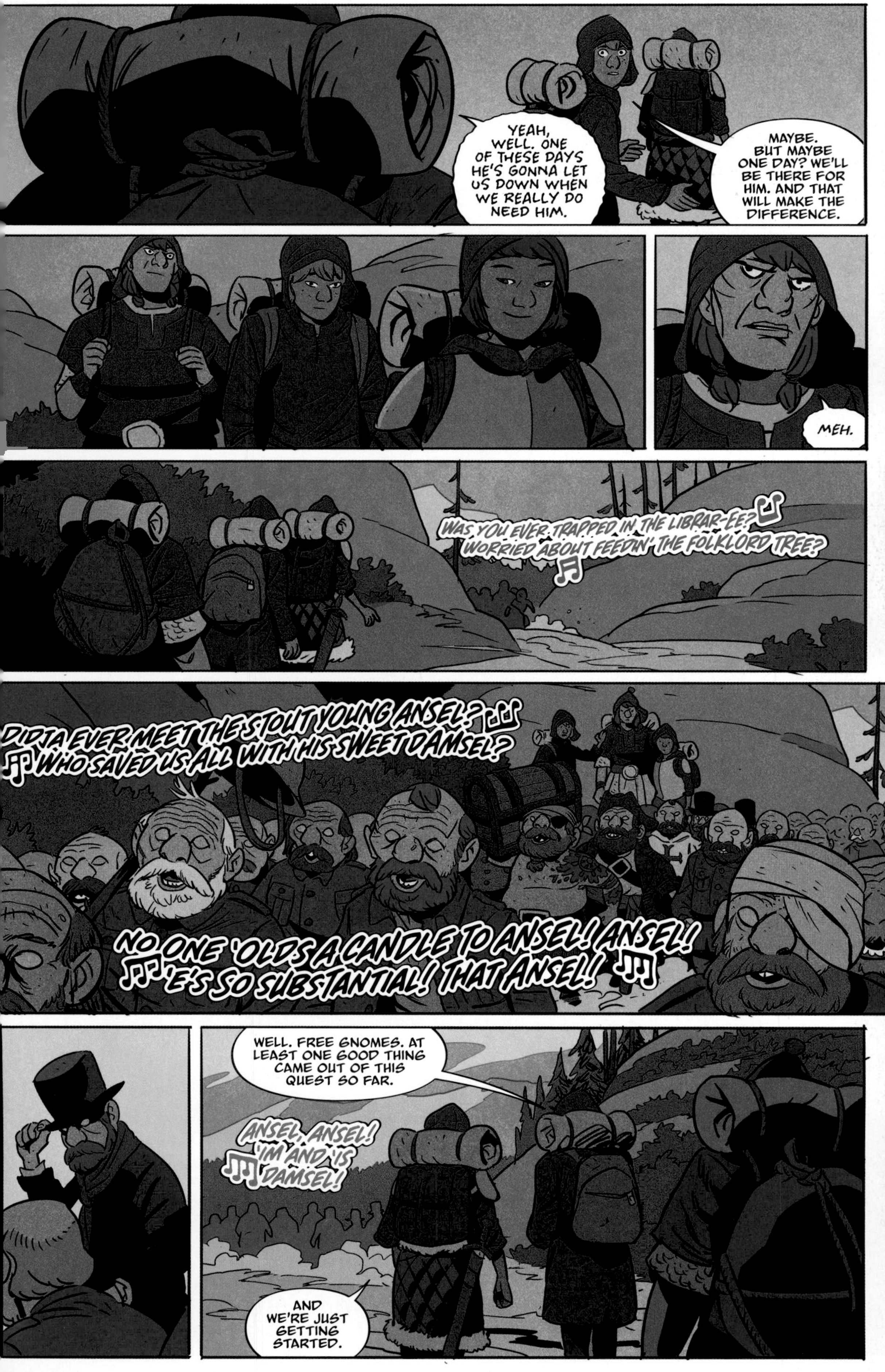
YEAH, WELL. ONE OF THESE DAYS HE'S GONNA LET US DOWN WHEN WE REALLY DO NEED HIM.
MAYBE. BUT MAYBE ONE DAY? WE'LL BE THERE FOR HIM. AND THAT WILL MAKE THE DIFFERENCE.
MEH.
WAS YOU EVER TRAPPED IN THE LIBRAR-EE? WORRIED ABOUT FEEDIN' THE FOLKLORD TREE?
DIDJA EVER MEET THE STOUT YOUNG ANSEL? WHO SAVED US ALL WITH HIS SWEET DAMSEL?
NO ONE 'OLDS A CANDLE TO ANSEL! ANSEL! 'E'S SO SUBSTANTIAL! THAT ANSEL!
WELL. FREE GNOMES. AT LEAST ONE GOOD THING CAME OUT OF THIS QUEST SO FAR.
ANSEL, ANSEL! 'IM AND 'IS DAMSEL!
AND WE'RE JUST GETTING STARTED.

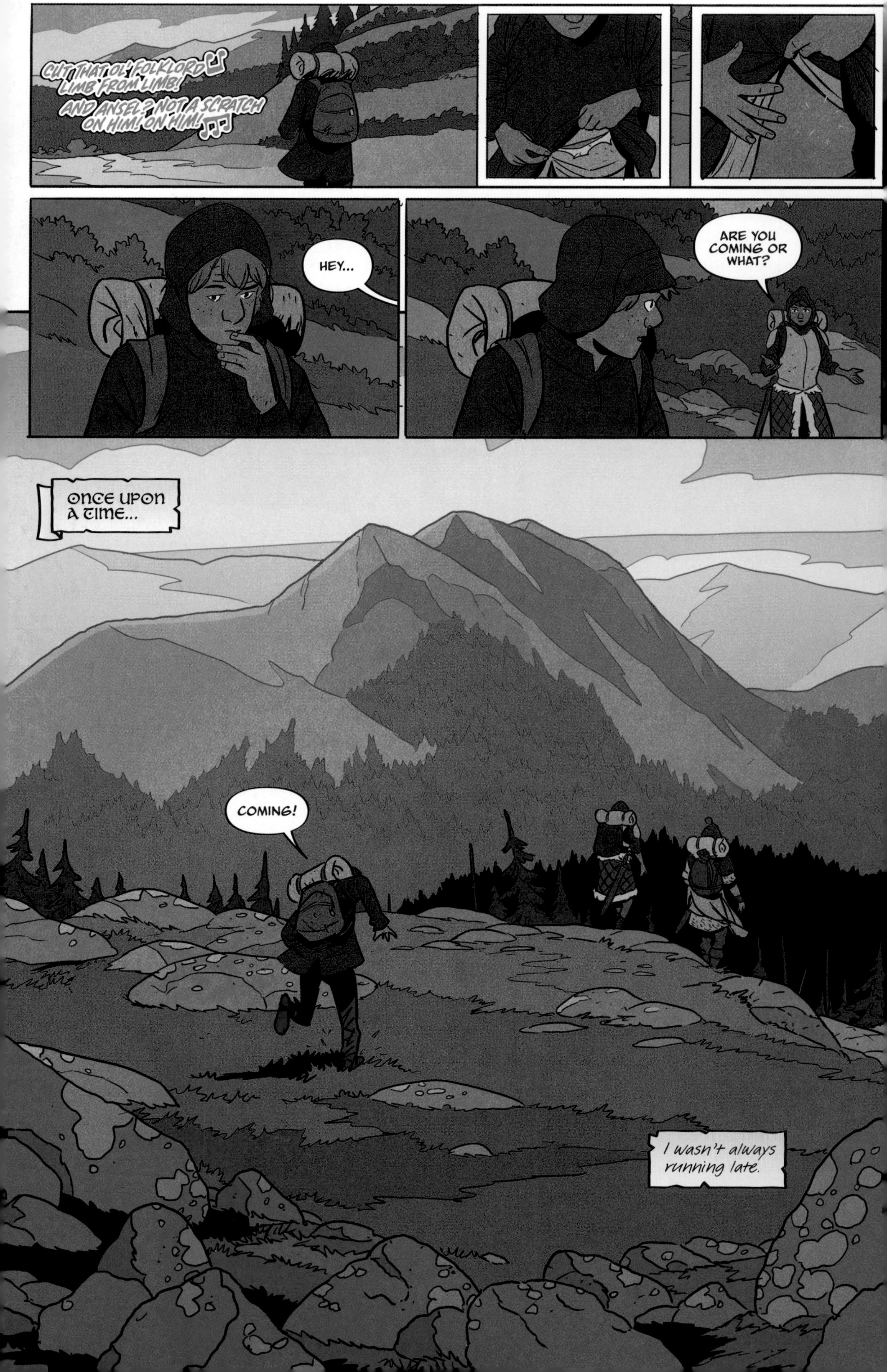
CUT THAT OL' FOLKLORD
LIMB FROM LIMB!
AND ANSEL? NOT A SCRATCH
ON HIM! ON HIM!
HEY...
ARE YOU COMING OR WHAT?
ONCE UPON A TIME...
COMING!
I wasn't always running late.

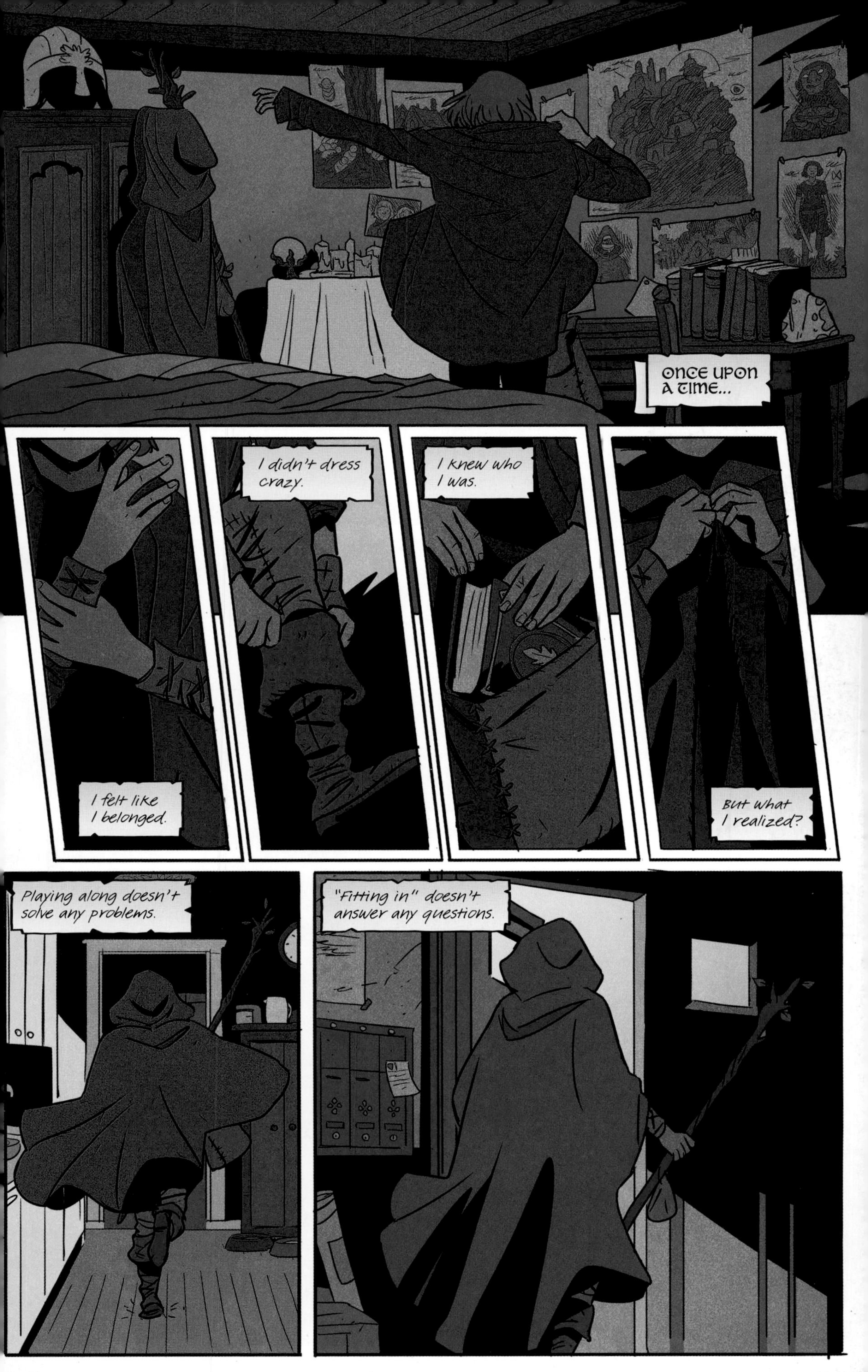
ONCE UPON A TIME...
I felt like I belonged.
I didn't dress crazy.
I knew who I was.
But what I realized?
Playing along doesn't solve any problems.
"Fitting in" doesn't answer any questions.

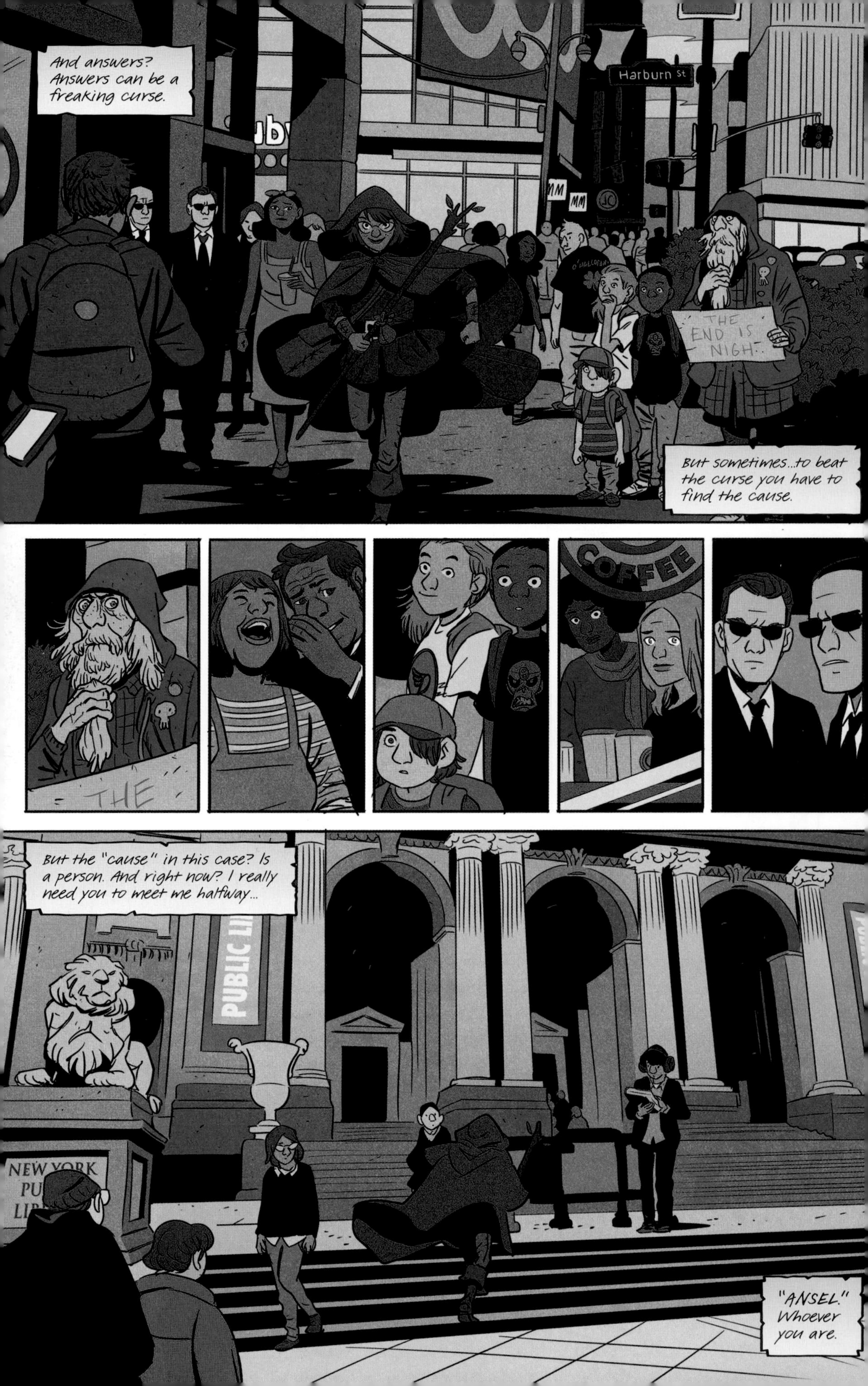
And answers? Answers can be a freaking curse.
Harburn St
THE END IS NIGH
But sometimes...to beat the curse you have to find the cause.
THE
COFFEE
But the "cause" in this case? Is a person. And right now? I really need you to meet me halfway...
PUBLIC LI
NEW YORK PU LI
"ANSEL." Whoever you are.

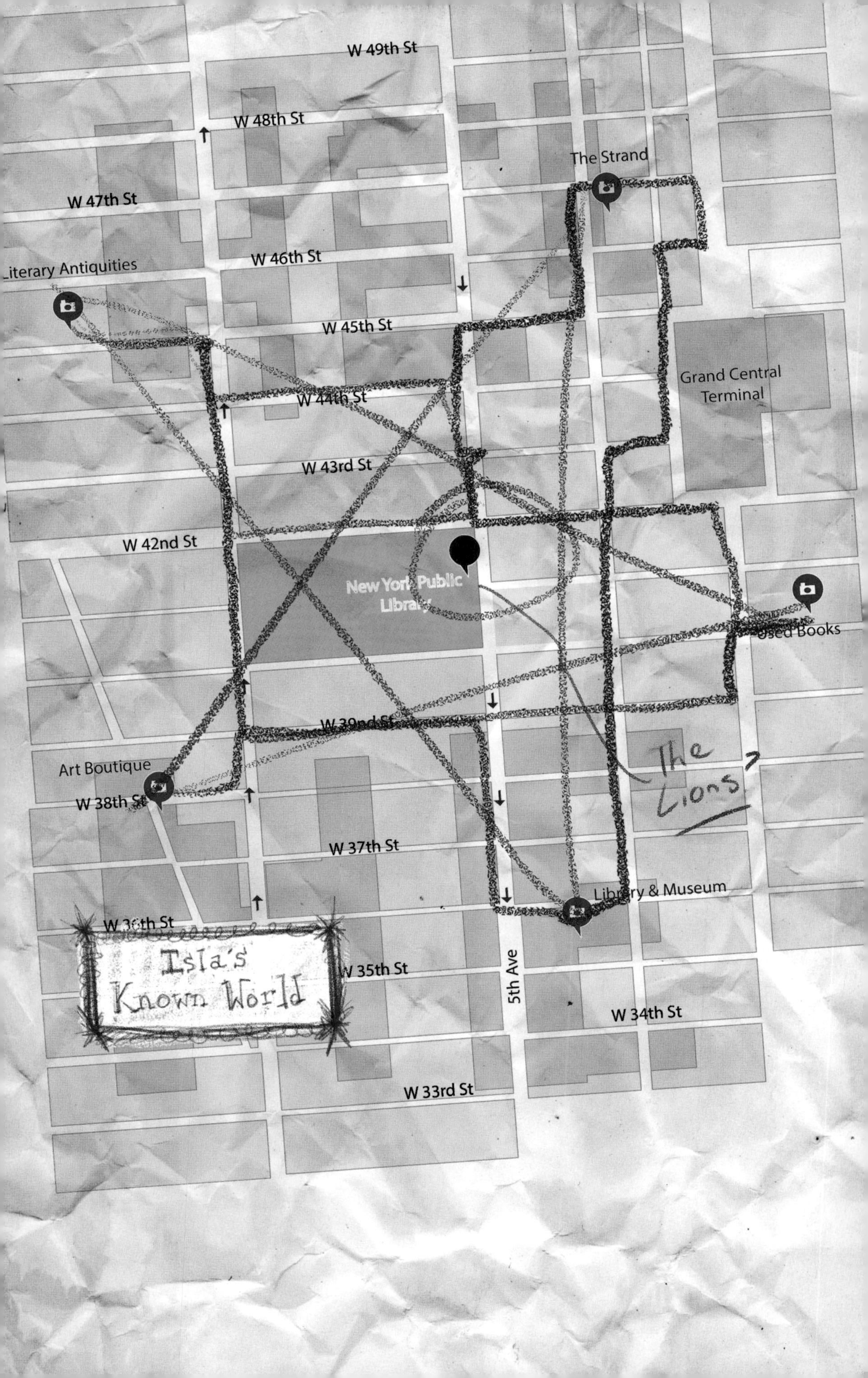
W 49th St
W 48th St
W 47th St
The Strand
Literary Antiquities
W 46th St
W 45th St
Grand Central Terminal
W 44th St
W 43rd St
W 42nd St
New York Public Library
Used Books
W 39nd St
The Lions?
Art Boutique
W 38th St
W 37th St
Library & Museum
W 36th St
Isla's Known World
W 35th St
5th Ave
W 34th St
W 33rd St

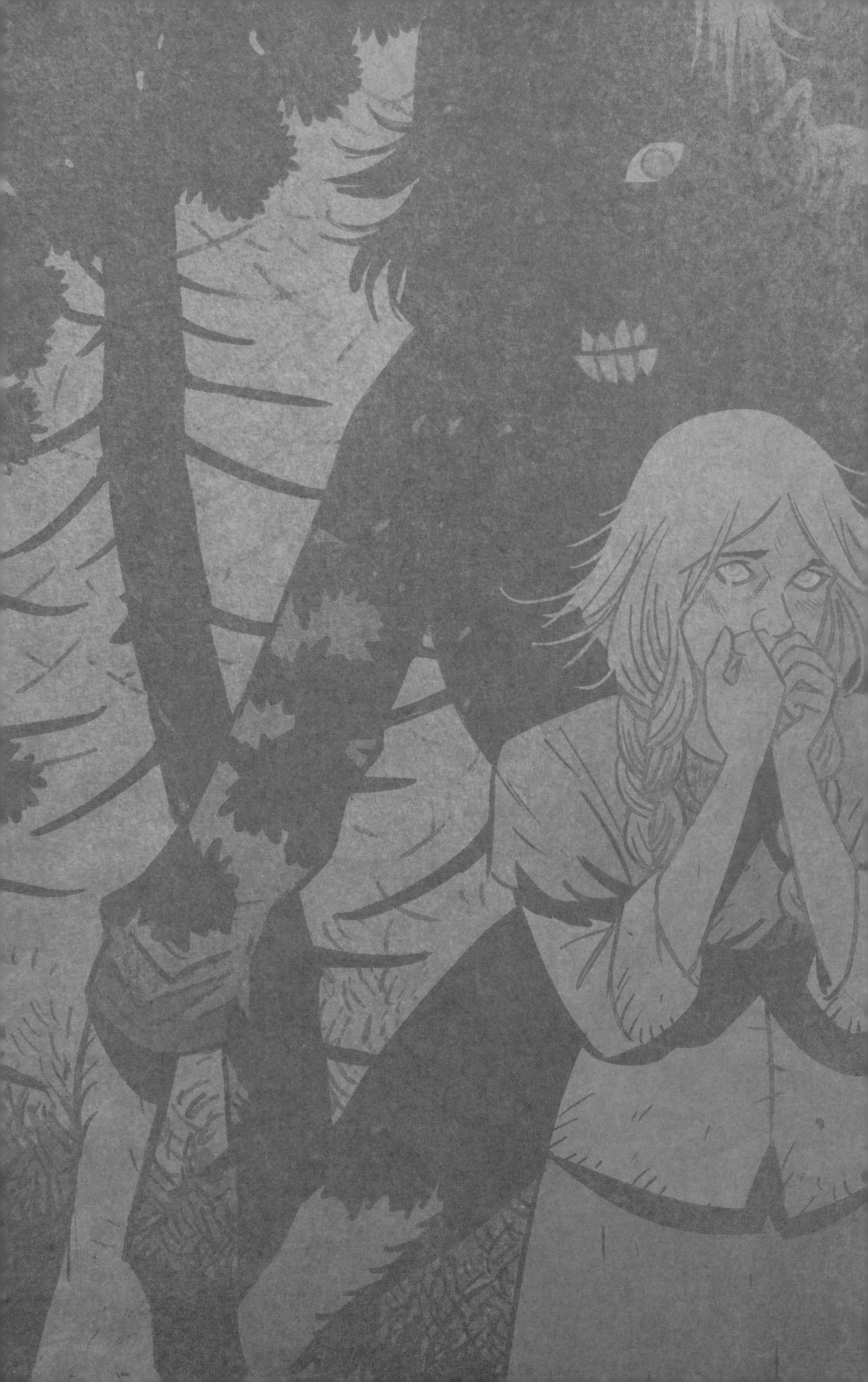

COVER
GALLERY

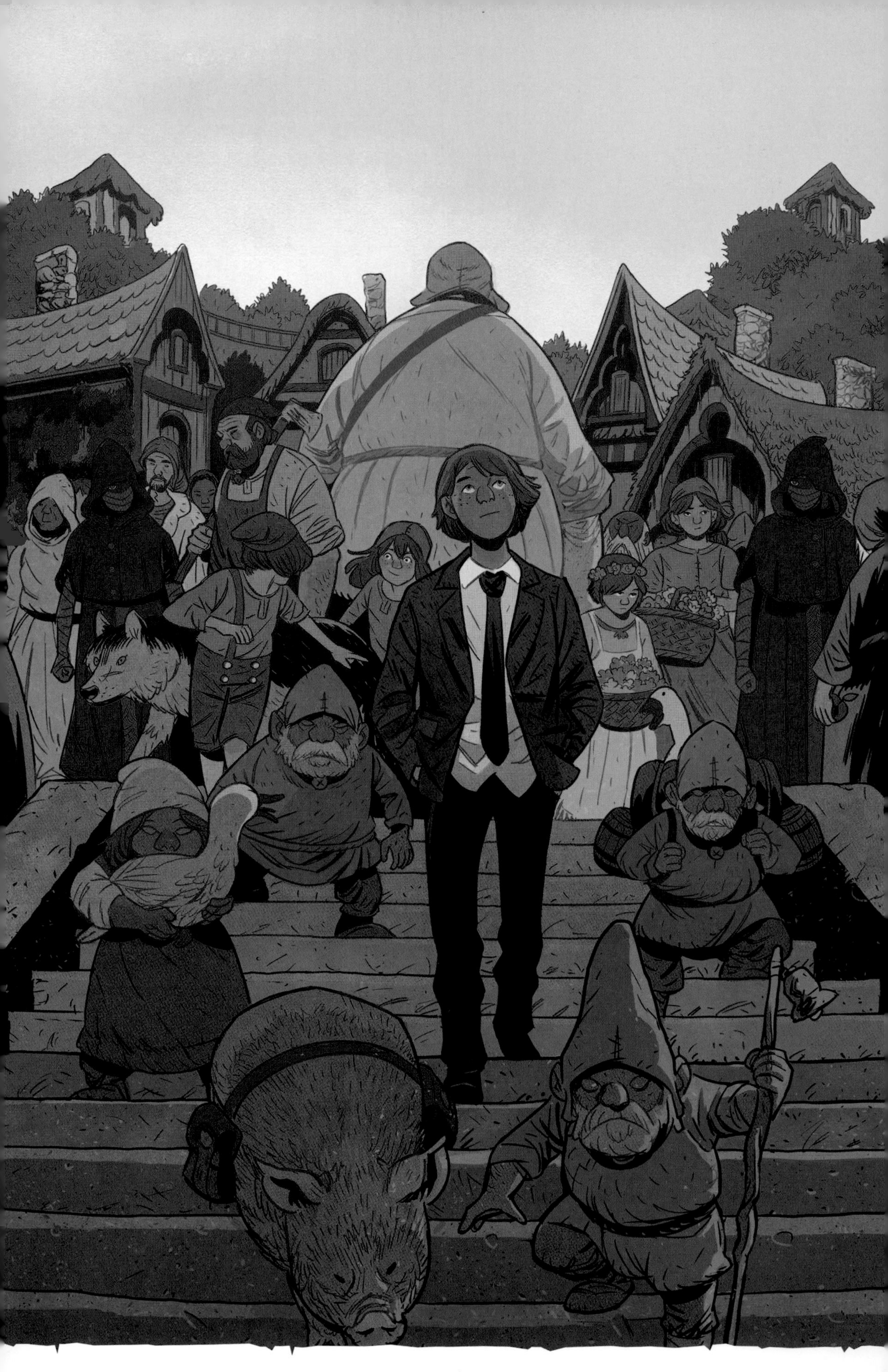

Issue One Cover by **MATT SMITH**

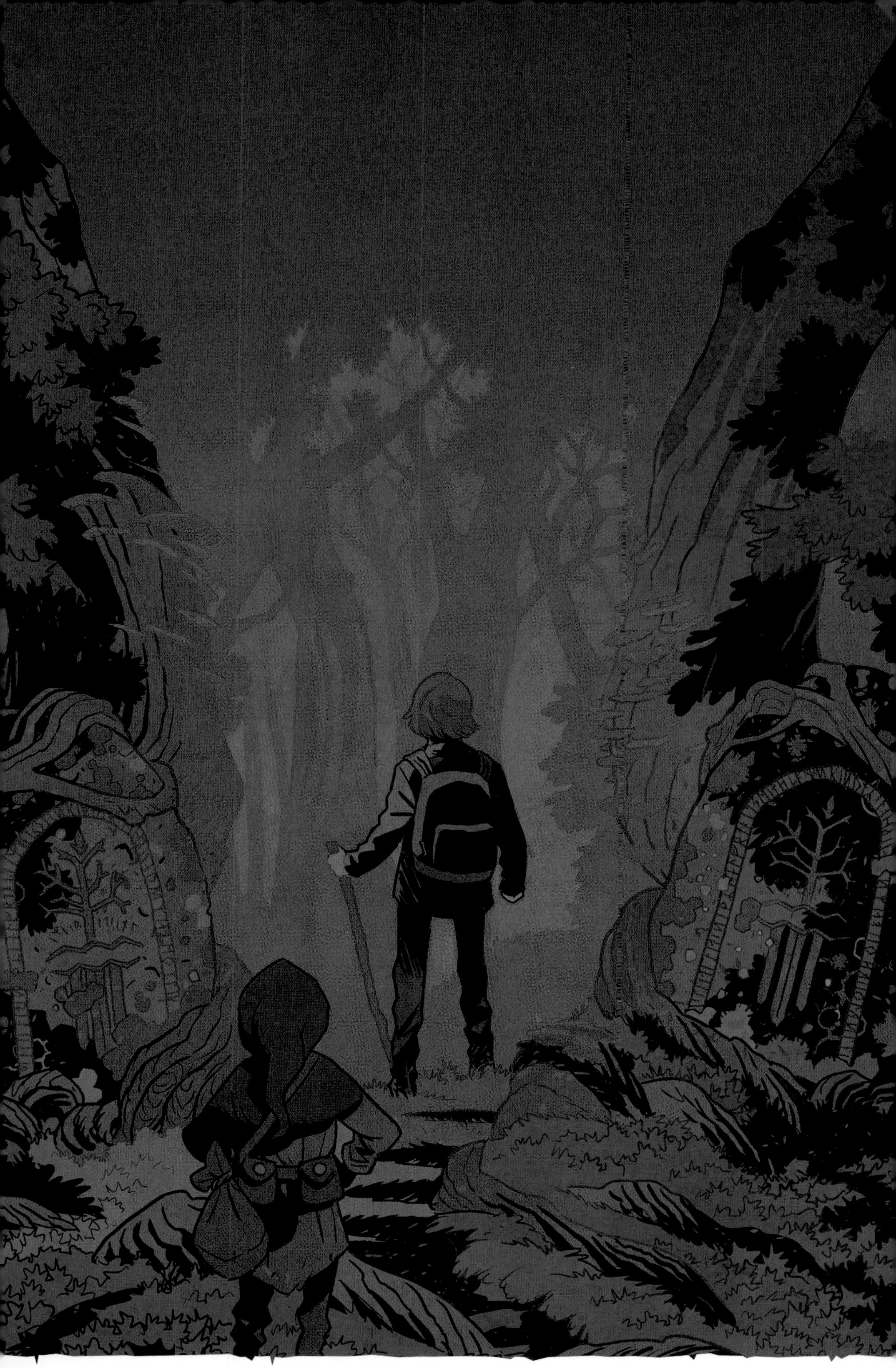

Issue Two Cover by **MATT SMITH**

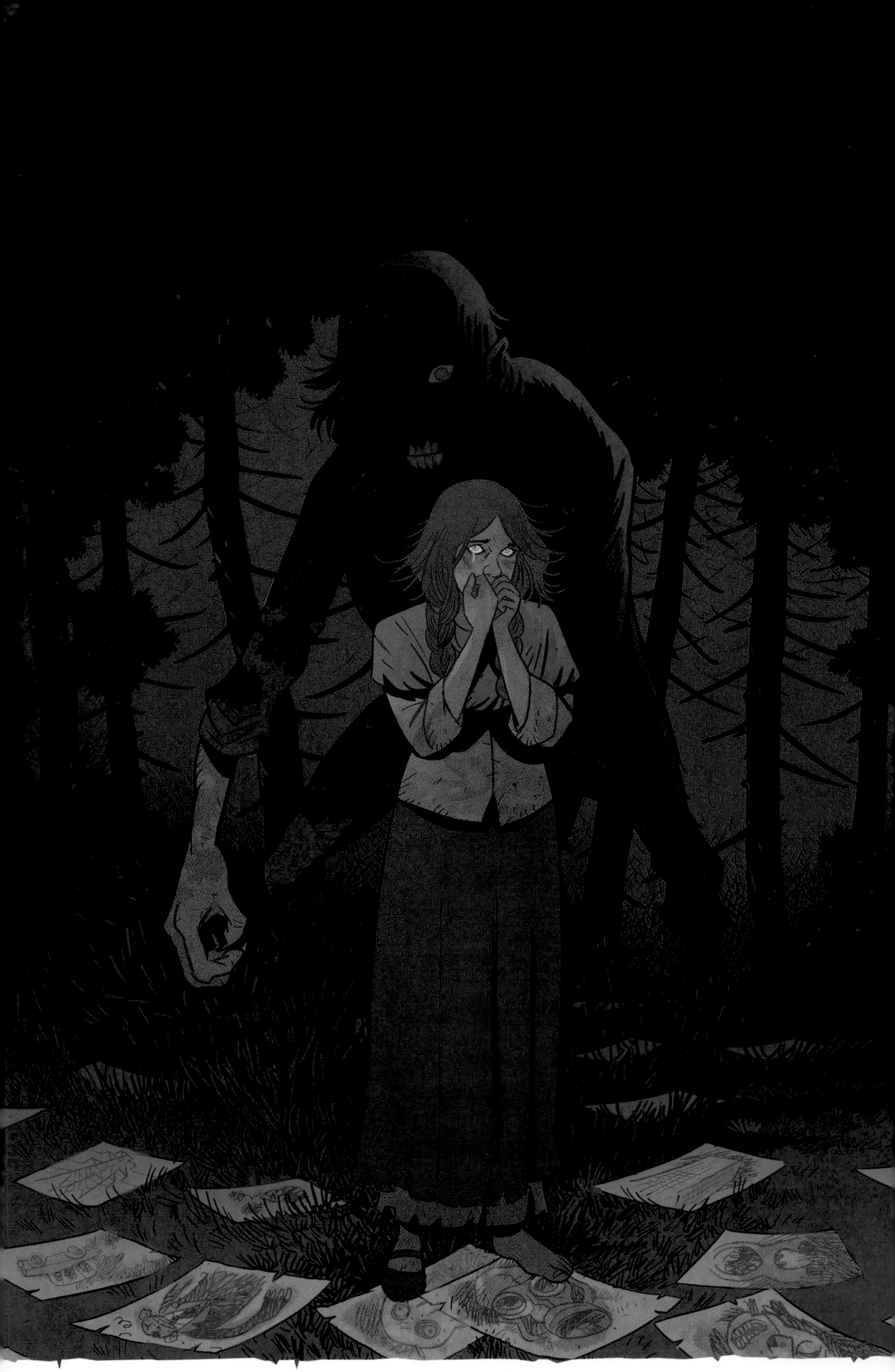

Issue Three Cover by **MATT SMITH**

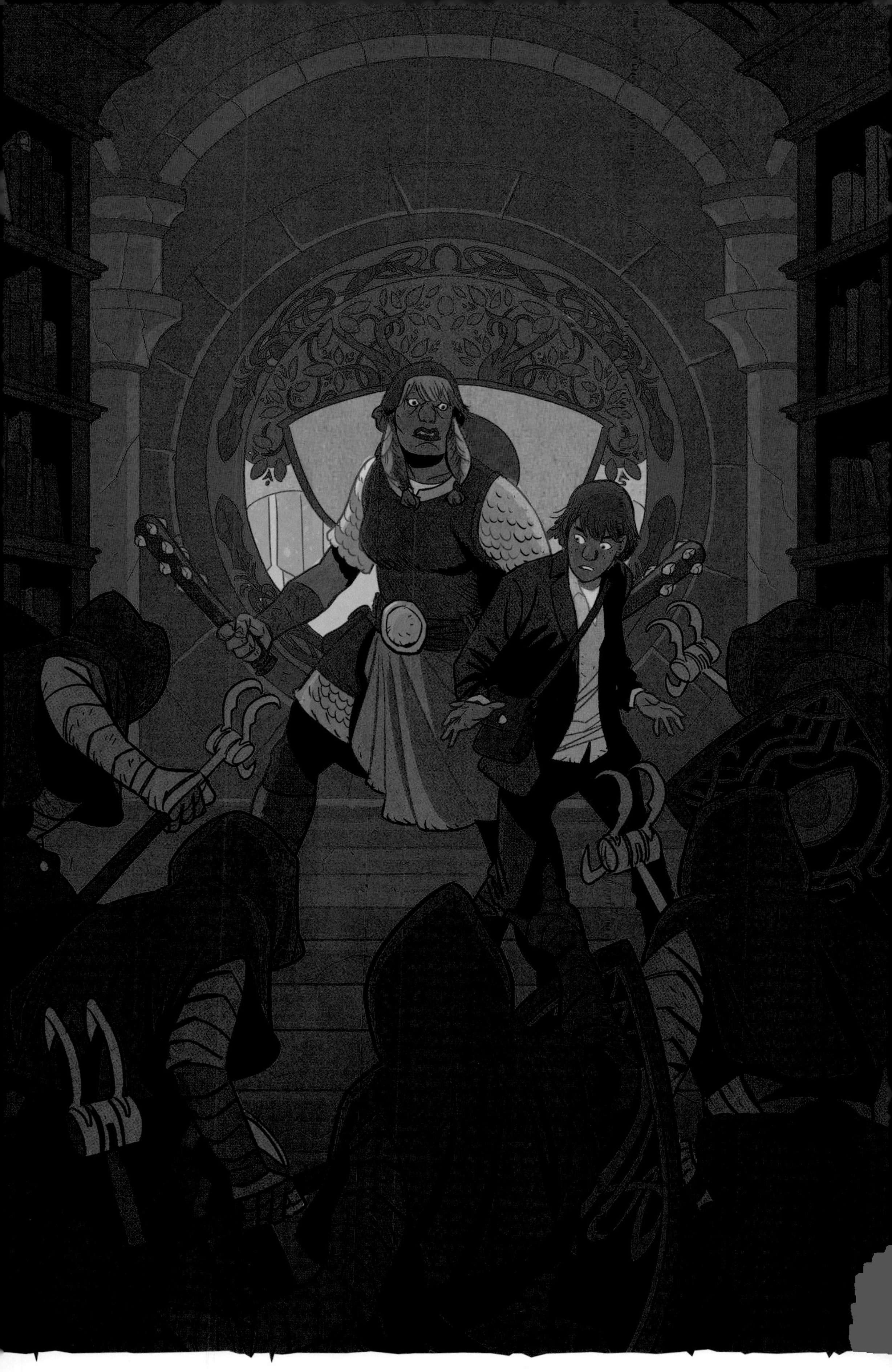

Issue Four Cover by **MATT SMITH**

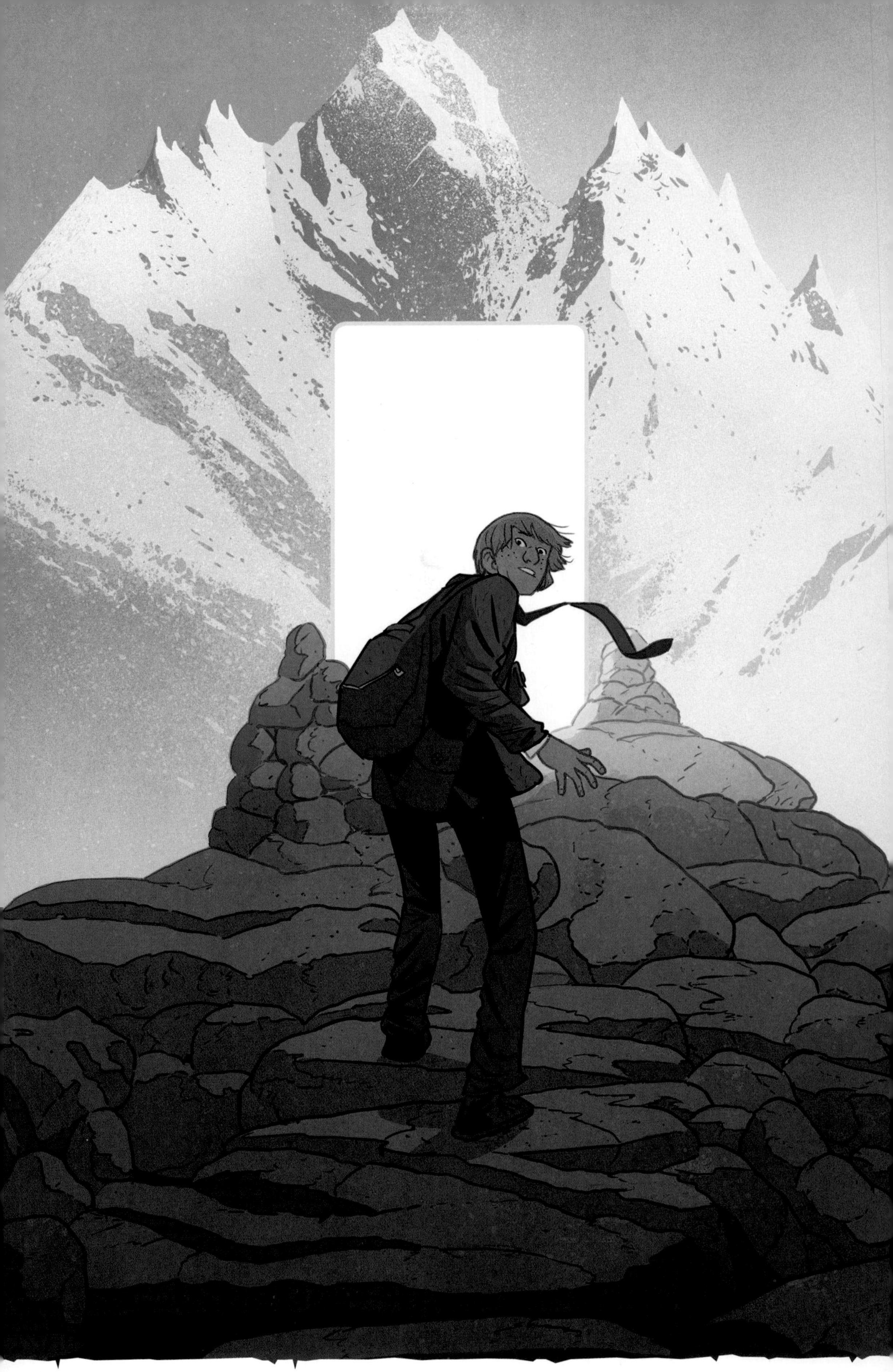

Issue Five Cover by **MATT SMITH**

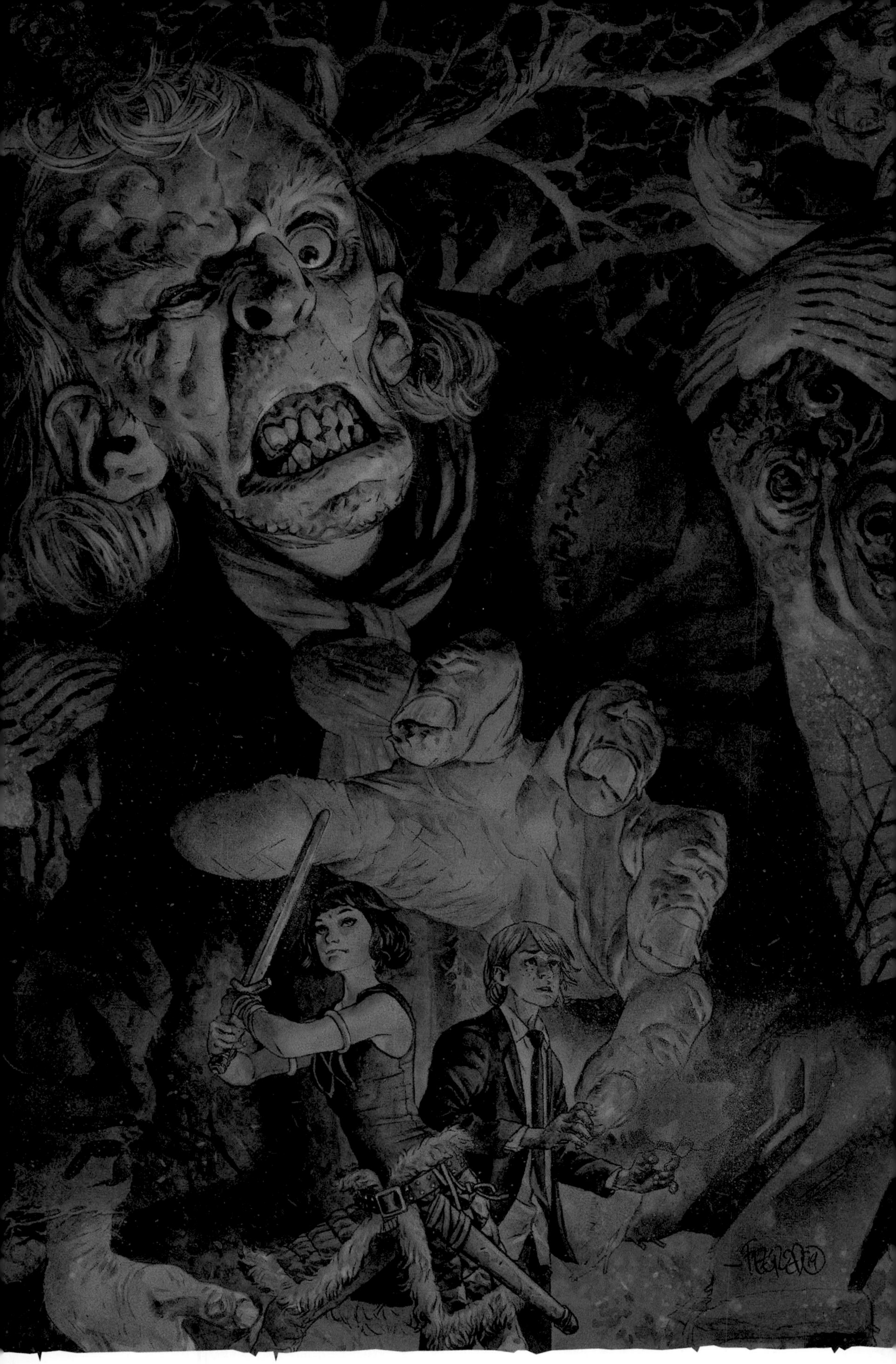

Issue One Variant Cover by **DUNCAN FEGREDO**

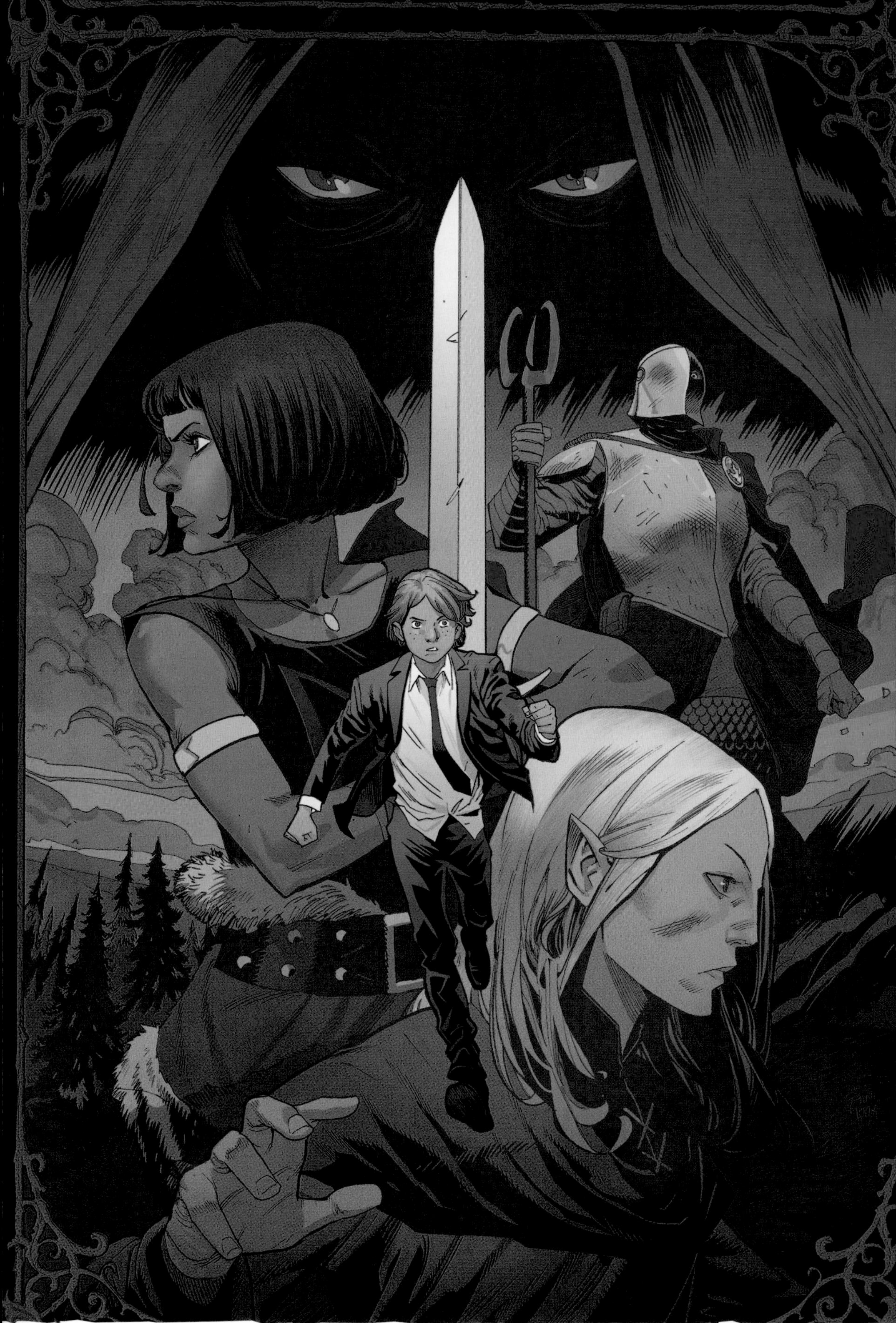

Issue One Unlocked Retailer Variant Cover by **DAN MORA**

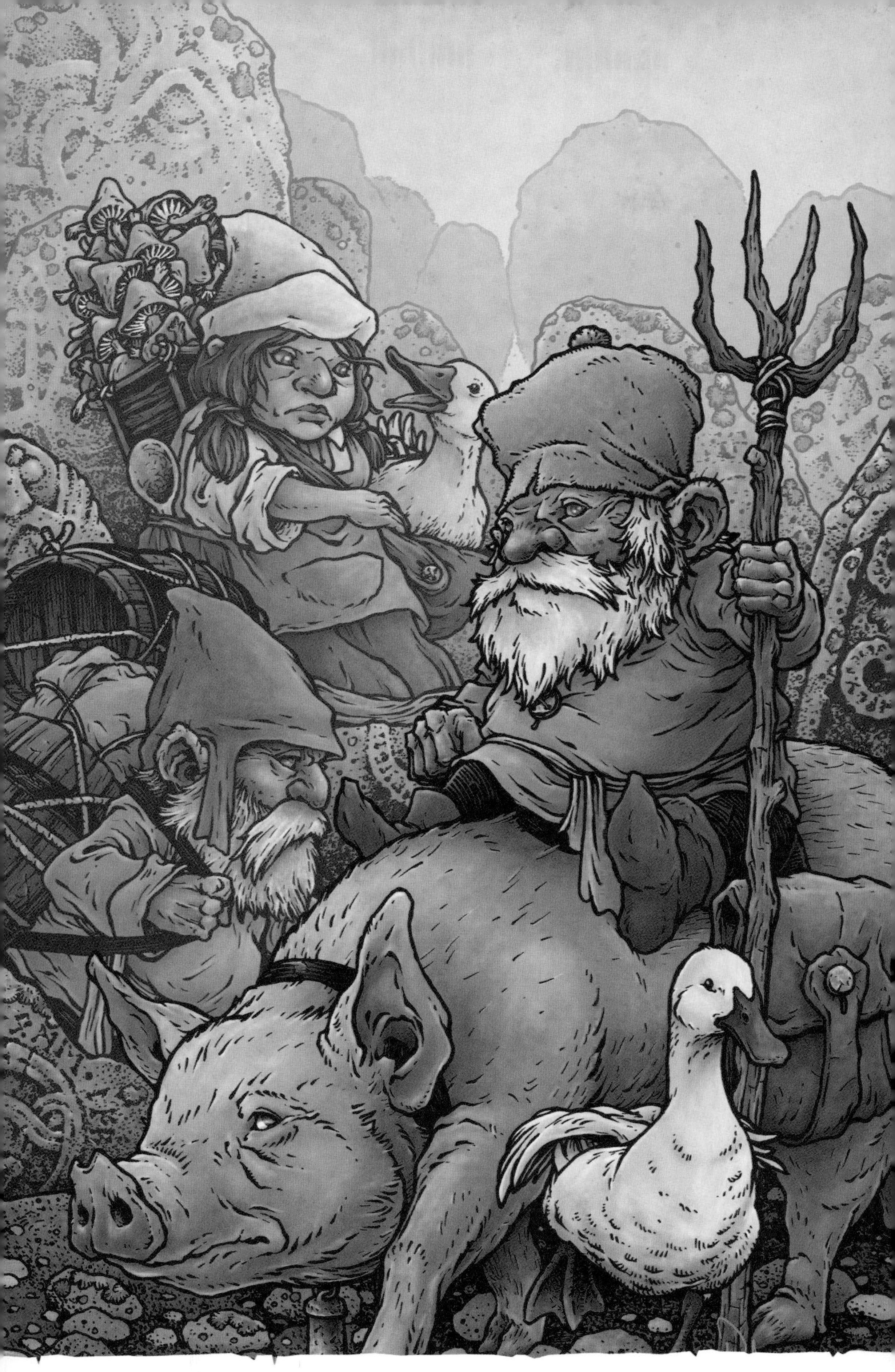

Issue One Jolzar Collectibles Exclusive Variant Cover by **DAVID PETERSEN**

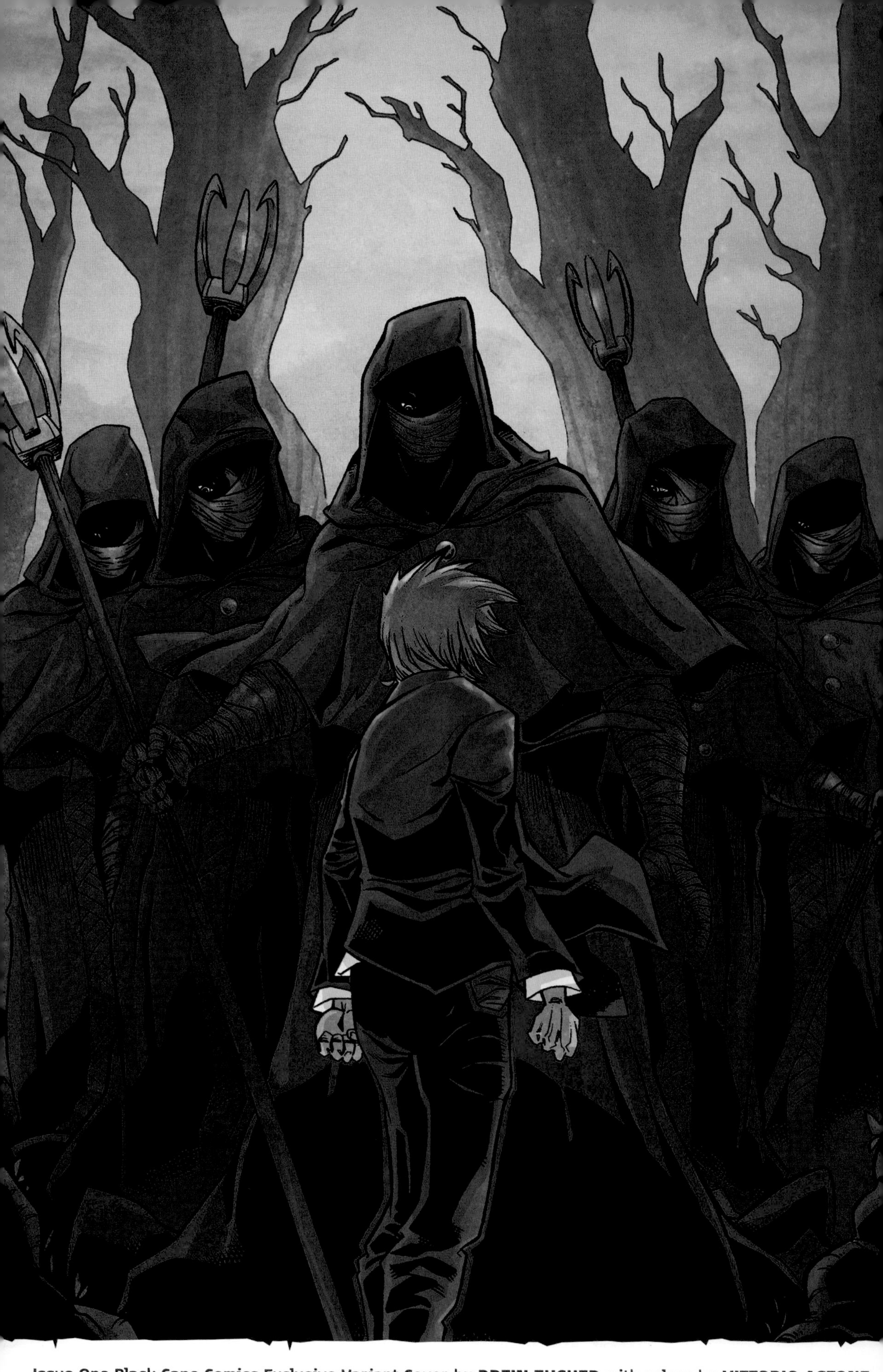

Issue One Black Cape Comics Exclusive Variant Cover by **DREW ZUCKER** with colors by **VITTORIO ASTONE**

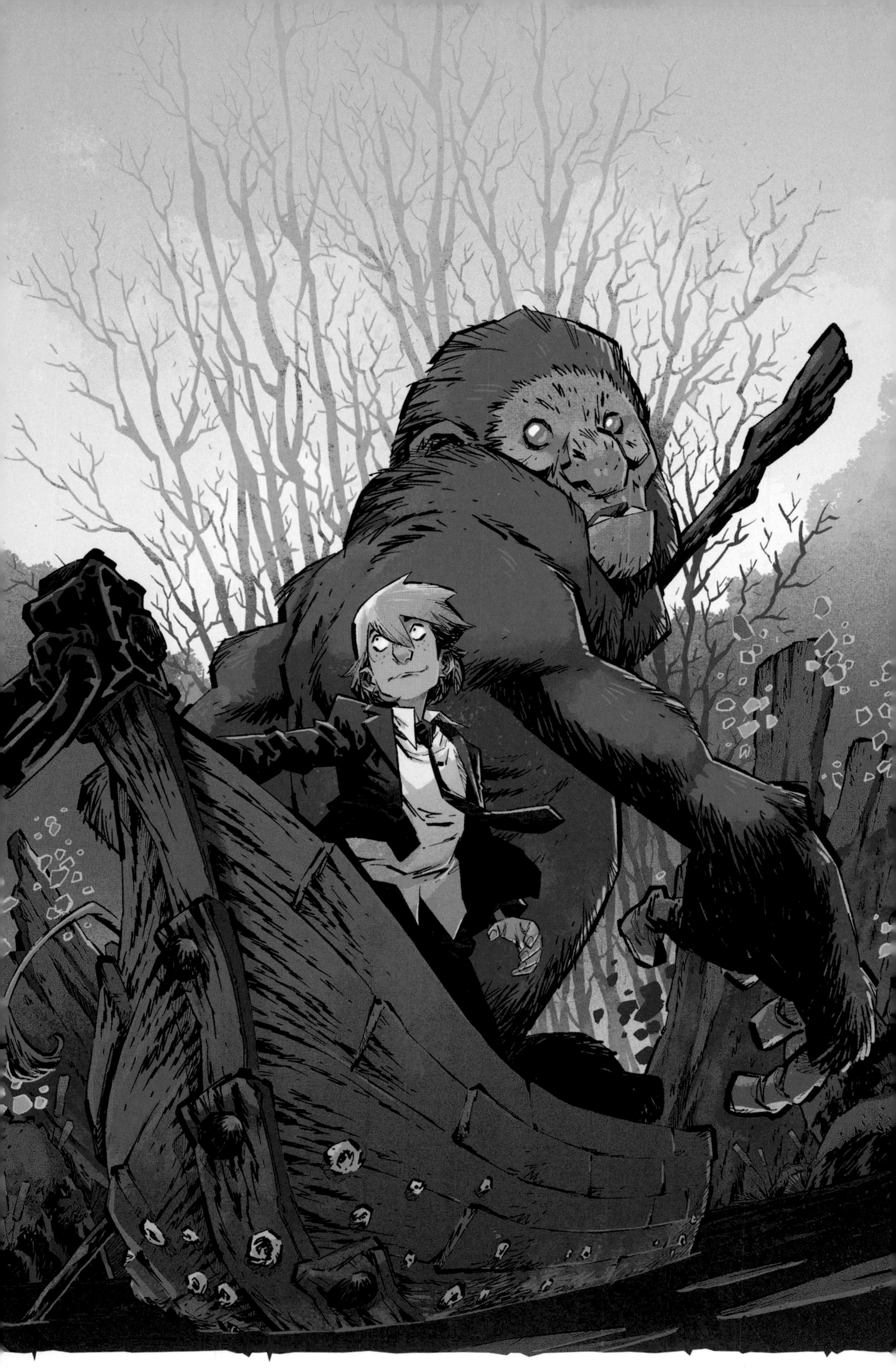

Issue One Second Print Cover by **JORGE CORONA** with colors by **SARAH STERN**

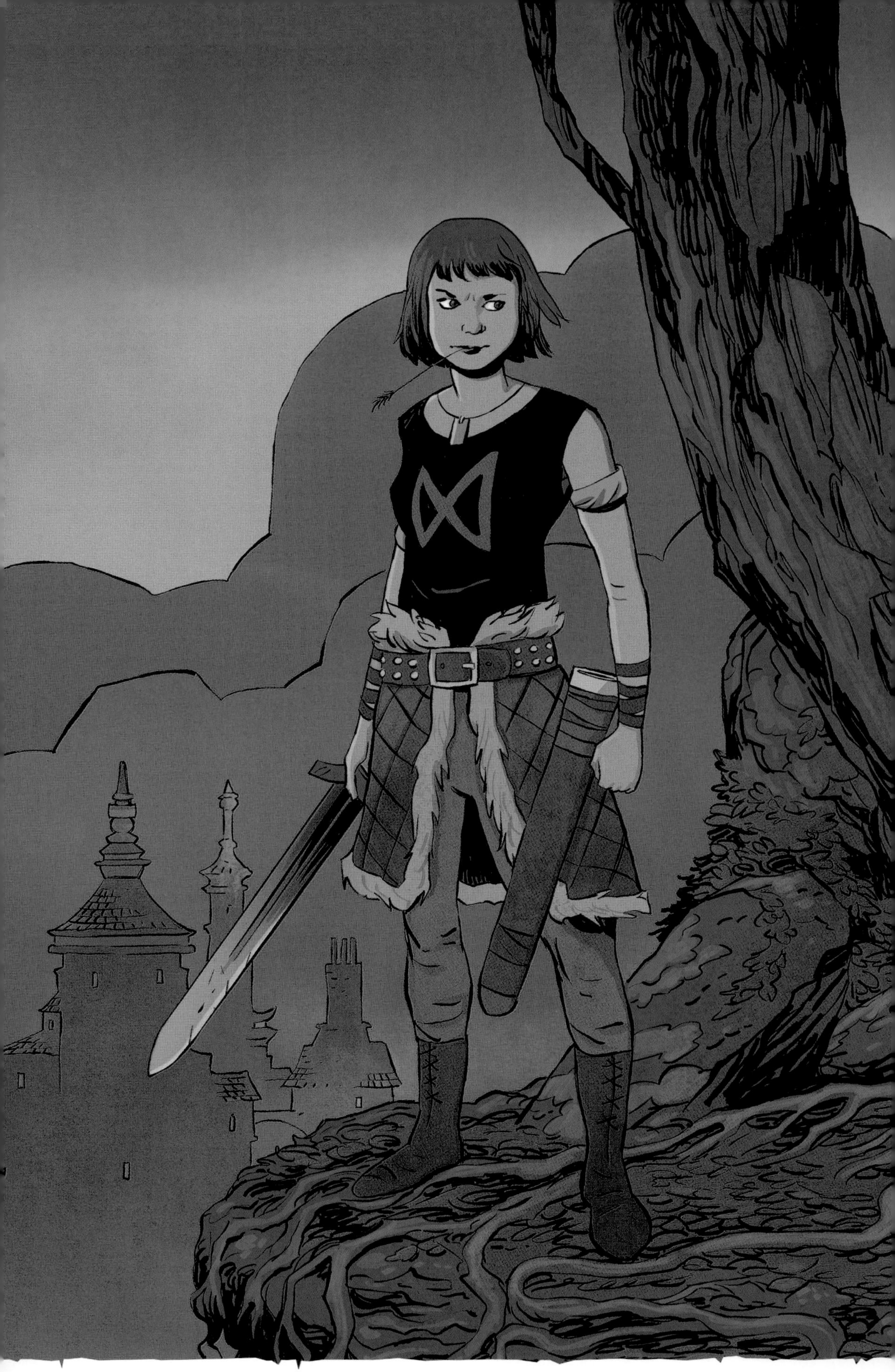

Issue One Third Print Cover by **PETER BERGTING**

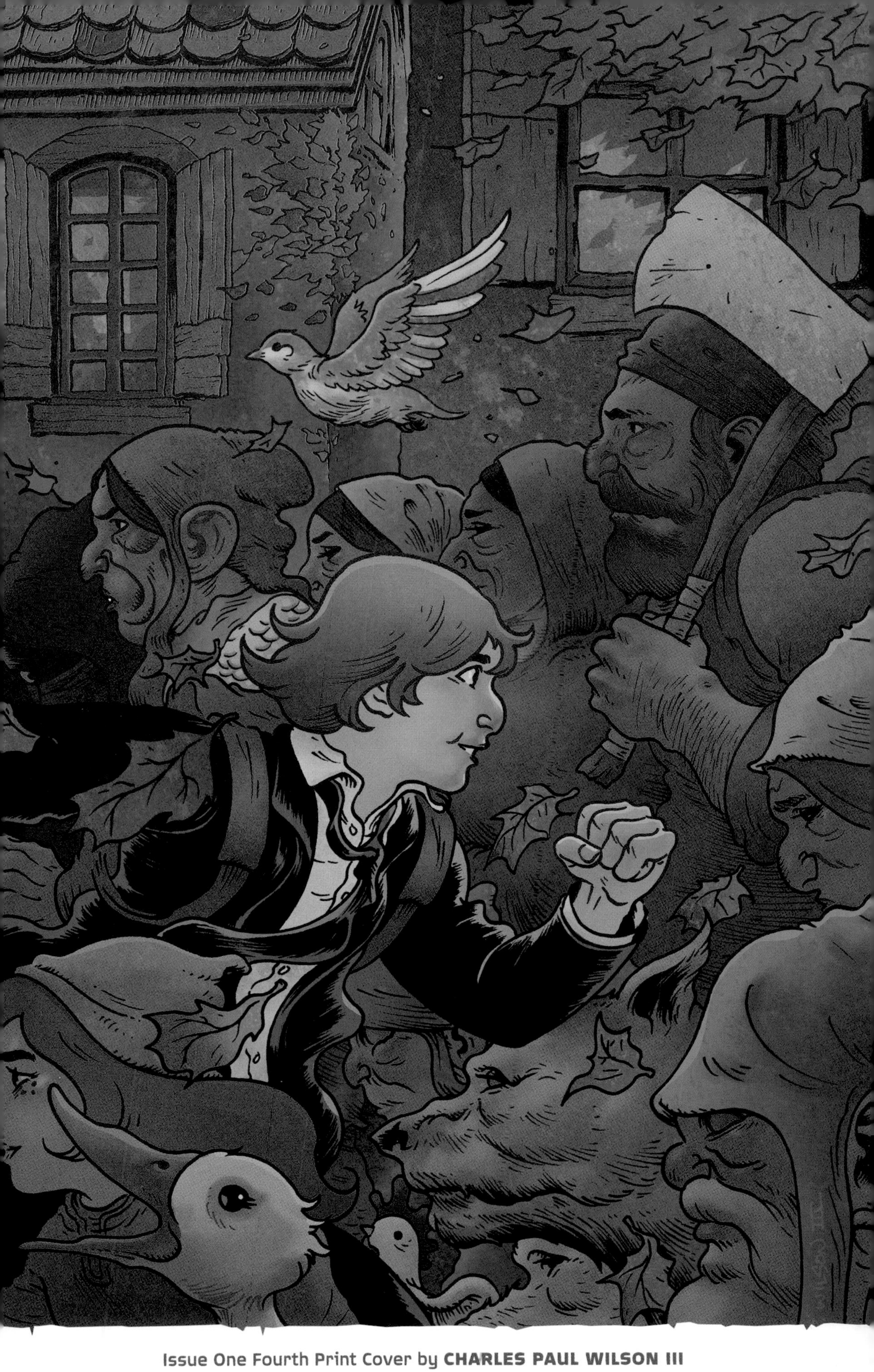

Issue One Fourth Print Cover by **CHARLES PAUL WILSON III**

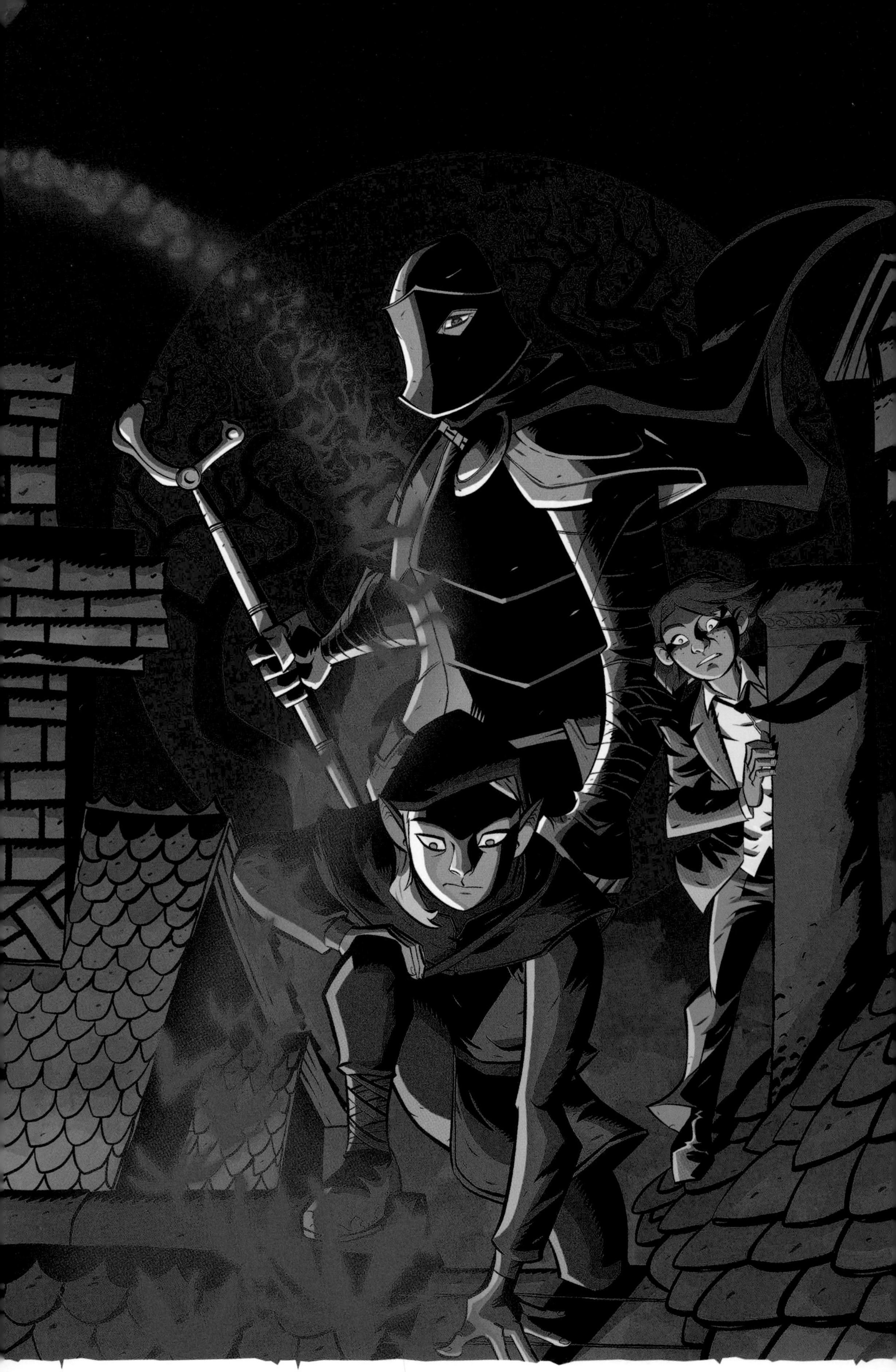

Issue Two Unlocked Retailer Variant Cover by **MICHAEL AVON OEMING**

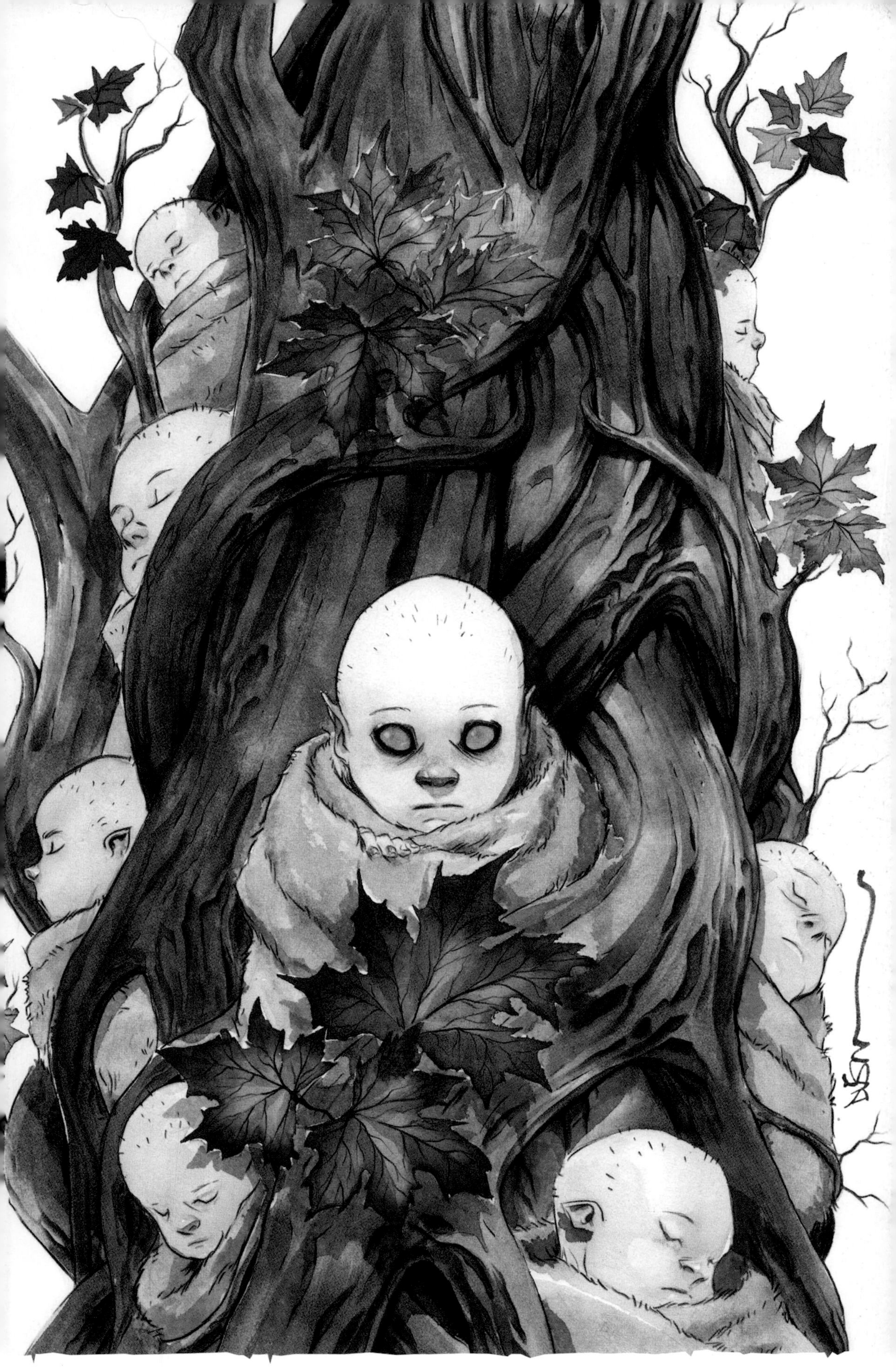

Issue Three Unlocked Retailer Variant Cover by **DUSTIN NGUYEN**

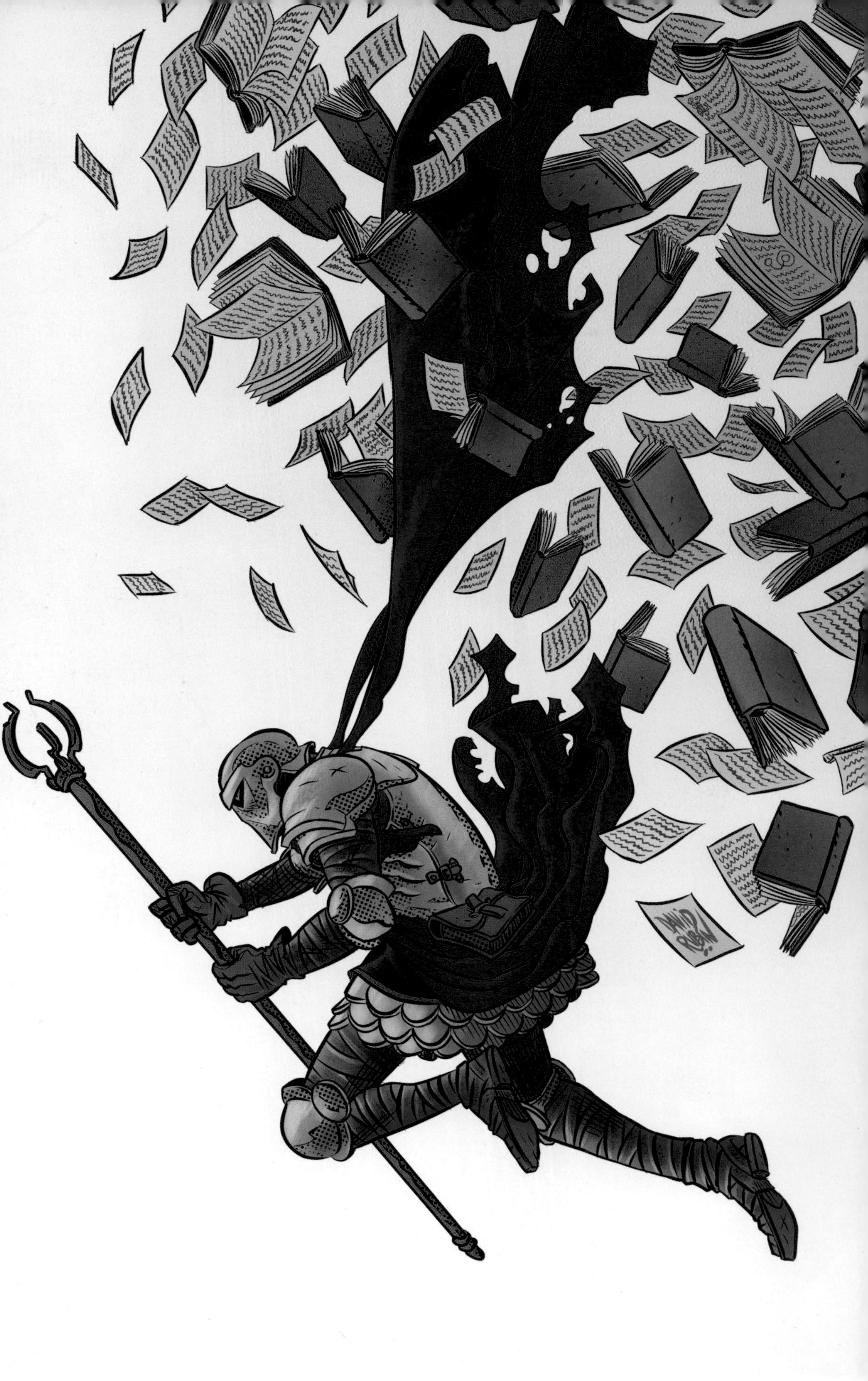
DAVID RUBÍN

Issue Four Unlocked Retailer Variant Cover by **DAVID RUBÍN**

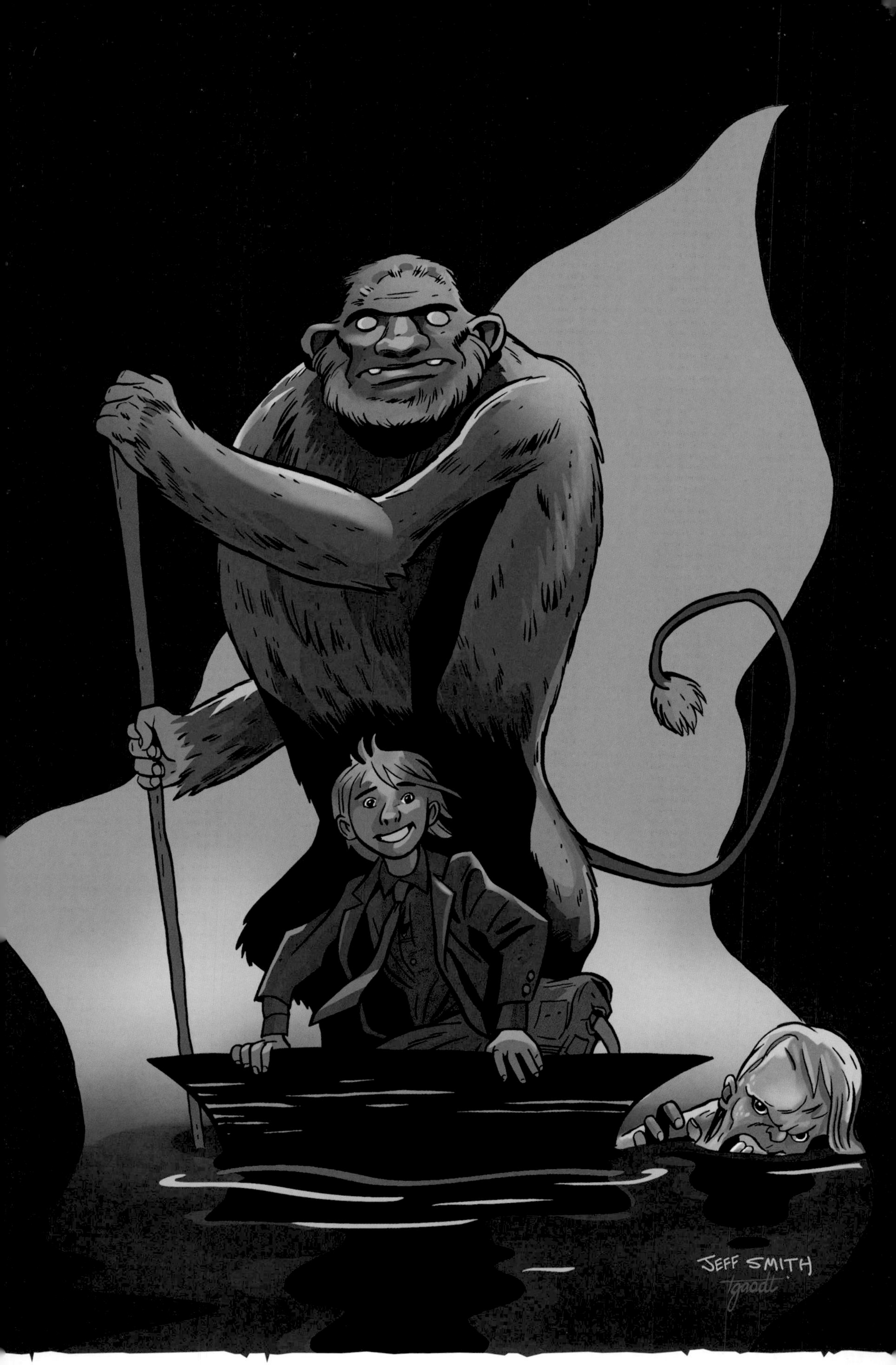
JEFF SMITH

Issue Five Unlocked Retailer Variant Cover by **JEFF SMITH**